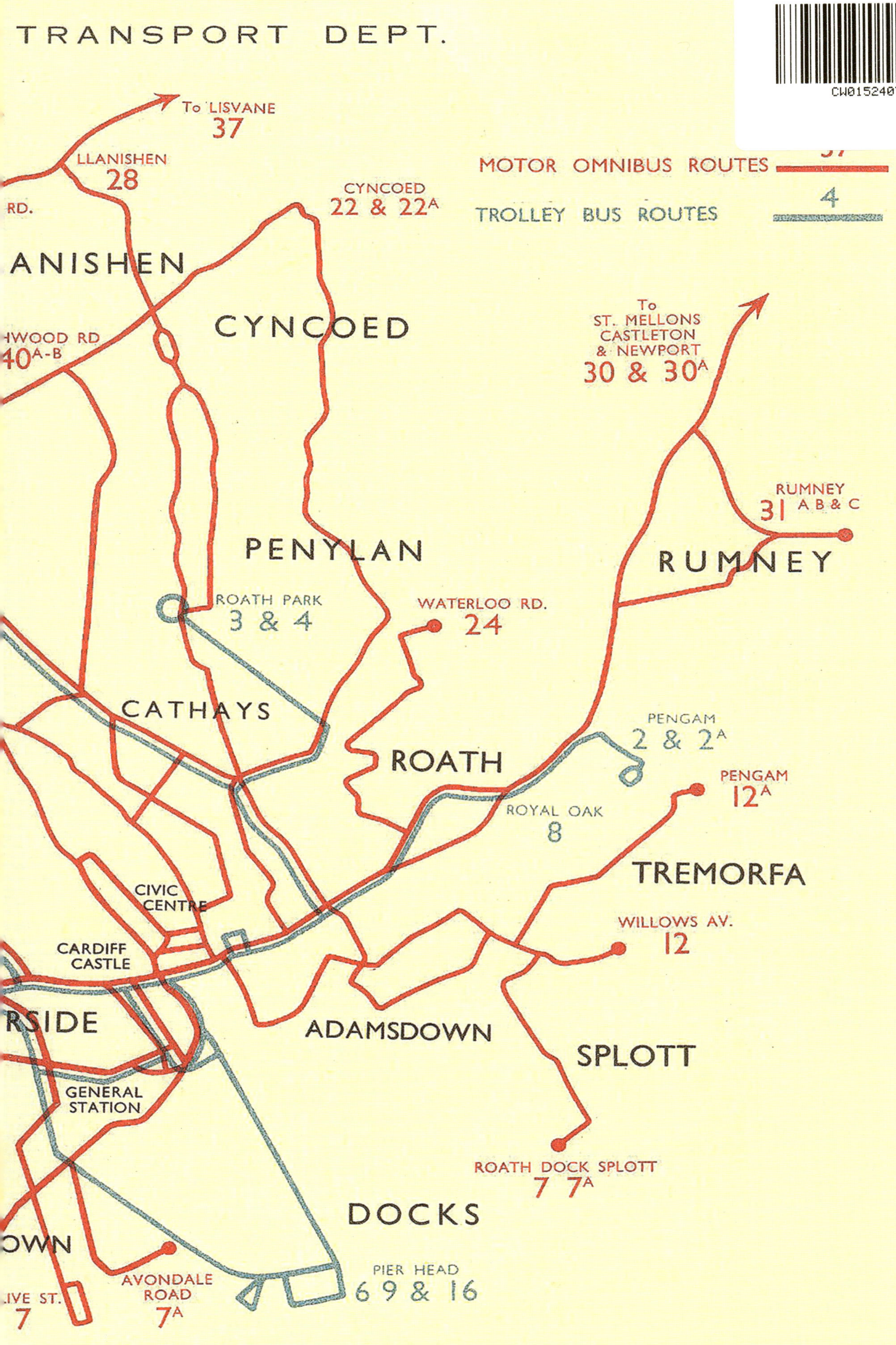
TRANSPORT DEPT.
MOTOR OMNIBUS ROUTES
37
TROLLEY BUS ROUTES
4
To LISVANE
37
LLANISHEN
28
RD.
CYNCOED
22 & 22A
ANISHEN
CYNCOED
HWOOD RD
40A-B
To
ST. MELLONS
CASTLETON
& NEWPORT
30 & 30A
RUMNEY
31 A B & C
RUMNEY
PENYLAN
ROATH PARK
3 & 4
WATERLOO RD.
24
CATHAYS
PENGAM
2 & 2A
ROATH
PENGAM
12A
ROYAL OAK
8
TREMORFA
CIVIC
CENTRE
WILLOWS AV.
12
CARDIFF
CASTLE
RSIDE
ADAMSDOWN
SPLOTT
GENERAL
STATION
ROATH DOCK SPLOTT
7 7A
DOCKS
OWN
AVONDALE
ROAD
7A
PIER HEAD
6 9 & 16
IVE ST.
7

Cardiff's Municipal Buses
Andrew Wiltshire

Posed on the forecourt of Sloper Road depot is 63 (CKG 422), the second of the Guy Arab utility double-deckers to join the fleet in 1942. It has a Park Royal body and here it is seen in original condition in the late 1940s. It was rebuilt by Longwell Green of Bristol in 1952, eventually coming out of service in 1958 and passing to a showman, possibly for use as a caravan.

(John Wiltshire)

First published August 2016 by
Bernard McCall, 400 Nore Road, Portishead, Bristol, BS20 8EZ, England.
Tel: +44 (0) 1275 846178
email: bernard@coastalshipping.co.uk. website: www.coastalshipping.co.uk
Design: Sarah Baber

ISBN 978-1-90295-378-6
Copyright © Andrew Wiltshire

The rights of Andrew Wiltshire to be identified as author of this work have been asserted by him in accordance with the Copyright, Design and Patent Act 1988. All rights reserved.

No part of this publication may be reproduced, stored in a retrieval system or transmitted in any form or by any means (electronic, digital, mechanical, photocopying, recording or otherwise) without prior permission of the publisher.

All distribution enquiries should be addressed to the publisher.

Printed by : Gomer Press, Llandysul Enterprise Park, Llandysul, Ceredigion, WALES, SA44 4JL.
Telephone : +44 (0) 1559 362371 Fax : +44 (0) 1559 363758
Email : sales@gomer.co.uk website : www.gomerprinting.co.uk

OTHER TITLES BY THE SAME AUTHOR

South Wales Buses - The First Decade of Deregulation
Independent Buses of South and West Wales
South Wales Buses and Coaches Remembered
Looking Back at PTE Buses
Looking Back at Independent Double-Deckers
Looking Back at Traditional Cargo Ships
Looking Back at Bristol Channel Shipping
Tugs in Colour - Worldwide
Looking Back at Refrigerated Shipping
Looking Back at Bulk Carriers

All available from www.coastalshipping.co.uk

FRONT COVER

The last surviving Crossley DD42 in the Cardiff fleet was 46 (EBO900) which is seen in Central Bus Station on 12 September 1964. It has an Alexander low-bridge body and upon withdrawal in 1966, the bus was sold to a group of enthusiasts for preservation.
(John Wiltshire)

BACK COVER

Scania OmniCity articulated bus 617 looks very smart in the standard fleet livery. Here it waits on King Edward VII Avenue in Cathays Park on 9 April 2014 having been recently refurbished. It will be heading off to Cardiff Bay (Porth Teigr) on baycar service 6, which runs from this stop every 10 minutes Monday to Friday (daytime). The impressive buildings behind the bus are those of the Welsh Assembly Government and were originally occupied by the Welsh Office, which was part of the United Kingdom government.
(Andrew Wiltshire)

INTRODUCTION

As the years have passed by, many volumes have been published covering the history of British municipal bus fleets both large and small. I often wondered when someone would get around to publishing a book covering the fleet I grew up with, namely Cardiff Corporation Transport (CCT). The trams had long gone by the time I was born, but as a small boy living in Llanrumney and later Rhiwbina I became fascinated by Cardiff's buses and trolleybuses from about the mid-1960s. My first recollections of bus travel were from Llanrumney into town on the 47 and 48 services as well as the odd run from St. Mellons (Bluebell Inn) to Newport on the 30. I also remember well, travelling on trolleybuses to Canton, Victoria Park and Wellfield Road, but at around nine years of age, failed to really appreciate the significance of the farewell trolleybus tour, which I participated in on a dark and miserable 11 January 1970. With encouragement from my father I eventually became conversant with the different types of motor buses in the fleet, and familiar with many of the services that CCT operated across the city. From the late 1960s my local routes were the 21 from Pantmawr and 22 and 25 from Rhiwbina into the city centre, terminating in Greyfriars Road. My grandmother lived in Broad Street, very conveniently close to the bus garage at Sloper Road and we would travel to visit her on the 37, or when it failed to turn up, the 16 would suffice, hopping off at Kitchener Road.

And so Cardiff became my adopted bus fleet which provided fascination for many decades to follow, as new vehicles arrived and old familiar buses departed. Cardiff as a city has grown in size with many parts changing beyond all recognition. Cardiff's municipal bus fleet has moved with the times to address the changes in the city, and continues to do so. There have been several changes of livery and vehicle policy over the years. It has gone from being a predominantly double-deck operation from the 1930s to one of largely single-deckers by the mid-1990s. Deregulation in October 1986 saw the fleet become an arms-length company, in which Cardiff Council still retained ownership. In 2016 the fleet still serves the city, and the Cardiff Bus brand has become a well-known household name. It operates a modern fleet of low-floor vehicles on a comprehensive network serving Cardiff, Penarth and Barry. Faced with ever increasing congestion on the roads of the city, the introduction of bus lanes and bus priority measures in recent years have kept the wheels of Cardiff's buses turning. As well as being a major shopping centre for the south-east Wales region which reaches its peak during the Christmas period, the City of Cardiff is regularly host to major sporting and cultural events. Many of the city centre roads are closed off, and Cardiff Bus plays its part in moving large numbers of people often under difficult conditions.

With no prospect of a book about Cardiff's buses on the horizon, in 2014 I decided that I should undertake the project myself. Having been a member of the Cardiff Transport Preservation Group since 2002, and having penned numerous articles on Cardiff's post-war buses for inclusion in their newsletter, I felt that I was in a good position to proceed. This book takes a chronological look at the types of vehicles operated by Cardiff's municipal fleet and its successor up to the present day and in particular the motor buses and trolleybuses. In order to do this we need to consider briefly how the history of local public transport services in Cardiff evolved, and how the municipal undertaking came into being. I have chosen to only give an outline history of the trams operated by Cardiff, as these have previously been covered in detail in other publications. The trolleybuses played an important part in the development of the municipal bus service network in Cardiff. They were introduced to replace the last of the trams, many years after the first motor buses entered service, and were themselves replaced by motor buses after just 27 years of operation.

For those readers who are unsure about the construction of a bus, this should help. The chassis of a vehicle as referred to in this book consists of an underframe complete with all running units such as engine, gearbox, wheels etc. Well known chassis builders include AEC, Guy and Leyland, with AEC and Leyland also building their own engines. The body of a bus would usually, but not always, be built by another company of the customer's choice and at a different site. They would build a frame on the chassis, add panels and then complete the body by adding windows, seats, lighting etc. Since WWII, bus construction has also included integral and semi-integral vehicles. These vehicles do not feature a separate chassis as such, as the body is constructed to incorporate the engine, suspension and other runnng units. They are usually built by one manufacturer at one location, and a good example of an integral bus is the Leyland National.

ACKNOWLEDGEMENTS

Without the help of many friends and acquaintances this work would never have been completed to a standard that I would be happy with. A very large thank you must go to John Jones, Mike Taylor and Peter Smith for their endless support and enthusiasm for the project and for their efforts in proof reading the draft. John has made available his archive files in addition to his photograph and slide collection; and has also taken much time to proof read the text. Mike has made available many images from the Cardiff Transport Preservation Group (CTPG) archive, as well as letting me borrow and indulge in the extensive archive of his late father Chris. My late friend Dave Thomas was very supportive when I announced this project in early 2015, and subsequently donated his archive of Cardiff material to the project. Sadly with his untimely passing, he will not get to see the finished result. I am most grateful to Mac Winfield, Glyn Bowen, Gareth Stevens, Simon Nicholas, John Woodward, Mike Street, Malcolm Keeley and Paul Hamley who have all taken time and trouble to respond to my numerous enquiries and questions. In addition I would like to thank those who have let me use their photographic material including The Omnibus Society, Cliff Essex, David Donati, Paul Dudley, Richard Field and of course my father John Wiltshire. David Harman of the Transport Ticket Society has also provided some useful information on the early ticket systems used, while Pete Brabham has digitally renovated a few of the early images.

Bernard McCall has once again given his enthusiastic support and backing for this latest project, while my wife Tracey continues to encourage me as I research and compile yet another volume.

Andrew Wiltshire, Cardiff, August 2016.

FOREWORD

When I was asked by Andrew to write the foreword for his latest book it was with ease and great pleasure that I said yes. From beginning to present day, and all that has happened in between, it makes for a fascinating and enjoyable read that will leave you thoroughly versed in the company's rich and fascinating history.

My interest in the company's operations began in the late 1980s in my early teens and, some may say, dreams became a reality when I became employed by Cardiff City Transport Services in 2000 soon after moving into the then Traffic Planning Department. These times from interest to my employment with the company are fantastically covered from Chapter 7 onwards. This time also saw the company's centenary celebrations in 2002.

I am sure there will be many people reading this book who can recall the history of the company before this time, and may even think the de-regulation era and the 'Orange' years were not as good as the years that went before. I hope you agree this shows the richness of the company's history and the vital part it has played in the evolution of our city. This era saw exciting times, for example, the expansion of operations much beyond traditional boundaries into Caerphilly and the Vale of Glamorgan on a large scale. With that grew my interest in how things were brought together. The vehicles were always interesting, especially at this time, but the network and how it all worked was much more fascinating to me.

I hope you enjoy the book and the excellent photographs, fleet and route history as well general insight that finely tell the story of Cardiff's buses. If you are out and about in our city there is no better way to see it, than from a Cardiff Bus.

Gareth Stevens

Cardiff Bus

CONTENTS

Chapter one
A TRANSPORT SYSTEM FOR CARDIFF — 6

Chapter two
OIL ENGINES AND THE SECOND WORLD WAR — 32

Chapter three
THE AUSTERITY YEARS AND THE END OF THE TRAMS — 49

Chapter four
FURTHER FLEET RENEWAL AND NEW-LOOK FRONTS — 63

Chapter five
TROLLYBUS REPLACEMENT, REAR ENGINES AND ONE-MAN OPERATION — 79

Chapter six
THE COLOURFUL SEVENTIES: DIVERSITY AND VEHICLE SHORTAGES — 103

Chapter seven
COMPETITION, DEREGULATION AND SMALL BUSES — 126

Chapter eight
THE RETURN OF THE BIG BUS — 140

Chapter nine
EASY ACCESS BUSES, STANDARDISATION AND ANOTHER NEW IMAGE — 155

Chapter ten
EVEN BIGGER BUSES AND STRONGER BRANDING — 174

Chapter eleven
SOME OTHER ASPECTS OF THE UNDERTAKING — 188

Chapter twelve
PRESERVATION — 207

Appendix 1
CARDIFF'S OVERALL ADVERT BUSES AND SPECIAL LIVERIES SINCE 1970 — 217

Appendix 2
LIST OF ALL BUSES OWNED — 222

Appendix 3
FORMER BUSES IN THE SERVICE VEHICLE FLEET — 232

Appendix 4
DEMONSTRATORS INSPECTED AND/OR EVALUATED IN SERVICE OR PURCHASED — 236

BIBLIOGRAPHY — 240

CHAPTER ONE

A TRANSPORT SYSTEM FOR CARDIFF

The early days

A settlement close to the mouth of the River Taff is believed to have been established in Roman times, and these lands were later occupied by Saxons, Vikings and later still Norman conquerors. By the beginning of the seventeenth century, the area which we now recognise as the centre of Cardiff had developed, with areas such as Working Street and St. Mary Street being identifiable on maps of that period. By the end of the eighteenth century the South Wales coalfield was being developed along with the iron industry at Merthyr Tydfil, and that brought the 25-mile long Glamorganshire Canal to Cardiff in 1798, and with it came prosperity. Cardiff grew rapidly in size during the nineteenth century from a population of 1,870 in 1801 to over 129,000 by 1899. The Marquis of Bute provided the finance for the first dock at Cardiff which opened in 1839, and two years later on 12 April 1841, the Taff Vale Railway began running from Merthyr Tydfil into Cardiff. By the late 1860s the port had expanded further due to the vast tonnages of coal being exported through Cardiff, and now there was a need for local public transport.

Horse-buses were known to be running on the streets of Cardiff as early as 1845 and there were a number of proprietors until 1863. At this point the Town Council drew up bye-laws and in 1865 initially granted licences to just three operators. By 1871 there were three proprietors running to Penarth and by June 1873 Solomon Andrews held five out of 15 licences that were granted by the Cardiff Town Council. Solomon Andrews was a baker and confectioner by trade having arrived in Cardiff in 1851. An entrepreneur, he was soon engaged in hansom cab operation as well as becoming a coach-builder.

In 1871 a horse tramway was constructed by the Cardiff Tramways Company Ltd from the Docks (Pier Head) to High Street. This was opened on 12 July 1872 and the cars were painted green. This was later extended in 1879, eventually serving Castle Road, Roath (now City Road) from 24 April. The Canton section opened from 1 August with red liveried cars followed by Cathays with yellow cars and finally Grangetown was served by brown cars. The track was to standard gauge (4ft 8½in) and consisted of 6¼ route miles. By 1873 a dozen trams were in use while this had risen to 16 by 1881. A second horse tramway company, the Cardiff District and Penarth Harbour Tramways Company Ltd. commenced on 28 November 1881, and operated a line just under 2½ miles long, from Clifton Street, Roath via Adamsdown (Moira Place), Bute Terrace, Penarth Road through to Clive Street, Grangetown. For this operation Solomon Andrews provided the horses, drivers and 11 tramcars.

This was a typical horse-bus operated by Solomon Andrews and marketed as Andrews' Improved Omnibus. Note the primitive ladder access to the top deck seating and the use of two horses.
(The late Chris Taylor collection)

An advertisement stated that from 1 September 1878, Solomon Andrews was running horse-bus services between:

St. Mary Street and Penarth

St. Mary Street and Roath (Elm Street)

High Street and Llandaff

High Street and Canton (Severn Road)

A later advertisement went on to state that from 2 December 1878, Solomon Andrews would be running a horse-bus service between: Castle Road in Roath and James Street at Cardiff Docks. Andrews would be using red horse-buses and charging a fare of 2d. By August 1882 he was running 26 horse-buses. Meanwhile, the extension to the Cardiff Tramways Company Ltd horse tram service from the Docks (Pier Head), mentioned above, was opened on 24 April 1879 to compete with Solomon Andrews. This was followed by the Canton extension on 1 August 1879.

Solomon Andrews continued to run a fleet of horse-buses on the streets of Cardiff until 1888 when his operations passed to the Cardiff Tramways Company Ltd, with the exception of the Whitchurch, Llandaff and Penarth routes. The last traces of Andrews in the Cardiff area were the horse-bus services to Penarth and Dinas Powis which came to an end in December 1905.

Enter Cardiff Corporation and the electric tramcar

During the 1890s, the quality of the public transport service being offered on the streets of Cardiff was poor and was regularly disrupted by strikes and disputes. As a result in July 1898 Cardiff Town Council (Cardiff Corporation) obtained an Act of Parliament which gave them the necessary powers to purchase the two tramway companies previously mentioned, to upgrade and electrify the network and to undertake the operation of trams thereon. In order to do this £190,000 was made available to relay track, construct a power station and a depot for the tramcars. Initial thoughts pointed towards a conduit system laid into the road for the collection of current, but after studying a number of other tramway systems, an overhead trolley wire was selected as being the most suitable for Cardiff.

By June 1900 the first route was under construction and the first section of the re-constructed tramway opened a year later in June 1901 using horse-trams. On 1 January 1902, the Corporation took over the Cardiff Tramways Company (now part of Provincial Tramways) for the sum of £65,644. The deal included 52 tramcars, 342 horses and all routes that lay within the town boundary, with the exception of a horse-bus service to Whitchurch. And so the municipal fleet was founded though, at this stage, the Cardiff District and Penarth Harbour Company line remained in private hands.

The reconstruction of lines and the erection of overhead wires continued, while a 3000kw power station was built on a site at Roath with a large 94-car tram depot erected adjacent to it. The new trams were delivered, partly assembled, by rail to Roath Sidings. On 25 March 1902 the first electric tramcar took to the streets of Cardiff, being driven from the power station at Roath to St. John's Square by the general manager Arthur Ellis. On 22 April the ten track miles (six route miles) was inspected and approved by Board of Trade officials in the presence of Corporation Officers, and a Certificate of Authorisation was issued six days later. The system was officially opened on 1 May 1902 when 12 new tramcars were gathered outside the Town Hall in St. Mary Street. The Mayor (F.J. Beavan) then drove car number 1 and its party to Canton and then Cathedral Road, and declared these routes open. Later the chairman of the Tramways Committee (Councillor Andrew) drove the tram out to Newport Road and Castle Road (now City Road) whereupon these routes were also declared open. By 13 June 54 tramcars were available for service.

The new tram depot on Newport Road, Roath was partially opened on 18 September 1902, while a smaller shed was opened in Clare Road, Grangetown at about this time. The horse tram depot in Lucas Street was closed in 1902.

ROUTES OPERATED DURING THE FIRST MONTH OF THE NEW ELECTRIC TRAMWAY		
Date	Route	Requirement
2 May 1902	City to Docks via Wood Street	12 cars
3 May 1902	Broadway to Monument	6 cars
	Penylan Road to Monument	9 cars
13 May 1902	Clive Road to Wood Street via Neville Street	5 cars
	Roath Park (Fairoak Road) to Monument	3 cars
25 May 1902	Roath Park (Fairoak Road) to Canton (Sundays)	12 cars
30 May 1902	Cathedral Road to Clarence Road (direct)	4 cars

The tramway offices were situated in the town centre at The Hayes. The very last horse-trams ran on 17 October 1902, and by the end of the year the Corporation had opened more new lines. On 10 February 1903 following a period of difficult negotiations, the Cardiff District and Penarth Harbour Company was taken over in a deal worth £12,000. This operation had since 1888 been in the ownership of Provincial Tramways after sale by Solomon Andrews. On 11 February a start was made on upgrading the Adamsdown to Grangetown line which would require single-deck trams. Initially trams began running between Bute Terrace and Splott on 20 May 1903 and the line was in full operation by 9 February 1904. At first, a number of double-deck trams cut down to single-deck were used pending delivery of single-deck tramcars from the batch 116 to 130. These double-deck trams were subsequently rebuilt to their original layout.

The first generation of trams consisted of 130 cars plus a service car. Details are given below.

Fleet no.	Builder	Running units	Body	Seating	Year introduced
1-20	Dick, Kerr	Brill 21E 4-wheel DK	Dick, Kerr Open-top	30/22	1902
21-40	"	Brill 22E bogie DK	" "	38/30	"
41-54	"	" DK	Dick, Kerr Saloon	34	"
55-74	"	Brill 21E 4-wheel DK	Dick, Kerr Open-top	30/22	"
75-94	"	Brill 22E bogie DK	" "	38/30	"
95-114	Brush	Brill 21E 4-wheel B.T.H.	" "	30/22	1904
115	G.F. Milnes	Brill 22E bogie B.T.H.	G.F. Milnes Saloon	36	1903
116-30	"	Brush bogie B.W.E.	" "	40	1904/05
131	Brush	Brill 21E 4-wheel	Brush Rail-cleaner	n/a	1905

DK = Dick, Kerr electrical equipment   B.T.H. = British Thomson-Houston electrical equipment
B.W.E. = British Westinghouse Electric Co. electrical equipment

In 1927 cars 3, 7, 19 and 98 were renumbered 138 to 141, and after a brief spell on a City Road shuttle service they became maintenance cars. They were joined by tramcars 15 (converted to a snow plough) and 61, all five gaining grey livery by the late 1930s and surviving until 1943. The rail-cleaning car was originally ordered from Dick, Kerr who in the event supplied the electrical equipment to Brush. It originally had a 1000 gallon water tank and was converted to a rail-grinder in 1920. In 1947 it received the electrical equipment from bogie-tram number 29. Many of the above cars were subsequently rebuilt to varying degrees over their life span.

In immaculate condition externally, Dick, Kerr bogie car number 90 stands on Newport Road outside the Roath depot in 1938. It has been rebuilt with an extended canopy and has gained windscreens, but is now somewhat dated with a totally exposed upper deck. *(The late Dave B. Thomas collection)*

A number of extensions to the new electrified network occurred between February 1904 and September 1906, but thereafter there would be no further expansion until 1928, although the tram fleet was upgraded. 28 October 1905 was notable as it was the day on which Cardiff became a city. This was granted by King Edward VII in honour of Cardiff's large contribution to the industrial and commercial status in the British Empire. After just three years of operation there were 19 different services, but this was simplified to just eight regular services in 1906, with additional peak-time specials. The routes were numbered for the first time from 1913, and these numbers were subsequently displayed on the tramcars.

125 is one of the first generation single-deck trams dating from 1905, and is seen at Clare Road depot.
(The late Chris Taylor collection)

ROUTE NO	ROUTE DESCRIPTION	TRAM TYPE
1	Whitchurch Road to St. Mary Street via Salisbury Road	Single-deck
2	Newport Road to Pier Head	Double-deck
3	Penylan Road to Pier Head	"
4	Roath Park to St. Mary Street	"
5	Victoria Park to Pier Head via High Street	"
6	Cathedral Road to Clarence Road via High Street	"
7	Carlisle Street, Splott to Grangetown via Bute Terrace	Single-deck
8	The Hayes to Splott via Glossop Road	Double-deck
9	Roath Park to Canton via High Street (Sundays only)	"

By 1910 a considerable amount of wear had taken place on the tracks, and therefore track renewal was urgently required. A parcels delivery service commenced on 11 August 1911 and proved very successful, and continued until 1942. The advent of the First World War resulted in only 80 tramcars being available for use, and during the war tram 101 was broken up for spares. With the war over, passenger traffic on the trams began to pick up and enough staff were available by 1920 to operate 100 trams out of the 130 owned. Eventually a large scale renewal of tram track took place between 1914 and 1923, and covered much of the network.

All-weather trams

The experience of having to ride on the exposed top deck of a tramcar in wet and wintry conditions must have been quite unpleasant for the travelling public. The undertaking was now looking to introduce a more modern totally-enclosed double-deck car, officially described as a "top-covered vestibule car". However in order to operate in Cardiff, with its numerous low bridges, it had to be built to a maximum headroom of 15ft. The Brush Company had a design that was based on a well-type underframe and used Peckham Pendulum P22 4-wheel trucks supplied by the Peckham Truck and Engineering Co. Ltd. These incorporated four smaller 26in diameter wheels as opposed to the more usual 32in., which were driven by small B.T.H. GE265 40hp motors. The trams had B.T.H. 510A controllers and featured electro-magnetic brakes. The second generation of tramcars consisted of 81 special low-height cars and 31 single-deck cars. Cardiff ordered the first double-deck car from Brush for 1923, who also supplied the bodywork, with the completed vehicle entering service in December 1923 at a cost of £1735. It had an overall height of 14ft 10in and an unladen weight of 10 tons.

FLEET NO.	BUILDER	RUNNING UNITS	BODY	SEATING	YEAR
101	Brush	Peckham 4-w truck	Brush closed-top	40/24	1923

The Transport Committee was impressed by this modern tramcar and as such, a further 25 similar examples were ordered from Brush for delivery in 1923/24. These took random fleet numbers vacated by earlier withdrawn tramcars: 2, 9, 20, 56, 57, 62, 66, 70, 95 to 97, 100 and 102 to 114.

These were then followed by a further 55 similar tramcars, again from Brush, that were delivered between February and October 1925 and continued the theme of taking random fleet numbers as follows:

1, 3, 4, 7, 8, 11, 14, 16 to 19, 21, 25 to 28, 31, 33, 35 to 40, 55, 58 to 60, 63 to 65, 67 to 69, 71, 73 to 75, 77 to 83, 85 to 89, 91 to 94 and 98.

In 1925 a design for a single-deck tramcar body was drawn up by Brush, based on Peckham P25 bogies and powered by B.T.H. electrical equipment including 506A controllers. After submission to the Transport Committee it was decided to place an order for a single tram.

Brush-built 101 was the first of the new "top-covered vestibule" tramcars. These fully-enclosed tramcars brought a new level of comfort for Cardiff's travelling public.

(The late Chris Taylor collection)

Brush/Peckham closed-top car number 2 is noted on Whitchurch Road in 1939, with the Allensbank Road junction on the right of the photograph. The Heath Hotel still stands today, now named simply The Heath, and has been a Brains pub since 1899. The tram lines and overhead have gone and the road is a lot busier, but location is otherwise instantly recognisable in 2016.

(John Jones collection)

FLEET NO.	BUILDER	RUNNING UNITS	BODY	SEATING	YEAR
53	Brush	Peckham 4-w truck	Brush saloon	44	1926

A further 30 similar tramcars followed between December 1926 and May 1927 at a cost of £73,650. They took fleet numbers as follows: 41, 44, 46, 47, 49 to 52, 54, 116 to 124, and 126 to 137.

These trams were for use on service 1 Monument via Windsor Place to Whitchurch Road, Cathays via Salisbury Road) and service 7 (Clive Street, Grangetown to Portmanmoor Road, Splott). The Salisbury Road tram route ended on 4 January 1930, and was replaced by a new service 39 (St. Mary Street to St. Athans Road, Gabalfa) using new Dennis double-deck motor buses. Lucas Street horse tram depot which closed in 1902 was re-opened in 1929 to accommodate these buses. As a result many of these modern single-deck trams became surplus and were offered for sale. The Grangetown to Splott route ended six years later which meant that all 31 were now surplus to requirements by October 1936. They were stored until 1940, when they were sold to a dealer, who it is believed exported, around 18 of these very serviceable trams to the State of Para at Belem in Brazil. There they lasted until about 1947.

Of the 130 trams introduced between 1902 and 1905, somewhere in the region of 104 were withdrawn between 1923 and 1929, having been replaced by the new generation of tramcars. Most were scrapped. In October 1926, six new tramway extensions were proposed, and eventually four of these were accepted which included a route to Grand Avenue, Ely. Two of these extensions were opened in August 1928. These were the extension to Llandaff Fields and from Whitchurch Road to Gabalfa, but the Ely route was never started. Under the leadership of General Manager William Forbes, the future expansion of municipal services within Cardiff was left to the motor bus.

Early thoughts on trolleybuses

As early as 1913 the Cardiff undertaking expressed an interest in trolleybus operation. A contingent of transport officers visited the newly-opened systems at Leeds and Bradford that year and reported favourably on their experience. They believed such vehicles would be useful in areas where the cost of new tram tracks could not be justified, and mentioned Whitchurch, Llanishen and Ely in their report. After giving the proposal careful consideration the ideas were laid to rest until a much later date.

The early motor bus operations in Cardiff

The first motor buses to grace the streets of Cardiff were six Dennis 40hp double-deckers introduced by the Cardiff Tramways Company Ltd in January 1907 on a service to Whitchurch. The City council was initially against the idea but eventually relented. By March 1909 three other operators (E. Gillard, F. Green and W. Thomas) had been granted licences to operate this route, but it is thought that none ever took up running the service. However until June 1910, motor buses were not permitted to enter the city on the Llandaff route and had to terminate at Cathedral Road. Following complaints from the Rural District Council about the Cardiff Tramways Company Ltd, the Llandaff route was licensed to Barton Brothers of Beeston, Nottinghamshire, from November 1910. Barton did not take up this operation though, and after the Cardiff Tramways Company Ltd left the Llandaff route in about May 1911, its operation passed to F. Meyer of Merthyr Tydfil who remained until November that year. From January 1913 and for approximately two years, Captain Beattie ran the Llandaff service with two motor buses, as an independent venture, even though he was on the staff of the Cardiff Tramways Company.

The Corporation's petrol-electrics

Dennis Bros Ltd was based in Guildford, and the business was founded in 1895 by John Dennis, a cycle maker. In 1898 they completed their first motorised tricycle powered by a single-cylinder De-Dion engine, followed in 1901 by a car which was promoted as a 3hp quadricycle. Two years later in 1903 they developed the worm-drive rear axle which replaced the conventional chain-drive system. The first commercial vehicle was built in 1904 and by 1907 a 40hp bus had appeared. In 1906 Maidstone-based W.A. Stevens had pioneered the petrol-electric method of propulsion which then appeared in the Tilling-Stevens range of buses. In 1916 Stevens Petrol-Electric

Vehicles Ltd entered into an arrangement with Dennis Bros. Ltd to launch a range of buses and lorries which were constructed in the Dennis works at Guildford. The engine drove a dynamo which fed current to an electric motor positioned at the forward end of the drive shaft.

Powers to run petrol-electric buses within the city boundaries were sought by Cardiff Corporation in April 1920, and these would be deployed on lightly-used routes as well as providing feeder services to the tram network. Having been granted permission to operate motor buses in October, Cardiff Corporation's first six examples, entered service on 24 December, and were put to work on a service from St. John Square to Monthermer Road, in Cathays - a suburb of the city. Cardiff's petrol-electric buses were numbered 48 to 53 (BO 3638-43). They were Dennis-Stevens 40hp A-type 4-ton saloons that were fitted with 28-seat Dodson CD19 bodies. The bodies featured rear entrances, illuminated destination boxes and clerestory roofs; with top-side vents giving ample ventilation and greater headroom. With a quoted price of £1550 each, they had White & Poppe 4-cylinder engines and featured a B.T.H. magneto and a Zenith carburettor. Delivered with Dunlop solid tyres as shown in the photograph below, all but number 50 had been fitted with pneumatic tyres by March 1926. 50 (BO 3640) was withdrawn in 1925 and the following year its body was transferred to a new Dennis 4-ton chassis, and emerged as 50 (UH 80). It ran as such until 1932. The bodies of the remaining five had been overhauled during 1926 and continued in service until withdrawal in 1929. 48 and 49 went on to become tower wagons in the ancillary fleet.

This was Cardiff Corporation's first motor bus 48 (BO 3638), a Dennis-Stevens petrol-electric dating from 1920. The Dodson body seats 28 passengers and we get a clear representation of the distinctive clerestory-type roof. With its solid tyres it is difficult to imagine anything other than an uncomfortable ride.

(The late Chris Taylor collection)

Three further motor bus routes commenced in 1922; running from St. Mary Street to Moorland Road, Splott, and St. Mary Street to Monthermer Road while another ran from the Taff Vale Railway Station to Cyncoed. In June 1922 the Cardiff Tramways Company's sole remaining motor bus-operated route to Whitchurch, and Andrews Road depot in Llandaff North were acquired by Cardiff City Council for £6000. Latterly Cardiff Tramway's bus fleet, which was not acquired by the Council, had included a trio of AEC YC double-deckers.

Meanwhile, six further Dennis-Stevens petrol-electric chassis were ordered by Cardiff Corporation, and entered service on 1 October 1922 on the newly-acquired Whitchurch route. They had Dodson CD22 type 52-seat open-top double-deck bodies with 28 seats on the top deck, 22 in the lower saloon and two beside the driver. They had open rear staircases, were 7ft 2in wide and were the only Dennis Stevens petrol-electrics completed as double-deckers. The batch was numbered 61 to 66 (BO 5221-6) and they were powered by White & Poppe petrol engines. The chassis cost £1175 each with the bodies being £462 11s with an additional £90 for lighting. These buses did not receive pneumatic tyres but the bodies were overhauled in the period 1924/25. All six were up for sale by November 1929, and 65 later went on to become an ancillary vehicle.

A driver and conductor pose with Cardiff 62 (BO 5222) which was a double-deck variant of the Dennis-Stevens petrol-electric. It was a fairly basic bus fitted with a Dodson 52-seat body.

(Roy Marshall collection courtesy of The Omnibus Society)

Christopher Dodson Limited was a passenger body specialist that traded from a base in Willesden in north-west London, and completed numerous bus bodies up until the early 1930s. The Dennis-Stevens petrol-electric was not a popular choice as a bus, and only one other municipal operator, Walsall Corporation, purchased them. Dennis-Stevens was more successful as a lorry manufacturer.

Early one-man buses

In 1923 two one-man operated services commenced, from Cathedral Road (Tram Terminus) to Llandaff North, and another from Canton to Ely. At a later date they were revised to run from Westgate Street to Llandaff North and Westgate Street to Culverhouse Cross, Ely. In October 1923 a batch of five Dennis 30hp 2½-ton buses were purchased primarily to compete with the Worrel operation on the Llandaff North, St. Fagans, Ely and Llanishen routes. These small buses were numbered 76 to 80 (BO 5862-6) and were fitted with Dodson CD 20-seat bodies with clerestory roofs and driver-operated folding doors. The chassis which cost £590 each featured 4-speed gearboxes while the bodies were quoted at £300 each. They received bad publicity as their bodies were not from local coach-builders, something that would be taken into consideration with future orders.

A Transport System for Cardiff

13 (BO 5862) was an early one-man operated bus intended for use in the less densely populated suburbs of Cardiff such as Llandaff North and Ely.

(Roy Marshall collection courtesy of The Omnibus Society)

They were all converted to pneumatic tyres by March 1926. All six had been withdrawn during March 1932 and passed to Leyland Motors that year in part-exchange for new buses.

THE NEWPORT SERVICE

On 15 April 1924 the business of G.Vernon Jones of Castleton was acquired together with the Cardiff to Newport service. An offer of £2500 was accepted in a deal which included the goodwill, four vehicles but not the garage premises. Jones had commenced on this route in January 1920 from a base at The Garage, Castleton. The acquired vehicles included a 20-seat Thornycroft (which may not have been operated) and three W. & G. du Cros buses new in 1922, AX 2083, AX 2931 and AX 5716. The W. & G. vehicles were one-man operated and later up-seated from 20 to 25 and finally withdrawn by 1926. Initially the route started from Broadway, Roath at the Cardiff end running to a terminus near the Cardiff Road/Commercial Road junction in Newport. From 11 August 1924 the Cardiff terminus moved to the Monument in St. Mary Street.

DENNIS 4-TON DOUBLE-DECKERS

In 1924 a further 12 Dennis motor buses were obtained. These were 4-ton 40hp models which were also very popular in a number of London fleets. The first six buses were obtained via James Howell and Co. Ltd in February 1924 and given fleet numbers 1 to 6 with registrations BO 6741-6. The chassis had cost £765 each and the body contract was awarded as follows: Dodson (4 at £511-4s each), W. Lewis (1 at £513-15s) and J. Norman (1 at £495), but the individual identities are not known. W. Lewis and John Norman were local coachbuilders in Cardiff. Lewis had premises in Tudor Lane, Grangetown, while Norman was located on Market Street in the Canton area. The two local firms were chosen following criticism from the local press. All six buses were open-top 52-seaters with an open rear staircase, and pneumatic tyres were subsequently fitted from November 1928. The bodies of 1 to 3 were overhauled around March 1926 while 4 to 6 were dealt with by March 1928. Upon withdrawal in 1934 they passed to AEC in part-exchange for new buses. The second batch of six was new in July/August 1924 and entered service as 7 to 11, 17 with registrations BO 7921-6 respectively. The chassis were slightly cheaper at £762 while the body contracts went to four coach-builders as follows: Buckingham (3 at £450 each), Dodson (1 at £531-8s-2d), W. Lewis (1 at £535) and J. Norman (1 at £525).

Both Dodson and Norman offered delivery within eight weeks while Lewis quoted nine weeks. They were to the same layout as the first six, and were extra vehicles intended for the Whitchurch route. Pneumatic tyres were subsequently fitted from November 1928, and all were withdrawn in 1934.

By May 1924 routes to St. Fagans and Capel Llanillterne had commenced, while the Radyr and Morganstown suburbs were being served by December, all in competition with Worrel. Three saloons were also added to the motor bus fleet, entering service on 10 October 1924. These were 25-seat Dennis 2½-ton 30hp models and the first vehicles in the fleet to be fitted from new with pneumatic tyres. They were numbered 113 to 115 (BO 8249-51) with two having W. Lewis bodies costing £375 each while the third was completed by J. Norman for £365, but the exact identities are not known. A fourth similar bus was given fleet number 16 (BO 8402) and entered service in December. This had a Dennis body and the complete vehicle was supplied at an agreed price of £1000. All had been converted for one-man operation by 31 March 1928 and could regularly be found working the Westgate Street to St. Fagans service. Upon withdrawal in 1932, all four passed to Leyland Motors in part exchange for new buses.

One of the Dennis 4-ton buses 11 (BO 7925) is seen at Gabalfa crossroads while working to Rhiwbina. Note the prominent advertising and the pneumatic tyres, which dates this view as post 1928.

(Roy Marshall collection courtesy of The Omnibus Society)

Northern Counties bodies

In 1925 a further six double-deckers were purchased and once again the Dennis 4-ton 40hp chassis was favoured. This was now described by Dennis as a London-type chassis, fitted with solid tyres. The first five were delivered in May as 67 to 70, 81 (BO 8746-50) and were 52-seat open-top buses with open rear staircases. They featured the first bodies supplied to Cardiff by Northern Counties Motor and Engineering Company Limited (NCME) which were obtained for £460 each. NCME had been founded in 1919 by South Wales industrialist Henry Gethin Lewis. The company was based in Wigan, Lancashire, and by 1929 its registered office had changed to Mount Stuart Square in Cardiff where it remained for many years, though the coach-building works was always in Wigan. Numbers 67 to 70 and 81 were subsequently fitted with pneumatic tyres in 1929, and when 67 was withdrawn in 1932, it became a lorry. The remainder lasted until 1934 whereupon they passed to AEC in part-exchange. The sixth Dennis 4-ton was 152 (BO 8751) which was bodied by Dodson with seating for 52, an open staircase and a covered-in driver's cab. It entered service on 24 October 1925 confined to the Whitchurch route, and was the first covered-top double-deck motor bus in the fleet. It had received pneumatic tyres by 1930.

69 (BO 8749) was a Dennis 4-ton and featured one of the first Northern Counties bodies supplied to Cardiff.
(Roy Marshall collection courtesy of The Omnibus Society)

Six saloons also joined the fleet in May 1925. They were Dennis 30hp 2½ ton models with a 15ft wheel base, which Dennis also described as their New Model. These had Northern Counties 30-seat rear-entrance bodies which cost £375 each. Numbered 117 to 122 (BO 8752-7), all had Michelin pneumatic tyres fitted from new, and were deployed mainly on the Cardiff to Penarth route. They later became 26-seaters and all were withdrawn in 1932 passing to Leyland in part-exchange for new buses.

117 (BO 8752) was a Dennis 30hp saloon with Northern Counties body for use on the Penarth route.
(The late Chris Taylor collection)

One-man operation was introduced on the service to Radyr and Morganstown on 23 January 1925 while a new route to Penarth commenced in the May. Two further routes in direct competition with Worrel were to Lisvane commencing in August, and to Rhiwbina via Llanishen in the following November. Meanwhile all-out competition with J.A. Rich within the City boundary led to practices such as racing and blocking-in at bus stops. Ultimately Rich invested in some superior vehicles, Palladiums with Dorman engines which he hoped would out-perform the City Council's buses.

Another covered top

A further nine Dennis chassis were acquired in 1926, comprising a pair of 4-ton models and seven 2½-ton models; delivery of the latter was required within seven weeks of the order being placed. One of the 4-ton models received the 28-seat Dodson body from Dennis-Stevens petrol-electric 50 (BO 3640) of 1920. It entered service in February 1926 with the same fleet number, but carrying new registration UH 80. The second example was 150 (UH 81) which received a new 52-seat Dodson covered-top double-deck body with open staircase, the cost of the complete bus being £1471-10s-4d. It also entered service in February, and as with 152 (of 1925), 150 was normally confined to the Whitchurch route. Both 50 and 150 had their steering altered at some stage to improve the steering lock and had received pneumatic tyres by March 1930. They were withdrawn in July 1932 and 1934 respectively, the chassis of 50 (UH 80) went on to receive a lorry body.

In this view we see 150 (UH 81) waiting at the Whitchurch Library terminus of the Whitchurch service. It is a Dennis 4-ton 52-seat double-decker to covered-top configuration. Most seats in the Dodson body were forward-facing, and there were anti-splash brushes fitted over the wheels.

(Peter Smith collection)

The seven Dennis 2½ ton chassis received 28-seat saloon bodies by Dodson, and entered service in July 1926 as 155 to 161 (UH 1351-7). They featured Dunlop pneumatic tyres and the final cost after extras, for the seven buses, was in the region of £8008. The position of the entrance is not known, but the buses had been re-seated to 26 by March 1933. They could often be found on the Morganstown and Radyr route as well as the Cardiff to Newport service. They were withdrawn between March and September 1935 and passed to AEC of Southall in part-exchange for new AEC Regents 11 to 20 (KG 5003-12).

Further take-overs

In November 1926 five vehicles were acquired for £1150 from George Worrel who was based at 10 City Road, together with the route from Cardiff to St. Fagans and Capel Llanilltern. He had been operating to Llandaff and later to St. Fagans from May 1921.

REGISTRATION	CHASSIS TYPE	BODY	SEATING	YEAR NEW
BO 1844	Trafford	?	?	1917
BO 4282	Leyland	?	?	1921

Plus three other vehicles, the identities of which are unknown.

In November 1926 five vehicles were acquired for £1250 from John Worrel whose address was 66 Cowbridge Road, Canton. With this came the routes from Cardiff to Rhiwbina (via Beulah Road), Llanishen and Lisvane. These had originally been introduced by Sydney Worrel in November 1914, passing to John Worrel in 1919.

REGISTRATION	CHASSIS TYPE	BODY	SEATING	YEAR NEW
NR 1145	Daimler CB	(Charabanc)	26	1922
AU 8316	Daimler Y	?	24	1923
BO 8199	AEC 2-ton	?	?	1924
BO 8552	"	?	?	1925
UH 1563	Morris	?	?	1926

All these former Worrel vehicles were withdrawn by 1927.

Former taxi operator Jack A. Rich commenced running a service to Rhiwbina in May 1920 using an old Commer. He was eventually based at the Rhiwbina Bus Garage in the Birchgrove area and traded as Rhiwbina Bus Service. In March 1921 he briefly ran a service to Whitchurch, and Cardiff Corporation then commenced running to Whitchurch in October 1922 after taking over the Cardiff Tramways Company Ltd. On 8 February 1927 six vehicles were acquired from Jack A. Rich together with the route from Cardiff (Kingsway) to Rhiwbina (Heol-y-Deri) via Caerphilly Road and Pantbach Road. This was the last of the suburban independents to be acquired and the Corporation paid £12,000 for the business and goodwill, and £7000 for the vehicles. In addition, they reluctantly agreed to take on the employees.

CARDIFF FLEET NO.	REGISTRATION	CHASSIS TYPE	BODY	SEATING	YEAR NEW
44	BO 6190	Palladium	Rich	O52RO	1922
43	BO 6921	"	"	"	1924
13	BO 7424	"	"	"	"
29	BO 8871	Commer 3P	Commer	"	1925
87	UH 1058	"	"	"	1926
89	UH 2190	"	"	"	1927

89 was ordered by Rich to replace Commer BO 9276 which was burnt out in February 1927, and it may well have been delivered new to Cardiff Corporation.

Palladium was originally a car maker based in west London, and started building commercial vehicles in 1913. They achieved some success with a Dorman-engine 3-4 ton chassis, a number of which were bodied as buses. A few Palladiums were bodied as double-deckers, but the firm closed down in 1924. The former Rich Palladiums were overhauled by Cardiff Corporation during 1928. The Commer 3P was a normal-control chassis often used for coaches. Delayed by WW1, it entered service from 1919 and was a great advance over earlier chassis, having worm rather than chain drive. Commer, by then based at Luton, were quite early into double-deckers, offering them from 1909, including some 3P types, but they were mostly saloons (buses), seating up to 29. An updated model on pneumatic tyres was introduced later in the 1920s (the 2P) but the post-war slump hit the company badly and from 1922 it was run by receivers. All six former Rich vehicles were advertised for sale by Cardiff Corporation in November 1929.

E-types

The Dennis E-type first appeared at the Commercial Motor Show in November 1925, and was the first forward-control chassis from this manufacturer, that is, the driver sat alongside the engine. The E-type featured a lower chassis frame, a rear axle with underslung worm-drive and pneumatic tyres fitted as standard. Power was from a White and Poppe-type 6.24-litre petrol engine of 70hp. Cardiff took 16 examples of the Dennis E in 1927 in two separate batches, all with 32-seat two-door bodywork and pneumatic tyres. Prior to the first ten being ordered in January, there was a plea for local coachbuilders to be involved in the construction of all ten. The chassis were obtained for £827 each and in the event Dodson was given the order for six bodies at £495 each while local builder W. Lewis gained the contract for four at £505 each. They were received as 164 to 173 (UH 2191-2200) in April 1927. It is known that Dodson built the bodies on 170 and 171, while 165 had a Lewis body, but the individual identity of the other seven is not known. In service these buses were initially plagued by braking problems. Following complaints from passengers about inferior vehicles, 164 was given a new Park Royal body in December 1930, for continued use on the Merthyr Tydfil service.

The remaining six Dennis E types were ordered in May and entered service as 174 to 179 (UH 3130-5) in July 1927. As before, it is unsure which bodies were actually built on which chassis. We do know that five of the bodies were completed by Dodson at a cost of £522-11s-6d while the sixth came from W. Lewis for £565.

170 (UH 2197) one of the 16 forward—control Dennis E- types new in 1927. We do know that this is a Dodson body, and note that it had a window bay forward of the front entrance, which the Lewis body lacked.

(Roy Marshall collection courtesy of The Omnibus Society)

165 received a Dorman 4JUR (4-cylinder 58bhp) oil engine in May 1933, which was replaced later that year by a larger Dorman 4HW 75bhp engine. 179 received a Crossley VR4 (4-cyl) oil engine in June 1933. The remaining vehicles 164, 166 to 178 were all to get AEC oil engines at a cost of £30 per vehicle. The entire batch (164 to 179) was renumbered 109 to 124 in 1935 (possibly not in order). 111 (UH 2193) was the first to be withdrawn in 1936 and was exchanged with Merthyr Tydfil Corporation 7 (HB 2244) in July that year. The remaining vehicles were taken out of service between 1937 and 1939, and most passed to AEC in part-exchange for new Regent double-deckers.

Having acquired all the independents operating in its suburbs, in May 1927 the City Council entered negotiations to purchase the businesses of Tresillian Motors, H.J. Cridland and Son and C.J. Vincent, which were all based within the city boundary. Tresillian Motors were offered £18,000 for six vehicles and Cridland £7000 for four vehicles, together with services from Cardiff to Barry Island, Pontypridd and Pentyrch. Vincent was offered £2700 for his Barry route, a Daimler bus and the goodwill that went with the business. However after a Ministry of Transport enquiry, licences were subsequently refused in the September, and the negotiations did not proceed any further.

BRISTOLS AND ALBIONS FOR 1928

In January 1928 tenders were sought for seven "low-loading" chassis and bus bodies with 35-seats.

The Bristol B was a 26-foot chassis that was announced in late 1926 and remained in production until 1934. Early on it was referred to as the Bristol Superbus. It featured a Bristol 4-cylinder 5.99-litre side-valve petrol engine coupled to a 4-speed gearbox via a single-plate clutch. It was very popular with over 100 entering service during its first year of production and eventually 778 chassis were completed. Cardiff bought four Bristol B saloons in April 1928, which would be its first Bristol chassis, and last Bristol saloons until 1976. They were numbered 180 to 183 (UH 4461/2/4/5) and had rear-entrance bodies with seating for 34 constructed by Buckingham of Birmingham, and formed an order worth £5188, for the four complete vehicles. From October 1930, two Bristol Bs replaced Dennis saloons on the Caerphilly route, while the other pair could well be found working to Merthyr Tydfil. They were eventually renumbered 125 to 128 in 1935.

185 (UH 4466) was one of three Albion PM28 saloons, the only Albion buses ever purchased by Cardiff Corporation. It had a Buckingham body and was outwardly similar to the Bristol Bs (180 to 183) which had a higher bonnet and larger radiator.

(Roy Marshall collection courtesy of The Omnibus Society)

Cardiff's Municipal Buses

The balance of the order for seven buses was also bodied by Buckingham, also entering service in April 1928. A trio of PM28 models were the only vehicles of Albion manufacture ever to be purchased by Cardiff Corporation. They too had 34-seat rear-entrance bodywork, and appeared as 184 to 186 (UH 4463/6/7) with route indicators over the front passenger window. Like the four Bristol Bs the bodies cost £525 each while the Albion PM28 chassis were £752 each. The Albion PM28 was first introduced in 1926 and featured the Albion 4-cylinder EN50D 4.54-litre petrol engine driving through an Albion 4-speed gearbox. It was of forward-control layout with a wheelbase of 16ft 3in and was intended for single-deck bodywork seating up to around 32 passengers. The Albion PM28 model had a brief reign being replaced by the PMA28, PMB28 and PR28 models in 1929. Cardiff's three PM28s were renumbered 129 to 131 in 1935. As was customary during this period, upon withdrawal, both the Bristols and the Albions passed to AEC in part-exchange, this being in 1937. Five of them went on to see some further service.

Buckingham Motor Bodies was founded in 1878 in Birmingham by John Buckingham Ltd. They completed their first new bus in 1915, and constructed a number of bodies for important customers like Birmingham City Transport. Following financial difficulties the business ceased to trade after 1934. In 1928 the Transport department's tram system reaches its peak with 142 tramcars running on 19 miles of routes, while the motor bus fleet stood at 75 buses, making it the ninth largest municipal fleet in the United Kingdom.

The Dennis HS double-deckers

The Dennis G and H series first appeared in 1927, the former being a bus version of a lorry chassis. The H was a purpose-built double-deck chassis based on the single-deck E type. The H was soon superseded by the improved 4-cylinder HS model which featured servo-assisted braking.

224 (UH 6994) was one of the 20 Dennis HS with 46-seat low-bridge bodywork by Brush. It was new in 1929 and later became fleet number 78 being withdrawn after nine years' service.

(Roy Marshall collection courtesy of The Omnibus Society)

Coach-builder Brush was based in Loughborough at the Falcon works established by Henry Hughes in 1864. Brush built their first tramcar in 1899, the first of many, and their first motor bus in 1904. In addition to railway locomotives and rolling stock, as tramcar production declined they started to build bus and trolleybus bodies.

In April 1929 Cardiff Corporation sought to obtain ten double-deckers for £1650 each. Two months later they were offered ten Dennis HS chassis at £830 each to be fitted with Brush bodies at £770 each which equated to £1600 per bus. However during July it was decided that the number of new vehicles would now include a further ten for the Salisbury Road route. With extras and a discount from Brush of £2-10s per vehicle, this resulted in an order worth £33,000. This would be the largest single order for the Dennis H/HS in the UK, and was approved despite there being initial pressure to buy local bodywork. The new buses were delivered from about October 1929 and numbered 210 to 229 (UH 6980-99). They featured 46-seat low-bridge bodywork with an enclosed staircase and two steps up to the platform. The seats were of a bucket type, arranged in a herringbone layout at 45° on the upper deck, so that passengers sat crab-fashion.

From 5 January 1930 they were regularly found working the 39 (St. Mary Street to St. Athans Road, Gabalfa) which replaced the tram route that had issues with the clearance under the Salisbury Road railway bridge. Apparently, patronage and therefore revenue on this service increased after the motor buses were introduced. With their 4-cylinder engines, they had a reputation for being slow, and were notoriously sluggish on Penylan Hill while working route 22 to Cyncoed. The Dennis HS double-deckers 210 to 229 were renumbered 64 to 83 in 1935. Eleven of them were withdrawn in 1938 and passed to AEC in part-exchange, while the remainder were taken out of service the following year. Only one example is thought to have seen further service.

Another addition this year was 179 (PK 3347), a former demonstrator that had been on hire since July 1929. It was a 48-seat Dennis H double-decker dating from September 1928 and with low-bridge Hall Lewis bodywork. Dennis and Hall Lewis had been working together to produce a lightweight bus to an overall height of around 13ft 6in and this was the result. PK 3347 was acquired from Dennis Bros, Guildford, for £200 in October 1929, and remained in the Cardiff fleet until it was withdrawn by 1936. It was claimed that this bus ran 2707 miles in 16 days, using 386 gallons of petrol at an average of 7mpg. The operating cost for this period was £64, the revenue £220 resulting in a profit of £156.

The Dennis E already featured in the Cardiff motor bus fleet and had been popular with a number of municipal fleets including Nottingham and Lincoln. Eight used examples were acquired from Lincoln Corporation in November 1929 for just £365 each. They had been new in 1926/27 and featured 32-seat rear-entrance bodies built locally by the Bracebridge Body Company of Lincoln. The allocation of fleet numbers was erratic and probably based on their entry into service, and was as follows:

241, 236, 239	FE 8518-20
238, 235, 237	FE 8625-7
234, 240	FE 8870/1

Upon arrival at Cardiff they were overhauled and painted. All eight went on to receive new 32-seat Northern Counties (NCME) bodies in April 1933. These had been built by Northern Counties for another operator and were offered to the Corporation for £280 each, fully painted and fitted. At the same time all chassis were converted to oil engine. This saw 241 (FE 8518) and 234 (FE 8870) receive AEC Ricardo 4-cylinder oil engines, while 235 to 240 received 4-cylinder Crossley VR4 oil engines at the same time. All eight were renumbered in 1935 as follows: FE 8518-20, FE 8625-7, FE 8870/1 to 101/6/3/4/7/5/8/2. During WWII numbers 101 to 105 and 108 were converted to Air Raid Precaution (A.R.P.) ambulances for the Medical Officer of Health at Cardiff.

Summary of services in 1929

TRAM SERVICES		
Route No.	Area Served	Comments
1	St. Mary Street to Gabalfa	
1A	Cathedral Road to Gabalfa	
2	Newport Road to Pier Head	
2A	Pengam and Newport Road to Victoria Park	
3	Roath Park to Pier Head	
4	Roath Park to St. Mary Street via City Road	
5	Victoria Park and St. Mary Street to Pier Head	
6	Cathedral Road to Clarence Road	
7	Roath Dock, Splott to Grangetown	
8	Roath Dock, Splott to Victoria Park	
9	Victoria Park to Roath Park	
13	Cathedral Road to Clarence Road via Lower Cathedral Road	Special journeys only
14	Victoria Park to Clarence Road via Neville Street	Special journeys only

MOTOR BUS SERVICES		
Route No.	Area Served	Comments
21	St. John Square to Monthermer Road	
22	St. John Square and Cyncoed circular route	
23	Kingsway to Whitchurch Library	
24	Kingsway, Whitchurch, Llandaff North, Cathedral Road, Westgate Street	Circular route
25	Westgate Street, Cathedral Road, Llandaff North, Whitchurch, Kingsway	Circular route
26	Victoria Park to Ely housing estate (Wilson Road and Archer Road)	
26A	Newport Road Car Terminus to Archer Road, Ely	Sundays only
28	Kingsway to Rhiwbina via Caerphilly Road to Llanishen return via Roath Park	Circular route
28	Kingsway to Llanishen via Roath Park to Rhiwbina return via Caerphilly Rd	Circular route
29	Kingsway to Capel Gwylim (Thornhill)	
30	St. Mary Street to Newport via Rumney	
31	Kingsway to Rumney village	
32	Westgate Street to St. Fagans, Peterston, Llanilterne and Creigian	
33	Westgate Street to Radyr and Morganstown via Llandaff	
35A	Lower Penarth, Penarth to St. Mary Street	
36	Kingsway to Caerphilly station via Tongwynlais and Nantgarw	
37	Kingsway to Lisvane school via Albany Road	
38	Kingsway to Rhiwbina Deri via Pantbach Road	

The Thornycroft Buses

Thornycroft began building cars at their Basingstoke factory in 1903 and production later turned to high-quality commercial vehicles including buses. They also manufactured their own petrol and diesel engines. The Thornycroft LC Forward was introduced from late 1929 and was based on the earlier forward-control BC Forward model. It featured a 4-cylinder MB engine of 6.97 litres and was available as a saloon as well as a double-decker, and a total of 160 were built. Cardiff took four Thornycroft LC models in 1930 and these are known to be amongst only 17 examples of this type actually completed as double-deckers. The chassis cost £796 each and they were fitted with 52-seat normal-height Hall Lewis bodies that it is believed were obtained second-hand and for about £500 each. These bodies were originally built in 1929 on four Leyland TD1s for Devon General, but they were identified as being too heavy, and were removed and replaced by low-height Hall Lewis bodies. The redundant bodies were offered for sale and passed to Cardiff Corporation by 1930. They were 14ft 6in high and had curious 'piano style' fronts. They entered service with Cardiff as 41 to 44 (UH 8231-4), but were soon renumbered 251 to 254. These buses suffered from poor braking, requiring continual adjustment (up to three times a day) and relining was undertaken at least once a week. All received Gardner 6LW oil engines in 1934 at a cost of £537-5s each, and supplied by Watts Factors of Lydney.

SUMMARY OF THE FOUR THORNYCROFT LC DOUBLE-DECKERS						
Fleet no. 1	Reg.	To service	Fleet no. 2	Re-engined	Fleet no. from 1935	Withdrawn
41	UH 8231	12/07/30	251	11/12/34	25	02/43
42	UH 8232	21/07/30	252	02/11/34	26	02/43
43	UH 8233	02/08/30	253	31/12/34	27	12/43
44	UH 8234	14/07/30	254	25/07/34	28	12/43

Hall Lewis was responsible for the rather top-heavy looking bodies on the Thornycroft LC double-deckers delivered in 1930. 253 approaches Kingsway on North Road, on a run from Whitchurch. Forming a back drop are the Cardiff Law Courts dating from 1906 and still in use in 2016 as Cardiff Crown Court, a Grade 1 listed building.
(Roy Marshall collection courtesy of The Omnibus Society)

Cardiff Corporation's second batch of Thornycroft buses were saloons and of the slightly earlier BC Forward model, which in turn was based on UB Forward design. The BC went into production in 1928 and featured a 6-cylinder ZB6 6.9-litre engine developing 82hp. It had an unusually high driving position and could also be made available as a double-decker, although was really only successful as a saloon. Cardiff ordered six saloons in October 1930 for use on the Merthyr and Caerphilly routes. They were delivered as 255 to 260 (UH 9001-6) with 256 to 260 arriving in December 1930 and 255 in March 1931. The chassis were £806 each while the rear-entrance bodies by Northern Counties were £405 each and came with Marshall seats. As with the double-deck LC models, these buses were plagued by brake problems. In 1934 they were fitted with 7.7-litre AEC oil engines at a cost of £491 each, and were renumbered 132 to 137 in 1935. During WWII they were all allocated to the Medical Officer of Health at Cardiff for use as A.R.P. ambulances and were all officially deleted from fleet strength by 1945. 135 (UH 9004) however lived on and was converted into a pole-carrying lorry for use in the service vehicle fleet from 1946 until sale in 1958.

Hall Lewis had its origins with the Lewis family in Cardiff who ran a haulage business. The same Lewis family were directors at Northern Counties (NCME) from 1919. Hall Lewis established its coach-building facility at Park Royal in London in 1924 and after its success went into liquidation during 1930. In the same year, the assets of Hall Lewis emerge as Park Royal Coachworks.

Crossley Condor

The Crossley Condor was a double-deck chassis introduced by Crossley Motors Ltd of Stockport in 1930 and featured a 6-cylinder Crossley 6.8-litre side-valve petrol engine and a 4-speed sliding mesh gearbox that was mounted amidships in the chassis. It remained in production until 1934. In January 1930 Cardiff was offered a brand new Condor on loan from Crossley for the rate of 3d per mile. This offer was taken up and the bus arrived the following month registered UH 7535. It had a low-bridge Crossley body which seated 50 passengers, and the bus was eventually purchased for £850 in March 1931. It did not receive a fleet number until 1935 at which point it became number 63. According to the Transport Department, this was a good vehicle, the only real issue being abnormal clutch wear due to a small flywheel. UH 7535 lasted until August 1939 when it was withdrawn and later sold.

Crossley was keen for Cardiff to try the Condor model and offered them this bus. UH 7535 is shown here when new, and joined the fleet in March 1931, eventually becoming fleet number 63.

(The late Chris Taylor collection)

A Transport System for Cardiff

A Leyland encounter

Compared to the AEC Regent, the Leyland Titan never featured in the Cardiff fleet in any great numbers. Just two examples of the TD1 were acquired, both having been built as demonstration vehicles. The Leyland Titan double-deck chassis was first announced in late 1927 as one of two high-specification designs by G.J. Rackham, the other being the single-deck Tiger. The Titan TD1 would have an overall length of 25 feet, a wheelbase of 16ft 6in and feature a 6.8-litre 6-cyl overhead valve petrol engine of 90hp. Other components included a 4-speed crash gearbox, all-round vacuum servo brakes and an underslung worm-drive rear axle. It could be offered as a complete package with a low-bridge 48 to 51-seat Leyland body and open staircase. From 1929 this combination also became available with an enclosed staircase and completed to a high-bridge layout, although some customers preferred to source their own bodybuilder.

In November 1929 a brand new TD1 demonstrator with a standard Leyland 48-seat low-bridge body was taken on loan from Leyland Motors Ltd, acquiring local registration number UH 7175. It was subsequently purchased from Leyland in March 1931 for £850 and given fleet number 66.

UH 7175 was the all-Leyland TD1 with distinctive piano-style front. Initially used as a demonstrator, it was then acquired in 1931 becoming number 66. It is seen here in St. John's Square. Clearly visible is the bold Shredded Wheat advert, a healthy breakfast cereal that originated in the United States and first appeared in the UK in 1926.

(Roy Marshall collection courtesy of The Omnibus Society)

It then received an overhaul in October 1934 at which point a Leyland E39 oil engine was installed. UH 7175 became number 52 in the 1935 fleet renumbering scheme and was eventually withdrawn, passing to Southern Vectis in 1946 where a new ECW body was fitted.

Tigers

Rackham's Leyland Tiger design was closely related to the Titan and incorporated a 6.8-litre 6-cylinder T-type petrol engine. The initial model was the TS1 which was introduced in 1927 with a 17ft 6in wheel-base, and an overall length of 27ft 6in. It too could be available as a complete vehicle with Leyland's own bodywork. Some local authorities would not allow vehicles of this length in their area and so in 1928 Leyland introduced the Tiger TS2 which had an overall length of just 26ft but using the same wheelbase which was not ideal for some customers. Leyland's response to this came in 1930 when the Lion LT2 underframe was modified and upgraded to take the 6-cylinder T-type engine, thus resulting in the TS3 model, a chassis with an overall length of 26ft but with a 16ft 6in wheelbase. In 1931 Leyland announced the TS4 which was an improved performance chassis with a bigger 7.6-litre engine, a new gearbox and rear axle, and triple-servo vacuum brakes. This was to compete with what was by now on offer from other manufacturers, and looking to the future, an oil engine version was announced in 1933.

During its final years in service, Leyland Tiger TS4 142 (KG 1145) is seen in Lower Penarth, reversing into Charteris Close from Lavernock Road, a manoeuvre it had performed many times over the years.

(The late Alan Jarvis courtesy CTPG)

In December 1931 Cardiff Corporation invited tenders for the supply of ten double-deckers and seven saloons. The latter was revised to five vehicles and would be Leyland Tiger TS4 models fitted with very smart rear-entrance bodywork by Northern Counties of Wigan. Delivered in June 1932, they had seating for 32 and carried registrations KG 1141-45. Photographic evidence shows that prior to 1935 KG 1143/5 carried fleet numbers 78 and 80, and so it seems likely that KG 1141/2/4 were numbered 76, 77 and 79. They were fitted with a large roof-mounted route number box and two side indicator boxes on both the nearside and offside roof line when new, which probably lasted until all the batch was rebuilt in 1937. All five gained fleet numbers 138 to 142 in 1935, the year in which they also received Leyland 8.6-litre oil engines. At this time they were usually to be found employed on services to Llandough, Penarth, Merthyr Tydfil and Markham. 138 to 140 were condemned by the Traffic Commissioner in June 1937 due to the very poor condition of their bodies and 141 and 142 were subsequently found to be in a similar state. As a result Cardiff Corporation carried out the rebuild on 138, while Northern Counties completed the remainder. From January 1942 they were all modified to perimeter seating configuration to increase their capacity, which allowed for 29 seated and 29 standing passengers.

Having all survived WWII, 138 would be destroyed by fire on 14 August 1947 whilst on Thornhill. By July 1948 their bodies were once again found to be in poor condition and a budget of £2100 was set aside to overhaul the four survivors in the Corporation's own workshops when there was capacity. 140 however was converted into a mobile canteen for the undertaking, and finally sold by 1951. At 17 years of age, the remaining three vehicles would be overhauled in 1949 in the Roath depot workshops. They survived for a good few years, with 139 and 142 bowing out in 1957, having put in an impressive quarter of a century's work. Meanwhile, 141 ended its days as a training bus from 1956 until 1958.

Titans

G.J. Rackham left Leyland in 1928 and took up a post at AEC where he set about developing amongst other things, the Regent model. From 1931 26ft length double-deckers on two axles were now permissible and so Leyland introduced the TD2, a revised and heavier-duty version of the successful TD1 model. It featured the 7.5-litre engine, a larger fuel tank and much improved braking which now used a three-servo (master and slave) vacuum system. Later developments from 1932 were the introduction of a Leyland 8.1-litre oil engine, a new gearbox and finally the option of Leyland gearless transmission (the TD2c model).

Cardiff Corporation took a batch of the Leyland TD2s in the summer of 1932 with 48-seat low-bridge 6-bay bodywork by Northern Counties. The chassis cost £880 each while the bodies were £645 each. They entered service during July 1932 as 113 to 122 (KG 1146-55) and were generally regarded as lively performers. The bodies featured a 'piano style' front and there were two destination boxes side by side with a route number box above. The purchase of these and the five Tiger TS4s was made possible by part-exchanging 15 older vehicles at £195 each. In 1935 the TD2s received Leyland 8.6 litre oil engines at a cost of £429 each, and were renumbered 53 to 62 the same year.

Leyland TD2 120 (KG 1153) of 1932 with original piano-front style NCME body. Later renumbered to 60, it lost this very dated looking body during WWII and received a new East Lancs 5-bay body in 1944.
(The late Chris Taylor collection)

In 1943/44 their bodies were removed and sold to Bristol Tramways and Carriage Co. Ltd for £110 each, and subsequently fitted to older vehicles. The chassis of 53 to 62 (KG 1146-55) were then overhauled locally by Leyland and received new 56-seat East Lancs bodies in 1944 (54, 56, 58 to 60), 1945 (55, 57 and 62) and 1946 (53 and 61). However, the fitting of larger, heavier bodies led to inadequate braking capability and heavy steering to such an extent that 56 was impounded by the Ministry of Transport in October 1947, which resulted in all ten buses being taken off the road in 1948. The bodies were removed for re-use on new chassis and the Leyland TD2 chassis were sold. Three chassis passed to Crosville Motor Services where two of them later received new ECW bodies.

More demonstrators

A three-axle 68-seat Brush-bodied Thornycroft double-decker, OU4264 was on loan for up to seven months in 1930. This was followed by OU 4028, a 2-axle Thornycroft BC double-deck demonstrator, new in December 1929, which Cardiff took on loan from May 1931. It was originally built with a Thornycroft WB6 petrol engine but this was replaced by a 46hp ZB6 unit in December 1930. It had previously been on loan to the municipal fleets at Hull, Nottingham and Aberdeen and by January 1931 had clocked up 31,000 miles. Cardiff subsequently acquired it from Transport Equipment (Thornycroft) Ltd of Basingstoke in March 1932, for the sum of £865. It had a 52-seat 6-bay Strachans high-bridge body that featured a destination indicator in the upper deck rear window. Cardiff was full of praise for this vehicle which had good steering and unlike their BC and LC models bought new, there were no real issues with the brakes. It was described as a good hill climber with easy gear changes from its four-speed gearbox. In 1935 it became number 29 in the Cardiff fleet, and it was withdrawn in 1941, becoming a training vehicle.

This Thornycroft BC was a former demonstrator that joined the fleet in 1932 to become 29 (OU 4028). It is seen loading passengers on Kingsway. Note the two registration plates and the unusual position of the rear indicator blind.
(The late Chris Taylor collection)

UB 4953 was a former demonstrator that was acquired from Daimler in May 1932 for £730, having been on loan since February 1931. Daimler had offered the new bus to Cardiff Corporation for 3½d per mile following a fortnight's free trial. It was 25 feet in length and had a 50-seat high-bridge Park Royal body with enclosed staircase. The body featured leather-finished seats on the upper deck while those in the saloon were moquette. In 1930 Daimler introduced two new models, the CG6 and CP6, both of which incorporated a fluid flywheel and preselector gearbox. UB 4953 was based on a Daimler CP6 chassis which was derived from the CG6 and featured a Daimler 6-cylinder 5.6-litre sleeve-valve 50hp petrol engine. UB 4953 became number 85 in 1935 and at some stage was thought to have been fitted with an AEC oil engine. It was withdrawn from passenger service in 1937 and became a tower wagon in the service fleet until its sale for scrap in June 1950 for £5.

Cardiff continued to obtain demonstrators on long term hire, often as new vehicles. They usually ended up purchasing them, no doubt at a good price, but the manufacturer did not always see subsequent orders as a result. MV 529, an AEC Regent 661 model fitted with a petrol engine, new in October 1931, was taken on loan from AEC Ltd at Southall in February 1932.

It had a Brush high bridge layout body seating 56 and was eventually purchased for £1000 in March 1933. MV 529 became fleet number 24 in 1935 and still retaining its petrol engine was withdrawn in 1941. It then passed into the service fleet as a driver training bus, gaining fleet number 28 in 1947. From August 1948 it was rebuilt into a general purpose van which was finally sold by 1950.

Arriving on loan as a new bus in July 1932 and in full Cardiff livery was AEC Regent KG 1251, which took fleet number 76 and had a Weymann 50-seat low-bridge body. This was the very first oil engine bus to enter service with the fleet and was eventually acquired from AEC Ltd of Southall in March 1934 for £800, following an overhaul. It was fitted with an AEC 8.8-litre engine of 130bhp and crash gearbox and was the first of many AEC Regents to work for Cardiff Corporation over the next 47 years. KG 1251 featured double gangway seating (on the upper deck) and the body had quite a deep roofline. It was often to be found working the Cyncoed route and became fleet number 23 in 1935. It was withdrawn in 1945 and advertised for sale, but was then used as a recovery demonstration vehicle. It took part in numerous righting exercises before being sold in 1947.

AEC Regent 76 (KG 1251) was the first oil engined bus to run in the Cardiff fleet and was originally on loan as a demonstrator. It is seen here prior to entering service. *(The late Dave B Thomas collection)*

Brief encounters

A Crossley Condor double-decker with a Crossley body to high-bridge layout, RG 1676, was taken on loan by Cardiff Corporation in January 1933 at the agreed rate of 3d per mile, and stayed until June.

A Morris Commercial petrol engined double-decker appeared at the Motor Show in 1932 in full Cardiff Corporation livery. It had a 50-seat Park Royal body and was intended for loan to the undertaking at the rate of 3d per mile. In the event it is believed Cardiff declined the offer as it was now looking to the economies of the oil engine for its future vehicles. It seems likely that this same bus eventually entered service with another operator, most probably Edinburgh Corporation, and registered FS 6340.

CHAPTER TWO

OIL ENGINES AND THE SECOND WORLD WAR

From 1930 we enter a period that witnessed the tram system in the early stages of decline as some routes were converted to motor bus operation. The undertaking was now starting to operate to residential suburbs not previously served and also to the new housing estates that were being built at this time. The oil engine offering many economies of operation came into favour, becoming the standard installation for new buses. Many conversions to oil engine were subsequently undertaken on older vehicles, and a diesel oil tank was duly installed at the Sloper Road depot.

CARDIFF AND THE AEC REGENT

The standard AEC double-decker of the 1930s was the highly successful Regent introduced in 1929. The first model was the petrol engined 661, and the first oil engine example appeared in 1933 as model O661 fitted with an 8.8-litre engine. The first of many new AEC Regent double-deckers started to appear from 1934. Cardiff received ten AEC Regent O661 models numbered 1 to 10 (KG 3701-10) which entered service in March and April. These buses featured the AEC A165 8.8-litre oil engine coupled to a crash gearbox, the chassis costing £1095-10s each. Nine of them had attractive 50-seat 5-bay Northern Counties (NCME) bodies to high-bridge layout. Strangely 9 (KG 3709) had a 6-bay body which it is thought may have been built for another customer's vehicle, possibly a Crossley Condor, before being transferred to and completed on the Regent chassis. The management described these early all-metal bodies as rough and noisy, the interior being spartan and purely functional. Due to the amount of smoke and fumes emitted from early diesel buses, it is said that councillors pushed for trolleybuses, but the General Manager William Forbes was always against this idea.

1 (KG 3701) in its original form with a Northern Counties body is seen in the late 1930s crossing the River Taff with Llandaff North in the background. The bus will now turn left on to Bridge Road and head towards Llandaff village. This river bridge was deemed unsafe in the 1970s and replaced by a new structure just downstream.

(The late Chris Taylor collection)

In March 1943 the bodies of 1 to 8 and 10 were scrapped, and the chassis were subsequently overhauled by AEC. New 56-seat East Lancs bodies were then fitted to these nine chassis between January and October 1944. This left 9 (KG 3709) with the odd 6-bay body as the survivor in its original form, and having received minor body attention in April 1946, it was eventually rebuilt by Cardiff Corporation in August 1949.

In November 1932 Leyland offered Titan TD1 demonstrator TF 6821 to Cardiff Corporation at a rate of 3d per mile. The bus was 12 months old at this point and entered service with Cardiff on 16 December 1932. It featured a low-bridge Leyland body of L27/24R layout, and had earlier been loaned to Hull Corporation in a crimson and cream livery. The bus was added to stock in March 1934 for £600, and in the October, a Leyland oil engine was fitted for £465 less a discount of 2½%. In 1935 TF 6821 gained fleet number 51 and was eventually advertised for sale in December 1943. It passed to Southern Vectis in 1945, who removed the original Leyland body and fitted a new 53-seat ECW body in 1945.

Up until 1935, all Cardiff Corporation buses continued to be numbered in a series laid down by the former Cardiff Watch Committee, a council-run body responsible to the Chief Constable of the Police. The 1935 renumbering scheme set things out in a more orderly fashion and can be summarised as follows:

NEW FLEET NUMBER	VEHICLE TYPE	COMMENTS
1 to 29	Oil engined double-deckers	
51 to 84	Petrol engined double-deckers	Although 52 to 62 were oil engine
101 to 142	Single-deckers	

The Mancunians

In September 1934 Crossley Motors offered Cardiff Corporation two of their latest double-deck buses with 48-seat Northern Counties bodies. These were the new oil engined Mancunian model and were delivered in April 1935, numbered 21 and 22 (KG 5001/2). The Crossley Mancunian was introduced in 1933 as a successor to the Crossley Condor, and remained in production until 1941. It was also available as a single-deck chassis. All were fitted with oil engines and the Mancunian usually featured the Crossley 6-cyl VR6 9.1-litre 90hp power unit with Ricardo indirect injection. Like the Condor, the gearbox was a 4-speed sliding-mesh type, but this time it was bolted to the main engine block. From 1938 a constant mesh and a preselector option was made available.

This is a good study of 22 (KG 5002), one of the pair of Crossley Mancunians. It is standing on Kingsway in the city centre with a departure to Whitchurch, and close to the spot where the Glamorganshire Canal passed under the road.
(Roy Marshall collection courtesy of The Omnibus Society)

Crossley offered the Gardner 6LW oil engine as an option in the Mancunian chassis, but the Cardiff pair had Crossley VR6 9.12-litre engines developing 100bhp at 1700rpm. Upon delivery they turned out to be 56-seaters, and one of their duties was on the Lisvane route. The pair soon earned themselves the nickname "motor boats", on account of their exhaust note which apparently sounded like a small motor boat. In 1943 they received the Gardner 6LW engines from withdrawn Thornycroft LC double-deckers 25 and 26. Both were withdrawn from service in 1949 and sold by 1950, 21 passing to a showman while 22 was converted to a goods vehicle.

More Regents

The Crossleys were joined the same year by a second batch of AEC Regents. These buses were also O661 models, but unlike the 1934 delivery, they were fitted with the smaller 7.7-litre AEC A171 oil engine, but again coupled to a crash gearbox. Numbered 11 to 20 (KG 5003-12), their 5-bay Northern Counties bodies seated 56 and featured a route number indicator box between the two front upper deck windows. They entered service between 10 August and 20 September and had an unladen weight of around 6 tons 15cwt. In 1943/44 numbers 11 to 13 and 18 were converted to run on producer gas for a short period but this was not a success. In 1949 the batch was re-numbered to become 37/38, 52, 134 to 138, 140 and 177 respectively, but were all withdrawn the following year and advertised for sale.

Seen here on Newport Road, 17 (KG 5009) wearing wartime livery is one of the 1935 AEC Regents with NCME bodies.
(The late Dave B Thomas collection)

During December 1935 a statement from the Transport Department was quoted as saying "Savings made by using oil engined buses has averted trading losses for the undertaking". In 1936 the Tramway Committee became known as the Transport Committee and a proposal to replace part of the tramway system by motor buses was discussed by them and met much opposition. This was a protracted debate during which alternatives such as battery vehicles, producer gas buses and trolleybuses were looked at. Eventually the first two types were ruled out. Meanwhile track on the Splott section of the Portmanmoor Road to Clive Street route was reported to be in very poor condition. As a result of this on 11 October motor buses took over the entire route. The track was retained between Glossop Terrace, Meteor Street and Adamsdown Square, and on the Moira Terrace, Adam Street, Bute Terrace to Custom House Street sections, which could be used for diversions. The track in Moira Place was removed. The negative outcome of this conversion to motor bus operation was that the relatively youthful single-deck trams were now surplus to requirements.

An experimental bus

The AEC Q was a very advanced side-engined bus chassis designed by John Rackham. The engine and radiator were located behind the offside front wheel and the prototype, a single-decker, appeared in 1932. By October that year a double-decker had appeared, but the concept was initially given a cold reception by the bus industry as offering few advantages over the conventional bus. Early models featured a petrol engine, although an oil engine was offered. The double-deckers tended to have the stairs over the off side front wheel and most had Wilson preselect epicyclic gearboxes and Metro-Cammell bodies. Cardiff Corporation had arranged to borrow Park Royal-bodied AEC Q demonstrator AMV433 in September 1934 at the rate of 3d per mile. In June 1935 Cardiff then ordered a single AEC Q for the St. Mary Street to Gabalfa via Salisbury Road service. It was one of only two AEC Qs to receive English Electric bodies and was ordered as a forward-entrance 60-seater at a cost of £2105, but this was revised to a 56-seater for £1990. It entered service on 4 April 1936 as 30 (KG 7750) and was the very last AEC Q double-decker built, with chassis number 0761023. It featured an AEC A170 7.7-litre oil engine and a Wilson preselector gearbox and eventually gained the nickname "Queen Mary". In service it was unpopular and was liable to skidding in wet weather, the cab was cramped, the driver's seat too narrow and the engine frequently over-heated. During its time with Cardiff, number 30 was used regularly used on the Whitchurch route 23 but also put in the odd appearance on the 38 to Rhiwbina and 24 to Llandaff North.

30 (KG 7750) the unusual and short-lived AEC Q when new. This view gives a superb view of the platform area and stairs which rose up over the engine. The platform was originally open, no doubt causing the lower saloon to be rather draughty.

(Roy Marshall collection courtesy of The Omnibus Society)

The AEC Q was last used by Cardiff in passenger service on 31 October 1943, and passed to well-known Oxfordshire independent operator Worth's Services Ltd of Enstone in December. They ran KG 7750 until 1956 by which time it was one of the last AEC Q double-deckers still in passenger use in the UK.

The tram replacements

The Leyland TD2 was superseded by the TD3 model which was announced in the spring of 1933, and was still offered as a complete chassis/body package if required. The TD3 featured a revised front end which was more compact and this allowed a larger lower saloon which could now in theory seat up to 26 persons. Also new was the restyled radiator, improved braking and power units. The petrol engine was now modified to give an output of 110bhp while the Leyland 8.6-litre oil engine of 94bhp was becoming an increasingly popular option for customers.

Finally, the TD3c was an option with torque-converter gearless transmission. By 1935 Leyland's oil engine had become very reliable and boasted a 98bhp output and the TD4 model was announced featuring hydraulic brakes that incorporated a single-vacuum servo and hydraulic master cylinder. Most TD4s were specified as oil engine vehicles, and the TD4c Leyland Gearless transmission model was to prove very popular with municipal sector fleets.

Cardiff Corporation sought 11 double-deckers to replace the tramcars on the Splott to Grangetown route from 11 October 1936, and with the likelihood of many tramcar drivers wishing to convert to motor bus drivers, they were looking for vehicles with more driver-friendly transmission. In 1936 Cardiff purchased some Leyland Titan TD4c double-deckers with 53-seat Northern Counties bodywork and an overall height of 14ft 3½in. Entering service between October and December 1936, they were numbered 31 to 35, and for some reason their registrations were issued out of order as KG 8904/5/3/2/1. They featured sloping windscreens, a "gearless" badge on the radiator and were the last new Leyland double-deckers for 25 years. As was the case with the 1934 Regents, their bodies featured route number boxes between the front upper deck windows. They were disliked by drivers and never strayed far from the routes for which they were originally intended. The TD4c Titans lasted in service until 1949/50 with 31 becoming a tower wagon in the service vehicle fleet in 1950, lasting until 1960/61.

35 (KG 8901) now looking rather scruffy is one of the five Leyland Titan TD4c gearless double-deckers. It is seen laying over in the late 1940s, with the former GWR station Cardiff General behind the bus.
(Roy Marshall collection courtesy of The Omnibus Society)

Also new in 1936 was another batch of AEC Regent O661 models, and yet another variation of driveline. Once again they featured the 7.7-litre diesel, but this time coupled to a Wilson preselector gearbox with fluid flywheel. These had been ordered in April 1936 at the same time as the Titan chassis, and entered service during October as 36 to 41 (KG 8906-11). Each completed bus cost £1800 and the Northern Counties 56-seat bodies were externally similar to the Titans, but with a higher seating capacity. The first of these AEC Regents to be withdrawn were 36 to 38 in 1949, but the last one, 41 did not bow out until 1957. After withdrawal 40 (KG 8910) was parted from its chassis which was sold, while its body passed to 1938 vintage AEC Regent 156 (KG 9810) in 1951.

Oil Engines and the Second World War

By now the last of its batch in service with its original body, and still in good shape, 41 (KG 8911) is about to leave Central Square for Snowden Road, Ely on the 26. This example outlived the other 1936 AEC Regents by at least five years. The taller of the two buildings in the background to the right of the bus is the Prince of Wales theatre and the building with the slightly lower roof line is the Pavilion cinema.

(The late Alan Jarvis courtesy CTPG)

A POOR CHOICE

Added to stock in September 1936 due to a temporary shortage of vehicles were five Crossley Condor double-deckers dating from 1930, which were acquired from Leeds City Transport, and were fitted with Crossley 6-cylinder 6.8-litre side-valve petrol engines. They had been withdrawn in 1935 and transport officials from Cardiff travelled to Leeds to inspect them. Entering service with Cardiff they became 42 to 46 (UA 5850-2/5, UB 2857). They had 48-seat high-bridge bodies by Dodson (42), Roe (43 to 45) and Crossley (46). These buses were allegedly acquired for just £50 each, and their bodies were soon found to be in a very bad condition and became unpopular on account of their very cramped staircases. They were withdrawn in 1938 and sold by March 1939, with 44 finding further use as a lorry.

Meanwhile Cardiff needed a normal control vehicle for driver training duties so that the instructor could sit alongside the trainee driver. A solution was found in July 1936 by exchanging Dennis E saloon 111 (UH 2193) for Merthyr Tydfil Corporation's HB 2244. This was a 1924-vintage Leyland A13 with a 29 or 30-seat BBW body, dating from 1921, which had been fitted in 1933. As Merthyr Tydfil number 7, it featured a full-width cab and had been withdrawn from service the previous December. HB 2244 was painted in service vehicle grey livery for its duties as a driver training bus at Cardiff.

In June 1936 20 AEC Regents were ordered for 1937 delivery, to replace the 20 Dennis HS double-deckers dating from 1929. These would mirror the 1936 Regents with AEC 7.7-litre oil engines Wilson preselector gearboxes and similar 56-seat Northern Counties bodies. They entered service as 47 to 50, 151 to 166 (KG 9801-20) from February 1937, with 158, 160/2 to 166 completing the order the following month. In part-exchange AEC took 20 saloons at £30 each. All 20 Regents were rebuilt between December 1946 and January 1949, but 166 was then withdrawn in February 1951 after involvement in a fatal accident, and was soon broken up.

A superb view of AEC Regent 161 (KG 9815) of 1937 with its original NCME body, in action at Tremorfa to the east of the city.
(The late Alan Jarvis courtesy CTPG)

A further 15 Regents were ordered at a cost of £1860 per bus, and were the first examples of the later more rounded style of Northern Counties all-metal body. They entered service between July and December 1937 and had an unladen weight of between 6t 14cwt and 6t 15cwt. Fleet numbers allocated were 167 to 181 with registrations ABO 970-84 respectively, and this brought the total number AEC Regents now in service with Cardiff to 63. Once again all had AEC 7.7-litre oil engines and Wilson preselector gearboxes, a noticeable feature being a much shorter radiator grill. The modern and stylish steel-framed bodies on AEC Regents 167 to 181 were, it is claimed, designed by the General Manager Mr William Forbes, and incorporated a number of flared panels and curved lines as well as a hand-beaten front roof dome. A trade advertisement went on to say that the windows were glazed with polished plate glass with Widney Stuart supplying the half-drop opening apertures. The interiors featured the use of Staybright stainless steel trim, while the scratchproof rexine panels were used throughout in shades of broken white or dark red. Lighting was provided by sunken chromium-plated lamps with chrome reflectors. The seating was of tubular frame with detachable chrome-plated top rails, padded backrests and Dunlopillo cushions. The lower-deck trim comprised moquette with leather facings while on the upper deck, first-selection hide was married to pleated cushions.

179 (ABO 982) is about to turn into the garage from Sloper Road in evening sunshine, sometime in the early 1950s. This is a superb study of one of the 1937 delivery of AEC Regents with the new style of NCME body as specified by General Manager at the time William Forbes. It has however been rebuilt, and subsequently lost its flared skirt panels.
(The late Alan Jarvis courtesy CTPG)

Oil Engines and the Second World War

On 11 November 1949, five of this batch, 167 to 169, 171/72 were withdrawn due to badly corroded bodywork, and ultimately received used 1944-built East Lancs bodies, taken from 1934 batch of AEC Regents.

AEC Saloons

By the early 1930s it was becoming apparent that the double-decker was the most suitable type of vehicle for Cardiff's motor bus requirements. The introduction of the AEC Regent and then the oil engine meant that the undertaking now had some powerful vehicles and was also starting to achieve some degree of standardisation and economy. There was however still a requirement for a handful of saloons for a number of routes with height restrictions such as Penarth and Llandough services.

In 1929 AEC established itself as the builder of high-performance chassis with the introduction of the Reliance 660 model which used the "6-type" engine. Meanwhile the AEC Regal 662 first appeared in 1929 and was developed as the single-deck option of a family of three similar chassis, which also included the double-deck chassis Regent 661 and 3-axle Renown 663. The 26ft Regal chassis incorporated single-servo vacuum brakes and the gearbox was mounted quite close to the engine. In 1930 a 4-cylinder 5.1-litre model, the Regal 4, was introduced while in 1931 AEC made the Regal available with an oil engine and as a 27ft 6in chassis. In 1935 a lightweight model with a 6.6-litre engine was offered and given the name Regal II, but by this time the standard oil engine being installed was the AEC A171 7.7-litre of 115bhp.

An order was placed by Cardiff in November 1936 for five AEC Regal O662 models which had Northern Counties bodies, but this raised objections. It was then decided in December to approach two local coachbuilders W. Lewis and J. Norman to supply 32-seat steel-framed bodies. However neither could initially oblige, but Lewis later came back and offered suitable bodies using Accles and Pollock metal frames sourced from elsewhere. The cost of each body was higher at £631, compared to £600 quoted by NCME. Construction was a rather protracted affair, and the chassis were said to be at AEC in April 1937, waiting for Lewis to collect. They eventually appeared between 17 July and 19 October as 143 to 147 (ABO 985-9). All the Regals had AEC 7.7 litre oil engines and Wilson preselector gearboxes. These were the last bus bodies completed by this Cardiff-based coachbuilder.

Having had its Lewis body rebuilt in 1947 AEC Regal 147 (ABO 989) is noted parked on the forecourt at Sloper Road on 15 February 1953. It was withdrawn later in the year and sold to Cardiff Corporation Waterworks Department and based in Merthyr Tydfil.

(The late Alan Jarvis courtesy CTPG)

As a result of these delays in delivery, and also because of the poor condition of the Leyland TS4s (138 to 142), it was announced on 12 June 1937 that there would be three additional AEC Regals added to the original requirement. Bodied by Northern Counties, they appeared as 148 to 150 (AKG 418-20) on 20 September and had seating for 35, the most noticeable feature being the lack of roof canopy over the bonnet area. Mechanically they were the same as 143 to 147 and had an unladen weight of 6tons 1cwt. 149 and 150 initially appeared in an ivory livery with a crimson Lake flash, for intended use on sight-seeing tours. This trio had bodywork that broadly followed the same method of construction as Regents 167 to 181. A novel feature of the platform doors was that they folded over the platform steps. The windows did however feature Triplex toughened glass, while the interior lighting was much more elaborate incorporating twelve flood lamps, two four-way Cenotaph lamps and a pillar lamp on the front bulkhead. During the Second World War all the AEC Regals (143 to 150) were temporarily fitted with perimeter-type seating giving them a revised capacity of 29 seated plus 29 standing. This was removed after the war, most probably when they were overhauled between June and December 1947. AEC Regals were also used on the Merthyr Tydfil service alongside the Leyland Tigers.

In January 1937 a 29-seat all-Leyland Tiger TS2 was purchased from Gelligaer Urban District Council for spare parts at a cost of £85. The vehicle, TX 6342, new as Gelligaer no. 1 in 1928, had been fitted with an AEC 8.8-litre oil engine in 1933, and was immediately broken up by Cardiff Corporation. The engine is believed to have been fitted in Daimler tower wagon (UB 4953).

For 1938 a further ten AEC Regents with AEC A173 7.7-litre oil engines and Wilson preselector gearboxes were received. These too had the revised NCME body style and featured a longer radiator grill. Numbered 182 to 191 (BBO 67-76), they were placed in service between 21 July and 10 September and were intended for use on the Waterloo Road extension, the total value of the order being £18,615.

AEC Regent 182 (BBO 67) sets off on Heathwood Road service 40. The engine compartment panel is propped open. Following a rebuild 182 has also lost its flared lower skirt panels, and was one of a few from this batch subsequently fitted with a shorter radiator. This photograph dates from 8 July 1953, the year of the Coronation, and the General station in the background is decorated for the occasion. Four years later in 1957, the bus was withdrawn.
(The late Alan Jarvis courtesy CTPG)

This batch of buses put in good service and it would appear that all were rebuilt in the years 1948/49. As late as 1956, 185 (BBO 70) received the similar-looking East Lancs body from accident-damaged AEC Regent 193 (CBO 702). This did seem a bit pointless, as 185 was withdrawn the following year. The final five survivors from this batch bowed out in 1958, and all were scrapped.

On 23 March 1939 a single-deck demonstrator was taken on a 14-day loan from Sentinel Waggon Works (1936) Ltd of Shrewsbury. It was AUX 296, a HSG model based on a Gilford 176 chassis and fitted with an American Hercules 6-cylinder petrol engine converted for running on producer gas. It was fitted with Cowieson 32-seat bodywork and was used in service to both Llanishen and Ely.

THE OUTBREAK OF WAR

By the late 1930s it was generally accepted that the whole of the tramway system would be gradually run down. However the outbreak of war in September 1939 meant that the remaining 13 miles of tramway would have to soldier on for a lot longer. Motor bus services to Newport, Merthyr Tydfil, Markham, Penarth, Llandough, Thornhill and Peterston-super-Ely were suspended from 8 September until after hostilities had ceased.

> The following first generation trams from the years 1902 to 1905 were still in use as of 1939.
> 5, 6, 10, 13, 15, 22, 23, 29, 30, 32, 34, 42, 43, 72, 84, 90, 99, 125, 138 to 141 (ex 3, 7, 19 and 98)

Shortly before the outbreak of war tenders were invited for the supply of 20 chassis with 6-cylinder diesel engines and suitable for 56-seat all-metal double-deck bodies. This resulted in a further 20 AEC Regents being ordered, to be delivered by 1940. However due to the outbreak of war, the Ministry of War Transport (MoWT) reduced the order to just seven vehicles. All had AEC 7.7 litre oil engines and Wilson preselector gearboxes and were delivered in March/April 1940 as 192 to 198 (CBO 701-7). They carried East Lancs 56-seat bodies to an overall height of 14ft 4in and featured the longer type of AEC radiator when new. It is thought that the change from NCME to East Lancs for bodywork may have been due to a dispute over prices, and so began a long relationship with the Blackburn-based coachbuilder that had entered the industry in October 1934. Of interest is that East Lancs were more than willing to produce bodies to the customer's specified design, and so 192 to 198 were finished to a style not unlike that of the previous NCME bodies. All were rebuilt by East Lancs in the years 1944/45 and again locally by Bruce in 1948/49. The last of this batch, 196, was not taken out of service until 1958.

East Lancs-bodied AEC Regent 195 (CBO 704) in the yard at Sloper Road depot with a Northern Counties-bodied example behind, making an interesting comparison.
(The late Alan Jarvis courtesy CTPG)

The Transport Department's central offices in Dragon Buildings, Paradise Place off Queen Street which it had occupied since August 1927, were completely destroyed by enemy action on 2 January 1941. Temporary offices in Womanby Street were then established and occupied until 1950. The first conductress was employed by CCT from 16 April this year. A notable achievement was the replacement of all petrol engined buses by 1941, though the two Bedford OWBs brought them back into the fleet the following year. Under the instruction of the Home Office, a number of elderly buses were converted into Air Raid Precaution (A.R.P.) ambulances from 1939 onwards for the Medical Officer of Health at Cardiff. These included former Lincoln Dennis E-types FE 8518/20, FE 8625/7 and FE 8870/1 together with the 1931 Thornycroft BC saloons UH 9001-6, but all were out of use by June 1945.

At last, trolleybuses for Cardiff

The operation of trolleybuses in Cardiff was subject to the passing of three Acts of Parliament described as follows:

1. *The Cardiff Corporation Act 1934* which granted powers to operate trolleybuses over existing tram routes plus a few minor additional sections.

2. *The Cardiff Corporation (trolley vehicles) Order Confirmation act, 1940* which extended the area above to also cover outlying districts of the city.

The third Act came later in 1946 and after initial trolleybus operation had begun.

3. *The Cardiff Corporation Act 1946* gave additional powers to allow operation along Churchill Way and any other street in the city to:
    i) Provide a turning point
    ii) Link up trolleybus routes
    iii) Gain access to depots, garages and other Corporation works

It was not until May 1939 that a decision was finally made as to whether motor buses or trolleybuses would replace the trams. It was made in favour of the trolleybus and things subsequently developed quite quickly. In 1940 a 30ft motor bus was borrowed and driven around various parts of Cardiff to establish the suitability of operating vehicles of this length at some future date, in other words trolleybuses. The bus was MV 2906, an AEC Renown 3-axle double-decker new in 1933 with a 65-seat Metro-Cammell body and loaned by Western Welsh in whose fleet it was 597.

Routes for conversion were drawn up and ten 70-seat 3-axle double-deck trolleybuses were ordered in October 1939. They were originally ordered as Leylands with GEC electrical equipment but, in June 1940, Leyland announced they would be unable to honour the order due to wartime restraints, and consequently the order was awarded to AEC in the August. They would supply the 30ft long, 7ft 6in wide 664T chassis with English Electric 80hp motors and electrical equipment at a cost of £1401 each. The electrical components would be specially modified to cope with operation on flooded roads. Northern Counties would supply the bodies at a cost of £1105 each, and significantly these vehicles would mark the end of the close association with this bodybuilder. They materialised as 201 to 210 (CKG 191-200) with 201/2 arriving in 1941, 203 to 209 in 1942 and finally 210 in 1943; and all were delivered in wartime grey primer livery. Of interest is that 201 was actually delivered as fleet no. 200 in error. They had an unladen weight of 9tons 8cwt and were to be the only trolleybuses ever to be bodied by Northern Counties. They featured a low-loading chassis to keep the overall height of the vehicle to just under 15ft and employed Metro-Cammell patent concealed gantries to support the trolley bases. The Clare Road depot was then adapted for the operation of trolleybuses, but the last of the trams did not finally transfer to Roath until 1946.

Oil Engines and the Second World War

202 (CKG 192) crosses onto the roundabout at Roath Park and will turn before proceeding back along Ninian Road and into town. 202 was one of the trolleybuses that was decorated with coloured lights in both 1963 and 1964 for the Cardiff Shopping Festival and Christmas festivities.

(Glyn Bowen courtesy Chris Taylor CTPG)

From 1 March 1942 trams no longer ran on the Wood Street and Clarence Road route. The trolleybus system was launched on this date by the Lord Mayor (Alderman James Hellyer) and the new vehicles entered service working route 6A Wood Street to Clarence Road (Avondale Hotel), Grangetown. A Pay-As-You-Enter (P.A.Y.E.) system was also introduced with a flat fare of 1d for a journey of any distance. From 3 May all remaining tram routes were revised so that all now terminated in the city centre. On 8 November 1942 it became possible to extend the trolleybus service through the city centre and out along Cathedral Road to Llandaff Fields, which ran as the number 6 when covering the full route, and also moved over to the P.A.Y.E. 1d flat fare at this time. Upon their first repaint after hostilities had ended, a number of these trolleybuses including 203, 204, 208 and 209 received a streamlined version of the crimson lake and cream livery.

A poster describing the P.A.Y.E. one penny fare collection system as introduced on the new 6A trolleybus service in March 1942. It even tells you which hand to use depending on whether you are heading upstairs or into the lower saloon.

An unfrozen Regent

Having recently been repainted, the solitary unfrozen AEC Regent 199 (CKG 325), waits in Mill Lane in the early 1950s. It is about to depart with a 39 service to Manor Way. Marments was a well-known department store located on Queen Street in Cardiff. Originally opening in 1879, it had closed by 1986.

(The late Alan Jarvis courtesy CTPG)

By the outbreak of the Second World War over 7000 Regents had been built by AEC which included 3764 for London alone. In 1941, AEC went on to build 92 "unfrozen" chassis using existing parts that were already held in stock and not subject to wartime restrictions. In addition to the 20 it had wanted for 1940, Cardiff had a further 20 Regents on order for 1941 that were to receive East Lancs bodywork. Having only managed to get seven for 1940, it was to be far less successful for 1941. In the event, only one example was completed, and this was delivered on 24 March 1942 as 199 (CKG 325). This bus had what was known as an "unfrozen" chassis, and featured a 7.7-litre engine and crash gearbox. It also had a 56-seat Northern Counties body to a pre-war design. After the war the bus was rebuilt by Bruce Coachworks in July 1947, and after withdrawal in 1958 became a driver training vehicle for about four years, getting a repaint in October 1959.

A FLEET SUMMARY FOR DECEMBER 1942 INDICATED 234 ITEMS OF ROLLING STOCK IN PASSENGER SERVICE				
Double-deck trams	High-bridge double-deckers	Low-bridge double-deckers	Single-deckers	Trolleybuses
89	95	12	29	9

Oil Engines and the Second World War

Between August and November 1943, the following buses were taken on loan from the London Passenger Transport Board (LPTB) with whom they carried fleet numbers ST879, 962/84. They were to cover for buses undergoing overhaul.

REGISTRATION	CHASSIS	BODYWORK	SEATING	YEAR NEW
GK 2055	AEC Regent	Tilling	H25/27RO	1930
GK 6238/60	"	"	"	1931

It should be noted that the initial success of the Pay-As-You-Enter (P.A.Y.E.) system led to it being adopted on the trams from 7 March 1943. It was also introduced to some motor bus services from 31 January 1944. The tram routes were converted as follows:

DATE	ROUTE NO.	ROUTE
7 March 1943	16	Pier Head to The Hayes
2 May 1943	5A	Victoria Park to St. Mary Street
"	8	Victoria Park to Windsor Place
1 August 1943	1A and 1B	Whitchurch Road to City Centre
"	2A and 2B	Newport Road to City Centre
"	4A and 4B	Roath Park to City Centre

What are Utility buses?

At the outbreak of war in September 1939, production of buses had more or less stopped as manufacturing concentrated on the war effort. As mentioned earlier, permission was given to use the large number of components in stock at the some manufacturers and for production to continue of "unfrozen" buses to exhaust these stocks. Examples of unfrozen double-deckers in the UK included AEC Regent, Bristol K5G and Leyland TD7, while saloons included the Bristol L5G and the Dennis Lancet II. In addition a number of buses and trolleybuses intended for overseas customers, and that were no longer able to be delivered, were requisitioned.

The Utility bus was a wartime specification vehicle to a design drawn up in 1941 and authorised by the Ministry of War Transport and Ministry of Supply. It would be a low cost common-specification bus, available as a normal-height body seating 30 upstairs and 26 in the lower saloon, or as a low-bridge layout seating 27 on the top deck and up to 28 in the lower saloon. The body would be of composite wood-framed construction, with no interior lining and minimal features. To cut costs there were few shaped panels and opening windows, while steel was used widely in place of aluminium.

CARDIFF CORPORATION'S UTILITY BUSES					
Fleet no.	Registration no.	Chassis	Body	Seating	Year
42/43	CKG 405/6	Bedford OWB	Duple	B32F	1942
29, 63	CKG 377/422	Guy Arab I 5LW	Park Royal	H30/26R	"
64	CKG465	"	"	"	1943
65 to 67	CKG 407-9	Guy Arab II 5LW	"	"	"
71 to 73	CKG 516-8	"	"	"	"
74 to 76	CKG 519-21	"	"	"	1944
77 to 79	CKG 581-3	Bristol K6A	"	"	"
80 to 82	CKG 584-6	"	"	"	1945
83 to 89	CKG 650-6	"	"	"	"
90 to 94	CKG 666-70	"	Duple	"	1946

The Guy Arab first appeared in 1933, a chassis that was designed for use with an oil engine. During the Second World War Guy was asked by the Ministry of Supply to produce a modified version of their Arab double-deck chassis for use as a utility bus. It was launched in March 1942 and soon achieved low running costs which resulted in its immediate success. The first 500 were retrospectively known as the Arab MkI and about 400 of these featured the Gardner 5LW engine. Special dispensation for the remainder allowed the installation of the 6LW engine, the length of which required the radiator to be moved 7in forward, thus making the overall length of the bus greater than 26 feet. The MkII version was introduced from mid-1943 and all were built with the forward-projecting radiator as standard, even though most were fitted with the Gardner 5LW engine. Both Marks were fitted with Guy 4-speed gearboxes with sliding-mesh on the lower gears. There was a change to constant-mesh on later MkIIs, the very final examples of which entered service in early 1947. From 1943 Daimler produced the CWG5 model, soon joined by the CWA6 which used the 6-cylinder AEC A173 oil engine. Bodywork in the main would be produced by Park Royal, Weymann, Brush and Duple with Massey, Strachan and Roe also contributing and Northern Counties concentrating on low-bridge bodywork. Cardiff took 30 utility double-deckers of both Guy and Bristol manufacture, all of which survived the war. They also took a pair of Duple-bodied Bedford OWB utility saloons in 1942.

72 (CKG 517), a 1943 Guy Arab II is seen parked opposite Cardiff's General station in more or less original condition (apart from livery). The bus was rebuilt in 1952 and eventually withdrawn in 1958.

(Roy Marshall collection courtesy of The Omnibus Society)

The Bedford OB was a semi normal-control single-deck bus that was introduced in August 1939, and based on the Bedford O-type lorry chassis. Production ceased soon after due to the war, but the OWB was later produced during the war, using basic materials. The 24ft 4in chassis still featured the 28hp 6-cylinder 3.5-litre overhead valve petrol engine and a 4-speed crash gearbox, and was mainly bodied by Duple. Cardiff was allocated a pair in August 1942 which emerged as 42 and 43. The latter was put into service in September 1942 followed by 42 on 3 October. Little is known about them, but they did have wooden slatted seats and an unladen weight of 3 tons 6 cwt. They were painted semi-gloss brown primer and do not appear to have been photographed at all during their brief time at Cardiff. They were used mainly on the service to Peterston-super-Ely and were deemed unsuitable for general stage carriage service. This resulted in their early withdrawal on 30 September 1943, and sale to Aberdare Urban District Council in whose fleet they became 29 and 30. CKG 405 ended its days in Ceylon while CKG 406 saw further service closer to home in west Wales.

Oil Engines and the Second World War

Guy Arabs 29 and 63 were ordered in March 1942 and entered service in October, while 64 was ordered in October and put into service on 1 March 1943. Number 29 had an unladen weight of 7tons 8cwt while its rear emergency exit was not glazed. All were 14 ft 5in hight. As MkI versions, these three had short bonnets and small mudguards, and the electrical system was 12 volts to save on weight and batteries. The cost quoted for all three buses was £2222. From the start of 1943 all double-deckers were to have wooden slatted seats, and it is known that the MkII Guy Arabs 65 to 76 had this feature. They were ordered during 1943 and all entered service between September 1943 and January 1944. All the Guy Arabs had Gardner 5LW engines, were delivered in wartime grey primer livery and none of them was popular with drivers. They were later rebuilt by Longwell Green in 1952 at a cost of around £900 each. The last survivors were retained in stock in order to cover for the British Empire and Commonwealth Games in July 1958, but 71 somehow managed to survive until withdrawal on 31 December 1961.

The original Bristol K was produced between 1937 and 1945. With an overall length of 26ft and a 16ft 3in wheelbase, it was intended to be bodied as either a high-bridge or low-bridge double-decker. It was available with the Gardner 5LW or 6LW engine, though no 6LWs were fitted. One of the K's distinctive features was the high-mounted KV-type radiator. Pre-war examples tended to have BBW or ECW bodywork, but Beadle and Brush also completed some Bristol Ks. Production ceased in 1942, but from 1944 the Bristol K6A was made available, featuring an AEC 7.7-litre A202 engine specially designed to fit in place of a Gardner 5LW in the Bristol K chassis.

Cardiff's first three Bristol K6As 77 to 79 entered service on 2 October 1944 followed by 80 to 82 on 17 April 1945. These buses had Park Royal bodies, an unladen weight of 6tons 19cwt and cost between £2362 and £2427 each. They were followed by similar buses 83 to 89 by October 1945, and these were obtained for £2374 each. The final batch had Duple bodies which featured aluminium external panels with 92 entering service in October 1945, while 86 and 89 followed by March 1946. It is thought that 83 onwards had sliding window vents from new. The Duple-bodied K6As were much heavier vehicles at 7tons 7cwt, despite the use of aluminium.

Bristol K6A 92 (CKG 668) crosses the old Wood Street Bridge. The body had been substantially rebuilt by D.J. Davies in 1952, and later by CCT in 1956/57 when it gained rubber-mounted windows. The high position of the radiator is most evident.

(The late Dave B Thomas collection)

Wartime re-bodying by East Lancs

In 1943 the bodies of A.E.C. Regents 1 to 8 and 10 (KG 3701-8/10) were scrapped, and following overhaul, the chassis received new 56-seat East Lancs high-bridge layout bodies in 1944 to a non-utility design. However, 9 (KG 3709) the odd one out, carried on working with its original 6-bay NCME body. In 1943/44 the bodies of 1932-vintage Leyland TD2s 53 to 62 (KG 1146-55) were removed and sold to Bristol Tramways and Carriage Co. Ltd. The chassis of 53 to 62 were then overhauled locally by Leyland, and went on to receive new 56-seat East Lancs bodies in 1944 (54, 56, 58 to 60), 1945 (55, 57 and 62) and 1946 (53 and 61).

Noted close to the General station in Central Square, and now wearing fleet livery, is Leyland TD2 53 (KG 1146) of 1932, with its new East Lancs body fitted in 1946. It is looking pretty shabby and the bonnet side panel is propped open. Upon withdrawal in 1950, its East Lancs body was fitted to new Daimler CVD6 chassis and emerged as 53 (EBO 10).

(Roy Marshall collection courtesy of The Omnibus Society)

Trials with Producer Gas

Producer gas was an alternative fuel to petrol that was manufactured from high-quality coal such s anthracite. In July 1940 a Worldwin Gasmaker Producer Gas trailer was acquired for £153 from Worldwin Products, and in November AEC converted a Regent to run on producer gas. This experiment was however abandoned within 12 months. In December 1942 the Ministry of War Transport later instructed Cardiff to put 12 producer gas buses in service although this figure was later reduced to six. It is known that AEC Regents 11 to 13 and 18 worked with gas trailers between March 1944 and March 1945, even though the whole scheme had been abandoned by September 1944. The trailers were subsequently sold.

CHAPTER THREE

THE AUSTERITY YEARS AND THE END OF THE TRAMS

Cardiff Corporation Transport emerged from the Second World War on 8 May 1945 relatively unscathed having lost no trams or buses, but they did suffer damage to buildings and infrastructure. The fleet at this point in time comprised 89 electric tramcars, 10 trolleybuses and 138 motor buses. The trams consisted of eight open-top cars (22, 23, 29, 30, 32, 34, 84 and 90) that were by now confined to the Newport Road to Victoria Park route. All had been rebuilt many years earlier and had gone by July 1947. The remainder were Brush/Peckham closed-top cars that were from the 1923 and 1925 deliveries as follows:

> 1 to 4, 7 to 9, 11/4, 16 to 19, 20/1, 25 to 28, 31/3, 35 to 39, 40, 55 to 59, 60, 62 to 69, 70/1, 73 to 75, 77 to 79, 80 to 83, 85 to 89, 91 to 98, 100 to 114

This wartime view at the Victoria Park terminus shows Brush/Peckham car number 94, which is a very presentable example in the traditional fleet livery. Note the P.A.Y.E. sign in the windscreen and the hood fitted over the headlamp.
(John Wiltshire collection)

The trams were in decline and the condition of the vehicles and permanent way was poor. The vehicles were now giving an inferior ride and were becoming unpopular with the travelling public. In 1946 the tram track in Neville Street and Lower Cathedral Road was lifted and Clare Road depot was closed to trams on 25 August, all cars now being housed at Roath. The ten AEC trolleybuses 201 to 210 on the other hand were a mere three years old and were giving good service.

Motor buses

The motor bus fleet at the end of the Second World War was entirely diesel-powered as follows:

PRE-WAR BUSES	
Leyland TS4	138 to 142
Leyland TD2	53 to 62
Leyland TD4c	31 to 35
AEC Regent	1 to 20 36 to 41 47 to 50 151 to 191
AEC Regal	143 to 150
Crossley Mancunian	21 and 22
WARTIME BUSES	
AEC Regent	192 to 199
Guy Arab Utilities	29 63 to 76
Bristol K6A Utilities	77 to 94

In addition, the following buses were in withdrawn status in 1945:

FLEET NO	REGISTRATION	CHASSIS TYPE	COMMENTS
135	UH 9004	Thornycroft BC	Became a pole-carrier in the service vehicle fleet
101 to 108	FE8518, 8871	Dennis E	Former Lincoln saloons of 1926/27 with new NCME bodies fitted in 1933. Some of these had latterly been in use as A.R.P. ambulances during the war.
52	UH 7175	Leyland TD1	
23	KG 1251	AEC Regent	

Changes to the fleet in the years 1946-49

In 1945 the Ministry of War Transport (MoWT) allocated 40 6-wheel Guy trolleybuses to Cardiff for 1946 delivery, but these did not materialise. This was a period when the Corporation, with a worn-out tramway system, would embark on replacing it with a new trolleybus fleet. In particular the track on the Bute Street section of the busy tram service 16 from The Hayes to Pier Head was in a bad way. The trams were withdrawn and replaced on a temporary basis by motor buses on 28 April 1946, pending the introduction of trolleybuses. The clearance under the Bute Street railway bridge necessitated the use of single-deckers, and five were specified as part of the large order placed by Cardiff Corporation for 75 vehicles.

The condition of the bodywork on many of the pre-war motor buses was also of concern, and so a programme of re-bodying and rebuilding had to be implemented. Air Dispatch Ltd was founded in 1934, and based at Croydon operated air services. For their wartime activities they relocated to Pengam Moors airfield at Tremorfa, Cardiff, in 1939. Initially involved in ferrying RAF personnel, they soon began repairing aircraft. After the war they moved into coach-building, carrying out repairs and rebuilds, and soon entered into an arrangement with Cardiff Corporation Transport. The first vehicle they rebuilt was Bristol K6A 84 (CKG 651) which was completed in October 1946. The company title Air Dispatch (Coachbuilders) Ltd was adopted from December 1947, and early on, a number of buses continued to be repainted in wartime grey cellulose, which resulted in many running in this guise until at least 1949. On 21 September 1948 the business was renamed Bruce Coach Works Ltd and by the end of 1949, the combined number of buses dealt with for the Cardiff fleet was around 50. Some of this work was quite extensive and involved replacing much rotten and corroded fabric of the existing lower sections of bodywork.

The Austerity Years and the End of the Trams

A summary of all vehicles rebuilt/overhauled during the period 1946 to 1949 is set out below:

CARDIFF CT WORKSHOPS	
1946	12/16/18 (KG 5004/8/10) 38 (KG 8908) 50, 156 (KG 9804/10) 169/180 (ABO 972/83)
1947	39 (KG 8909) 151/152/155/159 (KG 9805/6/9/13) 170 (ABO 973) 148 to 150 (AKG 418-20)
1948	41 (KG 8911) 47 and 49 (KG 9801/3)
1949	9 (KG 3709) 139/141/142 (KG 1142/4/5)
AIR DISPATCH, CARDIFF	
1946	84 (CKG 651)
1947	2 (KG 3702) 11/13/15/20 (KG 5003/5/7/12) 37 (KG 8907)
	154 (KG 9808) 168/70/73/81 (ABO 971/3/6/84) 199 (CKG 325)
	143 to 147 (ABO 985-9)
BRUCE COACH WORKS	
1948	1 (KG 3701) 16 and 17 (KG 5008/9) 40 (KG 8910) 48 (KG 9802) 152/153/161/164 to 166 (KG 9806/7/15/8-20) 174/175/179 (ABO 977/8/82) 185 (BBO 70) 192/193/195 (CBO 701/2/4)
1949	157 (KG 9811) 181 (ABO 984) 182/184/186 to 191 (BBO 67/9/71-6) 194/196 to 198 (CBO 703/5-7) 80 (CKG 584)
Year unknown	178 (ABO 981)
WELSH METAL INDUSTRIES	
1948	14 (KG 5006)

There are no recorded withdrawals of vehicles in 1946.

Doodlebugs

The Pier Head route was converted to trolleybus operation earlier than planned and in order to achieve this, seven second-hand single-deck trolleybuses were purchased from Pontypridd Urban District Council as a stop-gap measure. In November 1946 officials from Cardiff inspected TG 381/91 at Pontypridd and by April 1947 it was agreed to pay £200 each for five vehicles, £1000 each for the remaining pair which were undergoing a major overhaul at the time and £384 for a consignment of spare parts. They were 30ft English Electric SD6WTB models with English Electric 32-seat centre-entrance bodies and dated from 1930. The bodies were divided into three compartments with 12 transverse seats forward, a wooden 3-seater bench amidships and 17 in the rear section arranged around the perimeter of the body. They were 7ft 6in wide with an unladen weight of 7tons 12cwt, but were only capable of 18mph. Fleet numbers 231 to 237 were allocated to registrations TG 379/81/3/5/7/9/91, and all were placed into service between May and August 1947. 231 and 236 were the pair that were overhauled and received CCT crimson lake and cream fleet livery with gold lining, while the other five remained in wartime grey primer for their time at Cardiff. On 17 August 1947 the Pier Head service 16 became Cardiff's second trolleybus route when 231 to 237 took up duties on this service, but they also appeared as specials on other services. The P.A.Y.E. system was used for fare collection and at the same time the 6/6A trolleybus service was extended from Clarence Road (Avondale Hotel) to meet up with the 16 at Pier Head. 231 to 237 earned the nickname Doodlebugs, and remained with Cardiff until 1950 when all the new vehicles had been received.

This is a fine study of English Electric trolleybus 236 at Pier Head. It was one of the pair that benefitted from an overhaul and therefore gained full CCT livery upon entering service with Cardiff. Of particular interest is the mounting arrangement of the trolley booms, and also the centre entrance.

(Cardiff Transport Preservation Group collection)

Also inspected at Pontypridd Uban District Council by the engineering superintendent Felix Cunuder at this time was a pair of double-deck trolleybuses. These were 9 (HY 2391), a 60-seat Beadle-bodied 3-axle Bristol E model fitted with an 80hp B.T.H. motor; and 8 (UK 8948), a 56-seat Guy-bodied 3-axle Guy BTX trolleybus dating from 1930 and fitted with a 60hp B.T.H. motor. Both were in poor condition and it was estimated that it would cost in the region of £300 each to get them back on the road. The Bristol trolleybus was also considered to be underpowered for use in Cardiff.

OUTSTANDING ORDERS?

Prior to the Second World War, Cardiff had favoured AEC chassis and continued to do so, but when new vehicles were sought in the immediate post-war years, chassis supply was limited, and so the undertaking had to take what they could get. After the hostilities ended production of the AEC O661 chassis (with 7.7-litre engine and 4 speed crash gearbox) resumed as the Regent II and a total of 695 were built. In October 1945 it was announced that a number of AEC Regents had still been on order at the outbreak of the war, and delivery was never fully completed. As a result an order was confirmed for ten AEC Regent II chassis with the AEC A173 engine and a crash gearbox at £1450 each. The body contract went to East Lancs and four of these were to low-bridge layout. By March 1947 the cost of the chassis had risen to £1291-10s and the bodies were now £1700 each. The low-bridge examples were the first to arrive entering service between 14 March and 17 April 1947 as 101 to 104 (CUH 377-80) with 53-seat bodies. They had cream roofs and were said to be for route 24 and the Tredegar service. The six outstanding had high-bridge layout bodies that were built locally with 56-seat Air Dispatch bodywork assembled using East Lancs frames. The first of these to arrive were 95 and 96 (CUH 371/2) in December 1947 followed by 97 to 100 (CUH 373-6) in early 1948. Of note was that 95 was the first double-decker to be completed by Air Dispatch, while 104 made the headlines on 31 December 1947 when it skidded on ice and overturned.

The Austerity Years and the End of the Trams

What may have been the balance of outstanding chassis from the 1939 orders, (see above), were now due by March 1948. These were a further nine AEC Regent IIs and entered service between 24 March and 11 June 1948 as 105 to 113 (DKG 829-37). Like 95 to 100 they received Air Dispatch bodywork and a number of chassis had been stored locally in the Council-owned Llandaff Fields Pavilion from February 1948, awaiting delivery to the coachbuilder at Tremorfa. These were smart looking vehicles with an overall height of 14ft 5in and an unladen weight varying between 7tons and 7tons 4cwt. Some buses, including 95/6/8, 100 to 103/5/6 and 108 to 111/3, received shorter AEC radiators from pre-war Regents later on in their working lives. Upon rebuild, all the high-bridge Regent IIs received some rubber-mounted windows, while others also gained opening ventilators in the front upper deck windows and included 95, 100/5, 108 to 112. All the Regent IIs were taken out of service between 1962 and 1964. 96 and 104 went on to become training buses in the service vehicle fleet, while 108 (DKG 832) saw some further use after sale as a breakdown tender in the Cardiff area.

100 (CUH 376), an AEC Regent II passes along Wood Street. It has a high-bridge body completed by Air Dispatch, and it has yet to receive any rubber-mounted windows, but does feature a short radiator from a pre-war Regent.
(John Jones collection)

Vehicle shortage continues

Whilst trying to obtain as many new vehicles as possible, Cardiff was experiencing delays with supply, largely due to a backlog of work at the bodybuilder East Lancs. Still desperately short of motor buses the undertaking had to hire in seven buses from the privately-owned fleet of Hants and Sussex Motor Services for six months from November 1947. This was later extended by 12 months with the buses remaining on hire until May 1949. Details below:

HS2 to HS4 were actually brand new when taken on hire. Being of low-bridge layout HS5 was used on the Markham route, while HS1 was allocated to the Merthyr route. The buses were turned out in their owner's striking light red, dark red and cream livery enhanced by black mudguards and gold lining.

104 (CUH 380) one of the four low-bridge East Lancs-bodied AEC Regent IIs, and is seen at Sloper Road depot in the late 1940s.
(John Wiltshire)

105 (DKG 829) is one of the 1948 delivery of Air Dispatch-bodied AEC Regent IIs. It waits to depart Central bus station bound for Lisvane, a route that required 7ft 6in wide buses until 1962 when restrictions were relaxed.
(Dave B Thomas collection)

The Austerity Years and the End of the Trams

BUSES HIRED FROM HANTS & SUSSEX MOTOR SERVICES					
FLEET NO.	REGISTRATION	CHASSIS	BODY	SEATING	YEAR NEW
HS6	ECG 616	Leyland TD7	Brush	H30/26R	1942
HS7	EHO 586	Guy Arab I 5LW	Park Royal	"	1943
HS5	FCG 524	Leyland PD1	NCB	L27/28R	1947
HS1	FOR 837	"	"	H29/26R	1947
HS4	GAA 179	"	Leyland	H30/26R	"
HS3	GAA 180	"	"	"	"
HS2	GAA 181	"	"	"	"

In 1947, such was the need to obtain new vehicles that a pair of nearly-new Crossley double-deckers was acquired from Almondsbury Engineering Company Ltd (Streamways) of Almondsbury, South Gloucestershire, in December that year. Almondsbury had purchased these DD42/3 model double-deckers in 1947, which were registered GDF 58 and GDG 456 respectively. They had Crossley 7/1 8.6-litre engines and were fitted with 56-seat bodies from the Scottish Commercial Motor Company of St. Rollox in Glasgow. Scottish Commercial was a new coachbuilder and dealer who completed their first body in 1943 and produced 23 in the years up to 1950. They became agents for Crossley Motors Ltd in 1946. GDF 58 and GDG 456 were sold to Cardiff Corporation on 20 April 1948 for £7700 the pair, and entered service the following month as 23 and 24. On a positive note, they both featured Lush moquette seating, but the main drawback was their overall height of 14ft 8½in. As a result they were confined to a handful of routes such as the 26 to Snowden Road in Ely, the 23 to Whitchurch and the 38 service to Rhiwbina Deri. The destination boxes on 23 and 24 were rebuilt to make them suitable for use in Cardiff, and they received rubber-mounted windows in the period 1957 to 1959.

The only vehicle withdrawn in 1947 was 138 (KG1141) one of the Leyland Tiger TS4 single-deckers, which was destroyed by fire.

Former Streamways Crossley DD42/3 24 (GDG 456) waits on the perimeter of Central Bus Station bound for Snowden Road, Ely. The 7ft 6in wide body only accentuates the overall height of the bus. Note the modified destination box.
(John Jones collection)

Trolleybuses will replace trams

1948 saw the expansion of the trolleybus system gather pace. The first firm order for trolleybuses appeared to be in early 1946 for 75 8ft-wide AECs, five of which were single-deckers. On 21 June 1946 the joint company B.U.T. (British United Traction) was formed to build trolleybuses for AEC and Leyland, initially at the Leyland works at Kingston upon Thames. Cardiff therefore got B.U.T. trolleybuses.

The design for the new trolleybuses was the responsibility of the Transport Department's Chief Engineer W J Evans, before he became Transport Manager at Reading in 1946. They were B.U.T. 9641T models with GEC electrical equipment and 95hp motors. At this point it is worth mentioning that all new Cardiff trolleybuses were fitted with batteries to enable them to move under their own power for short distances whilst detached from the overhead wires. Their specially designed East Lancs bodies had a seating layout of H38/29D, and the completed vehicles had an unladen weight of 10tons 2cwt. The first of the order for 75 trolleybuses began to arrive and were numbered 211 to 230 (DBO 471-80, DUH 716-25). This now meant the next new route to Victoria Park via Canton could be introduced. The wiring was completed in May 1948 and from 6 June that year some of the new double-deckers began operating service 5A which ran from St. Mary Street to Victoria Park via Neville Street. The second service was the 5B which ran from St. Mary Street to Victoria Park via Castle Street, and both 5A and 5B deployed the P.A.Y.E. system for fare collection. The bodies which featured a dual-door/staircase system, were based on the Alcock design of 1927. Alfred Alcock at this time worked for Massey Bros and went on to form East Lancashire Coach Builders. This arrangement it was claimed would speed up boarding and disembarking times by eliminate congestion on the rear platform. The vehicles had a normal rear open-platform entrance and forward-ascending staircase with a front exit that had an air-operated sliding door controlled by the driver, and a rearward-descending staircase situated on the nearside, ahead of the doorway. Attached to the rear platform bulkhead was a seat for the conductor to observe passenger traffic and to ensure they placed their fare in the coin box.

218 (DBO 478) turns from Newport Road into City Road in about 1967, and appears to have come from the direction of Roath depot before taking up duty on the 3 from Roath Park. Behind the trolleybus is the splendid Cardiff Royal Infirmary which still stands in 2016. We also see the back of an Alexander-bodied Guy Arab V, while a Neepsend-bodied example waits at the traffic lights in Glossop Road. Note the complex nature of the overhead wires.

(Glyn Bowen courtesy Chris Taylor CTPG)

The Austerity Years and the End of the Trams

On 4 July 1948 service 5 was introduced, which took advantage of new wiring installed to Windsor Lane near Dumfries Place. This enabled a through service to Victoria Park running along Queen Street. By mid-1948 the expansion of the trolleybus network meant that only three tram routes remained. These covered the eastern side of Cardiff and were served by approximately 45 tramcars. Most of these were taken out of service between October 1948 and July 1949, and interestingly 13 of them were still in wartime grey primer livery.

Despite the drawbacks with the two Crossleys 23 and 24 obtained in 1948, a third example was obtained shortly after. This bus had been ordered by Almondsbury Engineering Company Ltd, and was due to have been registered HAD 141 in October 1947 but cancelled by 19 December. It was a DD42/5 model, also with a Crossley diesel, but featured some frame and engine mounting modifications. After purchase by Cardiff on 18 May, it was delivered on 20 July 1948, registered EBO 103 and given fleet number 25. It entered service alongside 23 and 24 with a modified destination box, and went on to receive rubber-mounted windows in June 1958.

New dimensions

When 8-foot wide chassis were permitted from February 1946, the Bristol K was made available as the KW model, an 8ft wide 26ft long chassis. Cardiff ordered 20 in July 1946 with Gardner 6LW engines which were designated KW6G. These were Cardiff's first 8ft-wide motor buses and as it turned out, were also the only examples of the KW chassis built. East Lancs were originally to body these, but the contract was passed to Air Dispatch in July 1947 who used East Lancs frames. The chassis were built and then stored from March 1948 in the Cardiff area for up to 12 months prior to bodying. The name of the coachbuilder changed to Bruce Coach Works in October 1948 during construction of these buses. Delivery commenced in October 1948 and continued through to March 1949. The batch was numbered 114 to 133 (DUH 301-20) with 119, 121/2/5, 127 to 129 and 131 to 133 being the 1949 arrivals. Their 4-bay bodies seated 59, and they had an overall height of 14ft 7in.

Bristol KW6G 115 (DUH 302) is seen out on driver training duties in about April 1966 with driving instructor Stanley Rogers in attendance. *(Glyn Bowen courtesy CTPG)*

Bristol KW6Gs 114 to 117, 120/3/4, 126 to 128 and 130 were rebuilt between 1957 and 1963, and it is known that 119, 123/4/6/8 and 131 received rubber-mounted upper deck front windows. 118 and 125 (DUH 305/12) were used as parts donors during the rebuild of this batch and were then rebuilt in June and January 1963 respectively. At this point they lost their elliptical lower saloon end windows, and also received rubber-mounted windows throughout, with new ventilators. 118 had been out of service for around 400 days. The Bristol KW6Gs were all withdrawn between November 1964 (128) and March 1968, with 131 being the last example in normal service.

Bristol KW6G 125 (DUH 312) is pictured on the forecourt at Sloper Road having received a major rebuild after being used as a parts donor for around a year. This bus was one of two of the Bristol KW6Gs to receive rubber-mounted windows throughout giving it a much more modern appearance.

(*John Jones collection*)

Spare bodies

The fitting of new 5-bay East Lancs bodies to the 1932-vintage Leyland TD2s 53 to 62 (KG 1146-55) in the years 1944 to 1946 was not deemed a success due to weight issues. This resulted in insufficient braking and heavy steering and, following issues with the Ministry of Transport, all ten buses were withdrawn in 1948. The plan was to buy new AEC Regent II chassis to receive these bodies, but Cardiff was informed by AEC that this model had just gone out of production. The only new chassis still available that were suitable to receive these East Lancs 56-seat bodies were from Daimler. Cardiff stated that it wanted Gardner engines, but these were not available, and so ten Daimler CVD6 models were ordered in December 1947 at a cost of £19450, and for delivery in April/May 1948. The Engineering and Rolling Stock Superintendent at Cardiff consulted with engineers at Newport Corporation and Rhondda Transport to report on the operation of Daimler engines.

The Austerity Years and the End of the Trams

On Kingsway we see an immaculate Daimler CVD6 61 (EBO 2) with its second-hand East Lancs body that came from Leyland TD2 61 (KG 1154). The result was an attractive and solid-looking vehicle.

(The late Dave B. Thomas collection)

Following modification the East Lancs bodies were gradually transferred to the new Daimler chassis over the years 1948 to 1950, and the Leyland chassis were then sold. The completed vehicles were given fleet numbers in the series 52 to 61 and were registered as they entered service, resulting in out of sequence fleet/registration numbers which was never corrected. The batch was:

FLEET NO.	REGISTRATION	CHASSIS	BODY	YEAR BODIED	BODY FROM
58	EBO 1	Daimler CVD6	East Lancs	1948	KG 1151
61	EBO 2	"	"	"	KG 1154
59	EBO 3	"	"	1949	KG 1152
57	EBO 4	"	"	"	KG 1150
55	EBO 5	"	"	"	KG 1148
54	EBO 6	"	"	"	KG 1147
52	EBO 7	"	"	"	KG 1155
56	EBO 8	"	"	1950	KG 1149
60	EBO 9	"	"	"	KG 1153
53	EBO 10	"	"	"	KG 1146

The CVD6s had pre-select gearboxes, supplied as standard for many years and, perhaps surprisingly, retained their Daimler engines throughout their working life. These engines, though very smooth-running, were noted for burning oil and had a very high fuel consumption which, at 7mpg, was the worst in fleet in 1965. In 1957 the entire batch received new 8ft-wide 60-seat Longwell Green bodies on their 7ft 6in chassis.

Some statistics quoted in The Passenger Transport Year Book for 1948 stated that Cardiff Corporation Transport Department operated 75 trams (route mileage 9.34), 17 trolleybuses (route mileage 4.99) and 147 motor buses (route mileage 127.48).

New for the Tredegar route

The final new motor buses in this period were a batch of six Crossley DD42/7 double-deckers for the Cardiff to Tredegar route with delivery by May 1949. They were supplied by Scottish Commercial Motor Company of Glasgow and were originally specified in October 1948, and finally ordered in March 1949. Scottish Commercial quoted a price of £4035 each for a low-bridge bus with composite-built bodywork. It later revised this to £4160 each for an all-metal body. An agreement was then reached by which they would all receive Alexander 53-seat bodies to the standard Leyland design used by Alexander at the time. The Crossley DD42 chassis was available between 1945 and 1951 and was particularly popular in the municipal sector in this period and over 80% of them were bodied by Crossley. The six DD42/7 models for Cardiff would have probably featured the Crossley HOE7/5 8.6-litre down-draught engine of 112bhp and a constant-mesh gearbox. They entered service in June 1949 as 42 to 46 and 51 (EBO 896-901). These fine-looking vehicles were the last new buses purchased by Cardiff with traditional low-bridge bodies, complete with sunken offside gangway in the upper saloon. Their delivery enabled the seven Hants and Sussex double-deckers to be returned off loan. They were normally used on the Tredegar route as well as the 32 to St. Fagans and Hensol Castle route, but their usefulness was somewhat diminished after the AEC Bridgemasters arrived in 1960. The appearance of 42 (EBO 896) was later altered as it received new rubber-mounted upper deck front windows with opening ventilators. All six vehicles went on to receive modified destination apertures with rubber-mounted glazing. These Crossleys were withdrawn between 1963 and 1966, and 46 (EBO 900) was sold to the Cardiff 46 Group in September 1966 for preservation.

45 (EBO 899) with a large destination box, is in original condition when pictured at Tredegar on the service for which it was originally purchased. It is a Crossley DD42/7 with a low-bridge Alexander body.
(Author's collection)

Motor buses withdrawn in 1949 included 3 (KG 3703), the first of the 1934 AEC Regents to go, together with similar 36 to 38 of 1936. The two Crossley Mancunians (21 and 22), further Leyland TD2s, and all five of the 1936 Leyland TD4c double-deckers (31 to 35) were also taken out of service. The remaining AEC Regents of 1934, 1, 2, 4-10 were then briefly renumbered 21/2/6-8, 30-2/6 to free up their fleet numbers for forthcoming new buses.

The Austerity Years and the End of the Trams

More delays

It was originally planned to close the tram system in June 1949, but unfortunately delays to the delivery of new trolleybuses meant that this event had to be postponed. However some minor sections of track continued to be abandoned. It was announced that in order to speed up deliveries, the contract for 25 double-deck trolleybus bodies, would be transferred from East Lancs to Bruce Coach Works at South Park Road in Tremorfa, Cardiff. As a result of these delays, new trolleybus chassis had to be securely stored in the Cardiff area. The programme to replace Cardiff's ailing trams with trolleybuses continued into 1949 with three new routes planned. Tram service 4 from Roath Park to St. Mary Street ran for the last time on 3 December, operated by tram 107, suitably decked out for the occasion. The trams were replaced on 4 December 1949 with a new trolleybus service 3 which terminated at Roath Park (Ninian Road/Fairoak Road) and turned on the new roundabout at this junction. New B.U.T. 9641T trolleybuses received in 1949 were 238 to 242 (EBO 891-5), the five saloons with 38-seat East Lancs bodies for the Pier Head route. These were in effect a scaled-down version of the double-deckers 211 to 230, and they featured a front exit. Once in service they allowed the withdrawal of the elderly ex-Pontypridd English Electric saloons 231 to 237.

242 (EBO 895) is numerically the last of the five B.U.T. single-deck trolleybuses new in 1949. It is seen at the terminus in Mill Lane with its forward exit door clearly visible. It would soon head off to Bute Street on the short run to Pier Head.
(John Wiltshire collection)

Also entering service in late 1949/early 1950 were double-deck trolleybuses 245 to 264 (EBO 902-21) which were basically similar to 211 to 230 of 1948. Of these, 248, 251 to 264 were the first examples with Bruce-completed bodies (using East Lancs frames), and in October, 264 had the distinction of being the first new trolleybus to be completed in Wales. Five of the East Lancs vehicles were actually completed by Yorkshire Equipment Co. Ltd of Bessingby near Bridlington using East Lancs frames. These were believed to be 245 to 247, 249 and 250. Finally, the flat fare used on the P-A-Y-E vehicles was raised to 1½d on most services from 5 June 1949.

B.U.T. double-deck trolleybus 245 (EBO 902) was delivered in 1950, and is seen at the Gabalfa terminus while working the service 9 to Pier Head, that was introduced in 1951. This vehicle has a body completed by Yorkshire Equipment Company on East Lancs frames, and of particular interest is the front exit in the open position.

(Roy Marshall collection courtesy of The Omnibus Society)

CHAPTER FOUR

FURTHER FLEET RENEWAL AND NEW-LOOK FRONTS

The year 1950 marked the start of a new decade, the year in which Cardiff's tramway system would finally close down. The last tram had run to Pier Head in 1946, while the last tram journey to Victoria Park took place in 1948, both being replaced by trolleybuses. With the trams having been withdrawn from the Newport Road services on 16 October 1948, and temporarily replaced by motor buses, the sole remaining tram route was that to Whitchurch Road at Gabalfa. The last tramcar number 112 ran in normal service on the evening of Sunday 19 February 1950. It had been decorated with ribbons, flags and messages by enthusiasts, and it operated service 1 from St. Mary Street to Whitchurch Road, before finally returning to Roath depot at 23.30. Trolleybuses then took over service 1 the following day. However tramcar number 11 was decorated by the Transport Department to operate a "special" service on 20 February between St. Mary Street and Whitchurch Road alongside the trolleybuses. Such was the demand by the public for one last ride, that tramcar 112 was brought out once more late in the afternoon as a relief. And so history was made, as a line was drawn under electric tramcar operation in Cardiff, after forty eight years. What is particularly unfortunate is that not a single passenger tramcar was saved; such was the desire by so many in the council to rid the city of this form of public transport. All the remaining vehicles were burnt and scrapped at the rear of Roath depot during the spring of 1950. The only survivor of the electric tramway system was the water car 131 that dated from 1905.

Tram number 11 was decorated to mark the end of the tram system in Cardiff and is seen here on Whitchurch Road at Gabalfa. It is working the "special" service on 20 February 1950, the day the trolleybuses officially took over, as is evident by the example in the background.

(The late Chris Taylor collection)

Fine-looking buses

This year also saw the arrival of some new AEC Regent III double-deckers, a model that had its origins in 1937 when London Transport developed a new chassis with AEC. Following the development of this chassis, AEC announced that it would be marketing a similar chassis for general sale. The "provincial" Regent III rolled off the production line complete with most of the lower cab section assembled, which was preferred by most bodybuilders at the time. A number of versions were made available by AEC including one with a manual crash gearbox and vacuum brakes. A further option featured the smaller 7.7-litre AEC A173 engine, while from 1950, a 27ft chassis was introduced. The AEC Regent III was replaced by the Regent V in 1954, but production did not finish until 1956.

Cardiff Corporation ordered 20 8-foot wide Regent III chassis in April 1948 at an initial cost of £40,000. They were late examples of the 26-ft long 9612E model, with AEC A208 9.6-litre engines of 125bhp at 1800rpm, four-speed air operated Wilson preselector epicyclic transmission and air brakes. 59-seat East Lancs steel-framed bodies at an initial cost of £41,208 were also ordered with delivery due late 1949/early 1950. In October 1949 in a somewhat surprising move, AEC informed the General Manager that the price of the 20 chassis would be reduced to £38,568. However, shortly after East Lancs announced that the price of the 20 bodies would rise to £43,007. In December 1949 East Lancs indicated that five bodies would be built by Yorkshire Equipment Co. Ltd of Bessingby at their Bridlington works. This company later became East Lancs (Bridlington) Ltd from about March 1950. However there was no mention at this time that the remaining 15 would actually be built by Bruce Coach Works in Cardiff using East Lancs frames. The batch was numbered 1 to 20 with registrations EUH733-52.

18 (EUH 750), a Bruce-bodied AEC Regent III in more or less original condition is parked at the side of Roath depot on Newport Road, and in the shadow of the adjacent power station. A most attractive bus. *(Glyn Bowen courtesy Chris Taylor CTPG)*

Delivery took place between February and April 1950, and they were the last exposed-radiator buses delivered new to Cardiff Corporation. When new they had large destination indicators which were modified over the years, and in their original form, these destination displays were never to be surpassed for information. They were the first motor buses in the fleet with air brakes and all carried a label on the windscreen "Caution Air Brakes". The Bridlington-built buses, 11, 14 to 16 and 20, differed in that they did not have louvres in upper deck front windows and also when new, had a cream band below the windscreen. Many were later rebuilt between 1958 and 1964 with rubber-mounted upper deck windows. 14 was completely rebuilt by Western Welsh in 1963 with rubber-mounted windows throughout, while on the other hand, 5 was not rebuilt to any extent, and remained in largely original condition with large front destination box but with a single panel route number box at the rear. 15 was the first motor bus to be painted in the revised livery introduced by General Manager E.G.A. Singleton in 1963.

The new Regent IIIs were used on most routes around the City with the exception of Lisvane and other semi-rural routes with a width restriction. They were regularly found operating the Cardiff to Merthyr Tydfil service 41, and even up to the mid-1960s they could be found duplicating the 17.30 Merthyr Corporation departure out of Cardiff. They were popular buses and did sound rather like London RTs, especially if they started from rest in bottom gear. Two members of the batch were involved in major accidents quite late on in their lives. Five went off the road and into the brook at Fairwater Green on 30 December 1966. It was withdrawn and donated its engine to sister bus 19. On 8 May 1967 number 3 was in the vicinity of Canton Bridge (opposite Green Street) during the morning rush hour, when it struck a power feeder traction post. The result was that it brought havoc to the trolleybus system on that section. The bus sustained considerable damage and was withdrawn as a result. Normal withdrawals had begun in 1966 and continued through to 1968. Sadly none of the buses saw any further service, with Bill Way at Cardiff East Dock taking the bulk of them for scrap.

New offices and more trolleybuses

The Transport Department moved from its temporary offices in Womanby Street to an old building in Wood Street which had been converted from a school, and opened for business at this location on 1 June 1950. With the end of the tram system, trolleybus overhead wiring was now erected through to Roath depot, and on 15 October 1950 trolleybus operation began on service 2. The route had been extended at the Roath depot end to run over the railway at Pengam Bridge to a new terminus at Clydesmuir Road, Tremorfa. The balance of the Bruce-bodied trolleybuses were delivered in 1950 as 265 to 274 (FBO 85-94), and were identical to the earlier deliveries. The P.A.Y.E. system was completely abandoned on 12 November 1950 as being uneconomical. With this system now deemed a failure, the front exits on the trolleybuses were sealed up from about 1954. They were later panelled over on all examples apart from 222. The double-deckers however retained their front staircases to the end of their lives. The Ultimate ticket system was then introduced across the fleet. Most trolleybuses in the 211 to 230, 245 to 274 series had their bodies extensively rebuilt, which included to varying degrees, the use of rubber-mounted windows and modified rubber-mounted destination apertures.

A large number of buses were withdrawn in 1950. This included the last of the Leyland TD2s that were donating their bodies to the new Daimler CVD6 chassis. Also taken out of service were the last of the 1934 and 1935 AEC Regents, and the first five of the 1937 Regents. Finally the first AEC Regal (146), a Lewis-bodied example and the second-hand pre-war trolleybuses (231 to 237) were officially taken off fleet strength. The AEC Regal 146 became a mobile canteen for the undertaking, fulfilling that role until 1956.

Further in-house body swapping

Cardiff Corporation Transport continued its well tried and tested practice of re-bodying chassis with sound re-used bodies in order to get a few more years out of a vehicle, at a time when new buses were still in relatively short supply. Having been withdrawn in 1949, the East Lancs body dating from 1944 was removed from the chassis of 3 (KG 3703) (new in 1934), and fitted in 1950 to newer AEC Regent 169 (ABO 972), that had been new in 1938 with a NCME body.

THE BODIES FROM:		WERE FITTED TO:	
21	KG 3701	172	ABO 975
22	KG 3702	162	KG 9816
26	KG 3704	167	ABO 970
27	KG 3705	163	KG 9817
28	KG 3706	160	KG 9814
30	KG 3707	171	ABO 974
31	KG 3708	168	ABO 971
36	KG 3710	158	KG 9812

Having been renumbered in 1949, and then as mentioned above withdrawn in 1950, the 1944-built bodies of a further eight 1934-vintage AEC Regents were removed, and fitted to slightly newer (1937) chassis in 1950/51. It gave these eight 1937-built chassis between four and eight further years in service with Cardiff.

AEC Regent 168 (ABO 971) of 1937 carries a 1944 East Lancs body from AEC Regent 31 (KG 3708). It is seen on 20 June 1953 at Custom House Street near the Monument. It is on its way from Splott to Grangetown on a 7A working.
(The late Alan Jarvis courtesy CTPG)

The original NCME bodies of 172 (ABO 975) etc were then sold for scrap. It is worth noting that the chassis of all but one of the 1934 Regents KG 3701-8/10 were sold for scrap, while KG 3709 with its original 6-bay NCME body passed to a showman. This whole process was carried out at a fraction of the cost of a new vehicle. The last three new Daimler CVD6s 56, 60, 53 (EBO 8-10) entered service in 1950, having received their second-hand East Lancs bodies removed from the 1932 Leyland TD2s.

An interesting double-decker was briefly received on loan during April this year from Foden Motor Works. It was KMA 575, a 1948 Foden PVD that was fitted with a 6-cylinder Foden FD6 4.09-litre super-charged two-stroke engine and Foden 4-speed constant mesh gearbox. In this respect it was unique as the only Foden double-decker so fitted. All other Foden double-deckers were PVD6 models with Gardner 6LW engines. KMA 575 had a low-bridge Willowbrook body dating from 1945 that had been removed from a Foden PVD6 demonstrator in 1948. It is known to have worked on the Tredegar route, but may also have seen use on the 30 to Newport.

Expanding the trolleybus system

In 1951 the Transport Department was quoted as saying "A trolleybus only has an advantage over a motor bus when passenger demand warrants a large vehicle". Within a few years motor bus dimensions would increase, and so this argument no longer carried any weight. At this point Cardiff still had 20 trolleybuses outstanding from the order for 75 B.U.T. vehicles, and in addition a substantial quantity of surplus overhead equipment was held by the undertaking.

A number of service revisions took place to the trolleybus system and three new through services were introduced on 21 October 1951 using the existing overhead. These were the 4 from Llandaff Fields to Roath Park and the 8 from the Royal Oak on Newport Road to Victoria Park, both running via Castle Street. The third through route was the 9 from Gabalfa (Whitchurch Road) to Pier Head running via St. Mary Street, Wood Street and Clare Road. Of note is that some morning peak journeys on the 2 from Pengam would run through to Victoria Park as service 8. In 1951 a proposal for three possible trolleybus extensions was submitted by the general manager for consideration by the Transport Committee. These were an extension from Victoria Park to Ely, one to Splott taking in Walker Road and Portmanmoor Road and finally a route to Willows Avenue, Tremorfa (via Splott) which would involve lowering the road under a railway bridge. No further decisions were made, but at this point East Lancs continued to offer motor bus bodies as an alternative, should no further trolleybuses be required. The motor bus fleet now stood at 174 vehicles.

In October 1951, two of the utility Bristol K6As (78 and 85) were taken out of service at the instruction of the Ministry of Transport, with major problems. Number 78 was later rebuilt at Roath works while 85 was dealt by a private contractor T. Hoskins. There were no new buses delivered in 1951 but AEC Regents 50 and 166 (KG 9804/20) of 1937 were withdrawn, the latter following an accident. Similar bus 156 (KG 9810) received the NCME body from 40 (KG 8910) of 1936.

SIZE DOES MATTER

At the start of the decade a small fleet of single-deck buses was still required for a few routes which were not suitable for double-deck operation. These included the 35 to Penarth which had an obstacle in the form of a low bridge in the Cogan area near the site of the Barons Court public house (as it is today), and also the route to Lavernock had a low bridge. The vehicles in use at this time were a mixed bag of pre-war saloons, the three remaining elderly and heavily rebuilt Leyland TS4s of 1932 and seven 1937 AEC Regals. In August 1950 Cardiff decided to replace some of these with five new saloons. Leyland Motors introduced the underfloor engine Royal Tiger chassis in May 1950 as an alternative to the integral Leyland Olympic. It incorporated many parts used in the Olympic and kept the same 15ft 7in wheelbase. The chassis was of channel section alloy-steel construction and was only available as a 30ft model in the UK, but in 7ft 6in or 8ft width. A spiral-bevel rear axle was fitted and a choice of vacuum or air brakes.

Tenders were received from six manufacturers for 18 model variations, but of these only four were under-floor engine vehicles. The lowest tender received was for Leyland Royal Tigers at a cost £1744 each. Five were ordered in March 1951, and extras which included auto chassis lubrication, alkaline batteries and electric speedometer brought the total cost to £1790 each. The bodywork was awarded to the lowest tender that could meet the specification and delivery date. Bruce Coachworks were chosen to build the 44-seat bodies in Cardiff, for £1710 per body, and they promised delivery within 12 weeks of receiving the chassis. This quote was cheaper than East Lancs, which was impressive as Bruce built their bodies on East Lancs frames. The cost of the chassis was increased in April 1951 and so Cardiff overcame this by revising the specification and deleting certain equipment. The revised price of £1727-17s-9d actually worked out cheaper than the original. Had all gone to plan Bruce Coach Works should have delivered the buses in September 1951, but in October 1951 Bruce announced that they would not be able to body the chassis, and East Lancs would now undertake the work. It is thought that Bruce actually commenced work on two bodies, but East Lancs went on to complete the five buses. The final body price was reported to be £2028-9s.

The five 44-seat Royal Tigers were delivered in 1952 as 134 to 138 and with registrations GKG 51-5. The chassis type was Leyland PSU1/15 and they were fitted with Leyland 0.600 engines and had four-speed gearboxes with synchromesh on the top three gears. On grounds of cost, Cardiff chose the vacuum triple servo braked model which, on buses with an unladen weight of around 7tons 17cwt, proved a constant problem in service. In order to accommodate them at Sloper Road garage, it is believed that the servicing pits had to be extended in length. One livery peculiarity was that when new, the cream bands did not have black lining. The Royal Tigers replaced four of the Lewis-bodied Regals, the fifth having been withdrawn a couple of years earlier.

Leyland Royal Tiger 137 (GKG 54) stands opposite the village school in Heol Pant Glas, Llanedeyrn village on a rather gloomy day. This is a service 54 and at the wheel is driver Alf Davies. He was one of the driving instructors, and they used to break off training for periods on Tuesdays and Fridays to operate this service. One of the trainees would act as conductor.

(Glyn Bowen courtesy Chris Taylor CTPG)

The main duties for 134 to 138 were to be on the Penarth route (35) and also on the 35A service to Lavernock via Redlands Road. Photographic evidence also records them in use on the 30 to Newport (evenings and Sundays), to Llanedeyrn village and to Capel Gwlym from Kingsway on the 29. At Capel Gwlym they would connect with the Caerphilly U.D.C. bus that had come over the mountain from Caerphilly. They were later used on the through service to Caerphilly via Thornhill and it is said that prior to the arrival of newer vehicles, these were the only CCT saloons capable of working up over Caerphilly mountain.

Further pre-war AEC Regents were withdrawn by the end of 1952 which left 41 (KG 8911), which was new in 1936, as the oldest double-deck bus in service. Also in 1952 it was announced that a number of the war time utility Guy Arabs would be sent away to East Lancs (Bridlington) Ltd to be refurbished, but this company went into voluntary liquidation before any Guys made the journey to Yorkshire. The contract then went to Longwell Green at Bristol. On 9 October 1952 the Cardiff Corporation Transport Department celebrated its Golden Jubilee and to mark this AEC Regent 155 (KG 9809) was fitted with a generator and decorated with lights, but did not enter passenger service as such.

New-look bonnets

For 1953 Cardiff received some early examples of Guy Motor's new Arab IV chassis and took up the option of Birmingham-style "new-look" bonnets assemblies, as supplied to Birmingham City Transport. This dispensed with the traditional exposed radiator and nearside front wing. In June 1951 Cardiff Corporation Transport ordered 15 Guy Arab IVs at a cost of £1742-15s each of which rose to £2054 as time went on. All-metal bodywork was supplied by Merthyr Tydfil-based coachbuilder D.J. Davies using Park Royal frames to four-bay construction and seating for 60 passengers, at a cost of £1780 each. The result was quite an attractive looking vehicle with a strong Park Royal resemblance. The lower-deck was of composite construction having wooden fillet inserts on the steel frame, while the upper-deck had the panels riveted directly to the steel frame. The two upper deck front windows were fixed panes, and the rear wheel arches had rubber mudguards, the first buses in the fleet to have this feature. Another feature was the internal window pan surfaces which were covered in a maroon-coloured leather cloth. The lower-deck front bulkhead was covered in brown linoleum, which was fixed in place by polished aluminium strips. This finish seemed a bit dated in 1953, as the previous two batches of double-deckers delivered to Cardiff had the front bulkhead finished in polished "chequer" plate.

They entered service as 26 to 40 with registrations GUH 931-45. They had an overall height of 14ft 6½in and were the last half cabs delivered to Cardiff to have hinged cab doors. Delivery was a somewhat protracted affair and took place between 3 February 1953 (32) and 23 January 1954 (37). The engine was the reliable Gardner 6LW 8.4-litre diesel of 112bhp driving through a Guy 4-speed constant-mesh gearbox while the braking system used was a vacuum-assisted triple servo. It was reported that some of these buses were returned to Davies early on due to bad workmanship. There were also issues over the livery, and varying shades of crimson lake not matching the correct specification. The report also says that black lines were omitted from the cream areas. These were the last locally-built bodies for Cardiff Corporation.

In late evening sunshine Guy Arab IV 39 (GUH 944) in original condition waits in Greyfriars Road, by the ruins of Greyfriars House. It will work the 28 to Llanishen via Roath Park. Its D.J. Davies body was built on Park Royal frames, hence the familiar and attractive styling.

(Roy Marshall collection courtesy of The Omnibus Society)

In service the new Guy Arab IVs could be found working throughout the City, and in their earlier days, were regular performers on the service 30 to Newport. Other favourite haunts especially in the latter years were the 40A & 40B to the Heath, 16 to Snowden Road and 21 to Pantmawr Road, Rhiwbina. As far as livery was concerned, all were delivered in crimson lake and cream and they were the last new double-deckers for a good number of years to have the cream carried below the windscreen. Cream was also evident on the surfaces below the engine canopy. The overall standard of finish by D.J. Davies must have been inferior as a number of the batch were to give bodywork trouble later on. All 15 were however withdrawn between 1967 and 1969 with 27, 34, and 35 joining the training fleet.

In February 1953, the go ahead was finally given for the extension of the trolleybus network to Ely which would require 13 new vehicles. These were B.U.T. 9641T chassis once again and utilise the electrical equipment which had been stored at Roath for a number of years now. 13 would be double-deckers while the remaining chassis was completed as an extra saloon for the Pier Head route. All 14 were bodied by East Lancs, but this time with rear entrances only, the double-deckers having just a single staircase. On 7 September single-deck trolleybus 238 re-entered service having had its seating layout modified to make it a "standee" vehicle. A number of seats had been removed to give it a revised seating capacity of 30 with standing for a similar number. However, this modification was to prove unpopular and it soon reverted to a 38-seater with standing for 8.

AEC Regals 143/5/7 were withdrawn in 1953 and interestingly 147 (ABO 989) would pass to the Cardiff Corporation Water Works department, replacing a lorry used to ferry workers between Merthyr Tydfil and Cwmtaff reservoir in the Brecon Beacons. It would be garaged and fuelled in the Merthyr Tydfil Corporation garage at Dynevor Street. Only three AEC Regals remained active after 1953 now that the Royal Tigers were in service. Other withdrawals comprised yet more pre-war AEC Regents plus the first of the 1940 delivery with East Lancs bodies (193). Meanwhile Guy Arab utility 29 (CKG 377) had been renumbered 62 to make way for the new Arab IVs.

There were no new buses delivered in 1954, but two AEC Regents, 165 (KG 9819), 168 (ABO 971) both of 1937 were taken out of service. Work erecting the overhead for the Ely trolleybus extension got under way this year. The other significant event this year was the opening of the new Central Bus Station opposite Cardiff General Station in Central Square. This would be the terminus for many of the Corporation's services including the joint services, as well as most out of town bus and coach services operated by the likes of Western Welsh, Rhondda, Red and White and Neath and Cardiff Luxury Coaches.

The last new trolleybuses

The year 1955 witnessed the arrival of the final batch of 14 trolleybuses, which included a solitary single-deck example. Changes in the law meant that the latter could have been a 2-axle vehicle, but for the sake of standardisation, it was the same chassis as the double-deck vehicles. The order for this batch of trolleybuses was worth £85,772 and was announced on 12 January 1954. All were based on the usual B.U.T. 9641T chassis and all had East Lancs metal-framed bodies.

The double-deckers were 72 seaters while the saloon seated 40. The chassis were completed at the Crossley works in Stockport between August 1954 and January 1955. The double-deckers arrived between January and March 1955 and were numbered 275 to 287 (KBO 948-60), while the saloon was delivered as 243 (KBO 961) on 15 April 1955. Number 243 was the last 3-axle single-deck trolleybus completed for service in the United Kingdom and the last new trolleybus delivered to Cardiff Corporation. All had entered service by early May and this now brought the total number of B.U.T. trolleybuses delivered to 69, out of the original commitment for 75 vehicles.

On 22 July 1968, B.U.T. trolleybus 278 (KBO 951) of 1955 crosses Canton Bridge on its way to Ely on a 10A.

(Cliff Essex)

Further Fleet Renewal and New-Look Fronts

The final extension through to Ely opened on 8 May 1955 as two routes. Replacing the motor bus route 27, these were the 10A which ran from the city centre (Havelock Street) via Victoria Park to Grand Avenue and Green Farm Road. The 10B followed a similar route but in Ely continued along Cowbridge Road West before turning into Green Farm Road and terminating. This was the first major extension to the trolleybus system beyond the former tramway limits. Minor extensions at an earlier date had been Clarence Road to Pier Head and Newport Road to Clydesmuir Road. The trolleybus system peaked at 79 vehicles running on 18 miles of routes. On 21 December 1955, the City of Cardiff gained official recognition as the capital of Wales.

DAIMLERS AND GUYS

For a number of weeks during early 1955 Cardiff Corporation operated the Daimler CVG6 demonstrator PHP 220 in service. The chassis of this bus had been built in 1952 as a CL-series lightweight prototype and in 1954 it received a lightweight NCME body. It was re-designated a CVG6 appearing at the Commercial Motor Show that year. The Daimler CV range had been introduced in 1946 and available with AEC, Daimler and Gardner (5LW or 6LW) engines, coupled to the usual fluid flywheel and pre-selector gearbox. As would be expected, the CVD6 was especially promoted by Daimler but was eventually dropped in 1954, sometime after the CVA6, leaving the very popular CVG5 and CVG6 models. The CVG6 required a bonnet six inches longer than other models. In 1950 the Birmingham City Transport "new look" front started to appear and eventually this became the standard configuration on CVG6s in 1956. From 1957 the electro-pneumatic operated Daimler Daimatic direct selection epicyclic gearbox became available.

In 1956 Cardiff took delivery of 30 East Lancs-bodied double-deckers, all with Birmingham-style new-look fronts. Unlike the 1953 batch of Guys completed by D.J. Davies, these 30 buses were of five-bay construction. A new number series was adopted for all deliveries of motor buses from 1956 beginning at 301, which continued in use until 1973/74. Previously all Cardiff motor buses had appeared with fleet numbers below 200, while trolleybuses occupied the 200 series.

East Lancs-bodied Daimler CVG6 308 (LBO 518) is performing a 3-point turn in Caer Wenallt at the Pantmawr terminus of the 21, on 2 December 1969. After a short break, the bus will return to the City centre via Rhiwbina village and Birchgrove.

(Mike Street)

The first in the new series were 15 Daimler CVG6s numbered 301 to 315 with registrations LBO 511-25, and had Gardner 6LW engines, coupled to a Wilson 4-speed preselect gearbox and centrifugal clutch. Daimler's quotation for 15 at £2404 each and a 16 week delivery was accepted, although it was only the second lowest. Leyland quoted £2035 each for PD2 chassis, but they could not meet the required delivery date. 301 to 310 had attractive East Lancs bodywork, the final cost of which came to £2338 per body. The first to enter service were 301 and 304 in February 1956 with the outstanding vehicles up to 310 following soon after. The bodies for the last five of the batch (311 to 315), were to have been supplied by D.J. Davies of Merthyr Tydfil as 60-seaters and at £2035 each. However, this coachbuilding company was in some financial difficulty, and in September 1956 asked to be released from the contract, resulting in a switch to East Lancs. The chassis for 311 to 315 were actually delivered to Davies's premises, and it is thought that work had actually started on one bus, but was then removed for use elsewhere. The chassis were not released for delivery to East Lancs as quickly as had been envisaged, and this resulted in the very late delivery of these five buses, which were not received from Blackburn until January/February 1957. 301 to 310 were ordered as 61-seaters from East Lancs, but all 15 eventually emerged from the coachbuilder with this revised to 63, adding an extra £14-8s to the cost of each bus.

Obviously happy with the 15 Guy Arab IVs delivered in 1953, a similar number were ordered in April 1955 for delivery in 1956, the order for the chassis being worth £33210, which was later revised to £34365. Originally just ten of these were to have East Lancs 63-seat bodies, with the final five (like the Daimlers 311 to 315) to have been bodied in Merthyr Tydfil by D.J. Davies. However, all 15 Guys numbered 316 to 330 ended up with East Lancs bodywork. They featured for the first time, matching registrations MUH 316-30, and the first examples 316 to 318 and 320 entered service in October 1956, with the balance by March 1957. These 30 buses introduced sliding cab doors, flashing trafficators to the fleet and they had an unladen weight of 7tons 14cwt. They were put to work from Sloper Road garage appearing on most normal city routes.

The 1956 Guy Arab IVs were regular performers on the Rhiwbina and Whitchurch services in the late 1960s, and 327 is noted in Queen Street in the evening rush hour on a 23 from Caer Wenallt on the Pantmawr estate. Note its sliding cab door in the open position. After withdrawal, 327 went on to become a driver training vehicle.

(Author's collection)

More AEC Regents were withdrawn in 1956 including the first example from the 1938 delivery 189 (BBO 74) and three more 1940 examples. AEC Regal 148 was also withdrawn following an accident. Cardiff borrowed an AEC Regent V demonstrator 88 CMV in January 1956 and used it in service. It was an MD3RV model completed in September1954 with a lightweight Park Royal 61-seat body, and the first Regent V chassis built. It had been an exhibit at the 1954 Commercial Motor Show on the Crossley stand. In time Cardiff bought AEC Regent Vs, but not the lightweight model with the smaller AV470 engine.

Further Fleet Renewal and New-Look Fronts

In 1956 Cardiff Corporation was responsible for operating 40 motor bus and 13 trolleybus services as well as an advertised works service from General Station to East Moors Road, and a hospital service from Fitzalan Road to Llandough. And finally, it is recorded that Leyland Royal Tiger 134 made a special journey to Vienna, Austria in December 1956. The purpose of this epic trip was to carry gifts for the Hungarian refugees who had fled Hungary after the Russians put down the uprising there.

Longwell Green and the Tiger Cubs

Cardiff continued to remain faithful to East Lancs for many years, but did source from Merthyr Tydfil-based D.J. Davies as well as Longwell Green, a coachbuilder based on the outskirts of Bristol. On 28 February 1956, it was decided that four single-deckers should be ordered for delivery the same year. These buses would replace the last of the pre-war single-deckers and would of course work alongside the Royal Tigers (134 to 138). The outcome of the tenders was that four Leyland Tiger Cub chassis be ordered, to receive bodies by Longwell Green. The chassis would cost £1880 each and the bodies would be £2150 each. The Tiger Cub was Leyland's lightweight answer to the Royal Tiger. The new generation of underfloor-engine saloons in the early 1950s suffered from poor fuel economy and most weighed in at over eight tons unladen. The Tiger Cub was unveiled at the 1952 Earls Court Show and a lot of the weight saving was achieved in the areas of mechanical units, wheels and tyres. The engine was a horizontal version of the 0.350 of 90bhp and the chassis was 30ft with a 16ft 2in wheelbase. In its PSUC1/1 form the Tiger Cub had a 4-speed constant mesh gearbox and was only available with air brakes.

1957 witnessed the arrival of the four Tiger Cubs 143 to 146 with registrations NKG 143-6. They had Leyland chassis code PSUC1/1 and their Longwell Green bodies had seating for 44. These buses had Leyland 4-speed gearboxes with constant mesh on 1st and 2nd gears and synchromesh 3rd and 4th gears. They had an overall height of 9ft 10½in and unladen weight of 6tons 1cwt. Unlike the Royal Tigers the bodies on the Tiger Cubs could perhaps best be described as distinctive rather than attractive.

On a sunny afternoon Leyland Tiger Cub 145 squeezes through the entrance to Cardiff Castle as it makes its way out onto Castle Street whilst engaged on a private-hire duty.

(Glyn Bowen courtesy Chris Taylor CTPG)

The Tiger Cub's duties closely followed those of the Royal Tigers which usually saw them on Penarth area routes, including Lower Penarth via Plymouth Road on a later variation of the 35. Other outings could include the 45 to Caeglas Road via New Road in Rumney, and later on the 29 to Caerphilly via Thornhill. They were occasionally used on numerous private-hire duties and duplicates. The low bridge in the Cogan area was removed in about 1959/60. It was not a railway bridge apparently, but a private bridge used for moving cattle to adjacent land. Consequently the requirement for single-deckers on certain workings disappeared although in practice double-deckers rarely ventured into Penarth.

Longwell Green was a coachbuilder who can be traced back to the early part of the twentieth century, being founded by the Bence family. They were based at Longwell Green near Bristol and following the Second World War, business really picked up with involvement in the rebuilding of existing bus as well as the construction of new bus bodies. They were also involved with lorries and vans and became masters in the use of fibreglass mouldings. Apart from Caerphilly Urban District Council, all of the South Wales municipal fleets took some Longwell Green bodies on either double or single-deck chassis, the last bus bodies built being a pair of AEC Regent Vs for Pontypridd Urban District Council in 1966.

The second batch of Daimler CVG6s was ordered in May 1956 and arrived during the autumn of 1957, taking fleet numbers 331 to 342 and registrations OBO 331-42. In most respects they resembled the earlier batch 301 to 315, but they were fitted with Kirkstall rear axles and their radiator filler cap protruded outside the front cowling. The main distinguishing feature of all the CVG6s was the chrome Daimler scroll across the top of the radiator grill. Internally the Daimlers had minor detail differences. 301 to 310 had metal window surrounds painted maroon in a similar fashion to the final batch of trolleybuses. 311 to 315 which were of course delivered late, had interior windows surrounds that were finished in a walnut-coloured plastic similar to the Guy Arab IVs 316 to 330. Daimlers 331 to 342 had white formica window surrounds and 312, 314 and 315 were later rebuilt by Cardiff to incorporate this feature too.

On 11 April 1970 there are still no leaves on the trees, as Daimler CVG6 331 (OBO 331) waits in the tranquil rural setting at the terminus in St. Fagans. The destination aperture has been masked and the blind poorly set.
(Mike Street)

The Splott Daimlers ... the last re-bodies for CCT

Also ordered in May 1956 for completion in 1957, were ten 8ft-wide Longwell Green 60-seat all-metal double-deck bodies that were fitted to the 1948-vintage 7ft 6in Daimler CVD6 chassis, which up until now, ran with used East Lancs bodies built in 1944. They cost £2410 each which later rose by £7-10s.

FLEET NO.	REGISTRATION	NEW BODY	SEATING	YEAR CHASSIS ENTERED SERVICE
58	EBO 1	Longwell Green	H30/26R	1948
61	EBO 2	"	"	"
59	EBO 3	"	"	1949
57	EBO 4	"	"	"
55	EBO 5	"	"	"
54	EBO 6	"	"	"
52	EBO 7	"	"	"
56	EBO 8	"	"	1950
60	EBO 9	"	"	"
53	EBO 10	"	"	"

The combination of an 8ft-wide body on a 7ft 6in chassis produced an alarming spectacle when cornering. As a result they were not popular buses with drivers, who also complained of engine fumes in the cabs. Once re-bodied, they did tend to cling to the Splott/Tremorfa area services (12 and 12A). This is why they became nick named the Splott Daimlers. Their fuel consumption was also heavy, hence their rapid demise, even though their bodies were only seven years old. They were all withdrawn between 1964 and 1966 and sold for scrap. 52 and 59 (EBO 7, 3) survived in Bill Way's Cardiff scrapyard at Cardiff East Dock for many years until sold to a Barnsley breaker in 1978 when they were towed to Yorkshire.

Daimler CVD6 number 54 (EBO 6) is noted laying over in Mill Lane adjacent to the open air market. It is engaged on service 12 to Tremorfa (Willows Avenue and Tweedsmuir Road) via Carlisle Street. The new 8ft-wide Longwell Green body does not seem to sit very comfortably on the 7ft 6in chassis.

(Glyn Bowen courtesy Chris Taylor CTPG)

Withdrawn this year was the last of the 1936 Regents 41 (KG8911), a truly remarkable survivor. Also on the way out were AEC Regals (149 and 150) and 1932 Leyland Tiger TS4s (139 and 142). Seven AEC Regents of 1937/8 and two of 1940 vintage were also removed from stock.

A summary of the Utility vehicles rebuilt/overhauled between 1951 and 1957 is set out below:

CARDIFF CT WORKSHOPS	
1951	78 (CKG 582)
1953	29 (CKG 377) 66/67 (CKG 408/9) 68 (CKG 503) 74/75 (CKG 519/20)
1956/57	76 (CKG 521) 78-80/82 (CKG 582-4/6) 83/85/87-89 (CKG 650/2/4-6) 92-94 (CKG 668-70)
T. HOSKINS, CARDIFF	
1951	85 (CKG 652)
LONGWELL GREEN, BRISTOL	
1952	63 (CKG 422) 64 (CKG 465) 65 (CKG 407) 69 (CKG 504) 71-73 (CKG 516-8)
D.J. DAVIES, MERTHYR	
1952	77/79 (CKG 581/3) 80-82 (CKG 584-6)

As can be seen, some of the Utility vehicles were rebuilt twice to varying degrees. Number 29 went on to become fleet number 62 after overhaul. The Transport Department's workshops fitted rubber-mounted windows to 62, 66 to 68, 74 to 76, 78, 79, 80, 82, 83, 85, 87 to 89 and 92 to 94. Longwell Green fitted rubber-mounted windows to 63 to 65/69 and 71 to 73. It is known that 81 and 84 still had original windows when withdrawn in 1958. D.J. Davies was awarded the contract to rebuild 15 K6As in February 1952 at a cost of £750 each. However the General Manager reported that in the opinion of the Ministry of Transport, any timber framework should also be replaced, which resulted in Davies increasing the cost of the work to £850 per bus.

East Lancs-bodied Guy Arab IV 344 (OUH 344) waits in the bus station on 6 September 1968, before heading off for Cyncoed via Roath Park. Behind is an Alexander-bodied Guy Arab V bound for Whitchurch, while an AEC Regent V is parked on the perimeter.

(Mike Street)

Further Fleet Renewal and New-Look Fronts

The final batch of Guy Arab IVs, 12 in total, were ordered in January 1957 and entered service between February and May 1958 as 343 to 354 (OUH 343-54). They were basically the same as 316 to 330, but their bodywork was built to a slightly lower height of 14'5" to enable them to pass under Penarth Road railway bridges. 348 was involved in a serious collision on Rumney Hill in 1960 and required substantial rebuilding, while 343 was de-roofed in 1965 under the infamous Virgil Street railway bridge which stands at 13ft 6in.. It had a new roof fitted. Number 344 was the first bus in the fleet to be rebuilt with a "folding pram" space cut into the rear nearside platform bulkhead.

In conclusion, all buses in the series 301 to 354 were delivered in fully lined out crimson lake and cream. Unlike the 1953 batch of Guys, they did not have the cream carried forward below the driver's windscreen, but at a much later date 327 did receive this embellishment. Liveries were all based on the various combinations of crimson lake and cream, and throughout their careers with Cardiff most carried three variations of the livery.

With nine underfloor-engine saloons now in service, the last front-engine saloon 141 (KG 1144), by now pushing 26 years of age, was finally withdrawn. The last seven pre-war AEC Regents were also withdrawn, together with East Lancs-bodied 196 (CBO 705) of 1940, the last of the batch to go. Withdrawal also commenced of the Guy Arab and Bristol K6A utility double-deckers with a dozen coming out of service. Of these 64 (CKG 465) was to pass to a showman while 91 became a traction pole-carrier. Number 77 became a training vehicle in March 1958, but was reinstated in July and withdrawn again in August. Following an encounter with the railway bridge in Fairoak Road on 15 November 1957, 95 (CUH 371), a 1947 vintage AEC Regent II paid a visit to Longwell Green's works where it received a translucent fibreglass roof, emerging in 1958.

A 30ft Daimler CVG6-30 with Willowbrook rear-entrance double-deck bodywork was demonstrated to the undertaking on 10 May 1958. This was most probably to evaluate its length, seating capacity and maybe its Gardner 6LX engine. Registered VKV 99 it had seating for 74 and had been new in 1957.

White stick Daimlers

Park visitors disembark from Daimler CSG6 357 (SKG 357) which stands under the wires at the Ninian Road terminus at Roath Park. It may be providing an afternoon duplicate to the trolleybus service.

(Glyn Bowen courtesy Chris Taylor CTPG)

In late 1957, and in an effort to attract new customers, Daimler announced the CSG chassis to be available in both 27 and 30ft lengths. For the first time since 1931 they offered a traditional "manual gearbox and clutch" transmission, on a derivative of its CVG chassis. It had a David Brown 4-speed gearbox which incorporated a Porsche synchromesh mechanism. The first example appeared in 1958 and most had Gardner 6LW engines. Cardiff ordered half a dozen 27 ft CSG6s in May 1958 at a cost of £2266-14s-11d per chassis, with a quoted delivery date of May/June 1959. They entered service in June 1959 as 355 to 360 with registrations SKG 355-60 and had standard East Lancs bodies. All Daimler CSG chassis had the Manchester style bonnet as originally specified by Manchester Corporation Transport Department. This feature made them instantly recognisable in the Cardiff fleet. Another interesting feature was their white painted gear sticks to highlight their different gearboxes, and it was not long before they became known as the "white stick Daimlers". Like Guy Arab IVs 343 to 354, their bodies were slightly lower in height (in this case 14ft 4in), to enable them to negotiate the Penarth Road railway bridges, and as a result the lower saloon ceiling was slightly recessed. They were the first buses in the fleet to be fitted with saloon heaters, a feature which was later adopted as standard.

It was not long before things went badly wrong with these six buses. The CSG6s started to suffer from gearbox failures at an alarming rate as well as differential and half-shaft problems, spending long periods of time off the road awaiting attention. A solution was eventually found by replacing the David Brown gearboxes with standard Guy 4-speed constant-mesh units, which were already common in the fleet. After this they settled down and soon earned a reputation for exceptionally good fuel consumption, and were in fact the best in fleet in 1965, returning around 11mpg.

Withdrawals for 1959 were restricted to just two Guy Arab utility buses, 68 and 69 (CKG 503/4), both of which went for scrap locally.

CHAPTER FIVE

TROLLEYBUS REPLACEMENT, REAR ENGINES AND ONE-MAN OPERATION

During the late 1950s and into the 1960s new residential areas continued to be developed throughout the city. These included housing estates at Llanedeyrn, Llanrumney, Pantmawr, Pentrebane, Radyr and Trowbridge as well as the expansion of Ely to the south of Cowbridge Road West. This resulted in many new and revised services being introduced to cater for these areas. The sheer variety of new buses purchased from 1960 to 1966 would not disappoint the enthusiast, but must have been a headache for the undertaking's engineering department, as little effort was made to standardise on a particular chassis. Traditional rear-entrance vehicles were very much the order of the day though, and a return to the AEC Regent model after 11 years added to the variety.

A NEW SOLUTION TO AN OLD PROBLEM

The first batch of buses received during this period arrived in 1960 and was rather special. Following the introduction of the revolutionary Bristol Lodekka and later the Dennis Loline, AEC began work on developing their own low-height vehicle in conjunction with Park Royal. It was of integral construction and had a drop-centre rear axle. Christened the AEC Bridgemaster, it made its debut at the 1956 Earls Court Show, though production did not begin until 1958, by which time several changes were made. The AEC AV590 engine was specified as standard from late 1958, and air suspension was also added to the rear axle at this stage in place of the coil springs. The body was to a new style, with a more upright blunt front end, and assembled using a steel frame. One major feature was the full-width rear-facing seat behind the driver and engine. This was not a gimmick, but was necessary to cover the gearbox housing which protruded into the lower saloon. The Bridgemaster was available in 27ft 8in or 30ft lengths and the overall height was now claimed to be around 13ft 4in.

Cardiff Corporation Transport ordered six short-wheelbase rear-entrance models in June 1959 for delivery in 1960, at a cost of £5436 each plus £300 worth of extras per bus. They were intended for the Tredegar route which had a low bridge at Maes-y-Cwmmer, and would in theory replace the famous low-bridge Crossley DD42s (42 to 46 and 51). These 11-year old buses were then transferred to less taxing duties including route 32 to St. Fagans and Hensol Castle. The new AEC Bridgemasters had saloon heaters, power-operated platform doors and curious "four and a bit" bay 27ft 8in bodies. They were delivered to Cardiff as 361 to 366 (TUH 361-6) in March 1960. They had a 4-speed AEC synchromesh gearbox, and the brakes were described as split front and rear air/hydraulic. The Cardiff Bridgemasters had an unladen weight of 7ton 18cwt, an overall height of 13ft 6in, with seating for 68. They were the first double-deckers in the fleet to feature platform doors.

Once in service they soon gained a reputation for an improved standard of ride. Their synchromesh gearboxes gave that distinctive AEC whine, and they were quite lively performers. On the down side their cabs were deemed cramped and platform staff often found the experience of air suspension and the accompanied bouncing and rolling a little nauseous. Number 366 sustained substantial damage to the front part of its upper deck in 1962 in a collision on Rumney Hill, and was rebuilt. All six were returned to AEC in February 1963 for modifications to the rear suspension, as it was found that some vehicles bounced so badly that the only cure was to bring the bus to a standstill.

A sad duty occurred in October 1966 when all six were used to transport medical supplies and personnel from Cardiff to the Aberfan disaster. They remained on standby until the threat of evacuation of the village had passed. From 1967 Daimler Fleetlines ousted the Bridgemasters from the Tredegar route, but they continued to be used for another year or so on the Cardiff to Merthyr Tydfil service, by then numbered 20. They were progressively used more on the 32 to St. Fagans and Hensol Castle service from 1965 after the ban on the use of 8-ft wide buses was lifted. This rural route did not require six vehicles though, and they gradually moved on to many city routes such as the 22, 25, 37 and 40A & 40B, and having platform doors were also a popular choice for school outings.

AEC Bridgemaster 363 stands in Castle Street, Merthyr Tydfil, about to depart for Cardiff on service 41, on which they were often found. Note the small window ahead of the staircase and the windscreen in the open position.
(The late Dave B. Thomas collection)

Memorable services 1: Cardiff to Merthyr Tydfil

Cardiff Corporation commenced running from Greyfriars Road, Cardiff, to Castle Street, Merthyr, on 8 September 1930. This was jointly with Merthyr Tydfil Corporation and by 8 November had settled down to a 90-minute frequency on weekdays and Sundays, increasing to hourly on Saturdays. Rhondda Tramways joined the service in November 1931 enabling an hourly service to be implemented with each operator providing one bus. Due to the outbreak of war, Cardiff and Rhondda withdrew from the service in September 1939, and Merthyr ran the service alone until May 1946 when the hourly service was restored. However, Cardiff was short of buses and Rhondda provided a second bus until Cardiff was able to resume running to Merthyr on 11 August 1946. In 1955, by which time the service had been numbered 41 by the Corporation, the Cardiff terminus moved to the new Central Bus Station, while in early 1960 the route was changed to include Aberfan. At the southern end of the route Northern Avenue was completed as a through road in 1961, which resulted in the 41 by-passing Whitchurch village from 14 May. On 6 January 1964 Cardiff Corporation renumbered the route from 41 to 20, and on 5 August 1968 it began running into the new Merthyr bus station. On 15 November 1970 one-man operation was introduced, while on 31 July 1971 after reporting an annual operating loss of £20,000, Cardiff withdrew from the service leaving Merthyr Tydfil Corporation to take over their timings. Rhondda Transport subsequently withdrew from the service on 27 November 1971.

In 1930 Cardiff initially used Dennis E saloons of 1927 vintage followed by the Bristol B saloons of 1928 moving on to the Leyland TS4s and AEC Regals. Double-deckers first appeared in the post-war years and the 20 AEC Regent IIIs of 1950 will always be associated with the 41 to Merthyr Tydfil. However the Guy Arab IVs made appearances too, until 1960 when the AEC Bridgemasters made their mark. They were ideal for this 25-mile route with their ample seating capacity, platform doors and saloon heaters. AEC Regent Vs, East Lancs-bodied Leyland PD2As and even the Alexander-bodied semi-automatic Guy Arab Vs were occasionally used on the Merthyr run. By late 1968 Metro-Cammell-bodied Daimler Fleetlines had largely taken over, with examples of the dual-door Willowbrook-bodied batch putting in regular appearances from the spring of 1970.

Far too advanced

An interesting double-deck demonstrator was on loan from Guy Motors in January 1960, and was apparently briefly used on the 30 service to Newport for a week. It was OHL 863, a 1959 Guy Wulfrunian with 77-seat Roe bodywork and in a red and cream livery. The Wulfrunian featured a Gardner 6LX engine mounted in line between the platform and the rather cramped cab area. It was 30ft long and offered a high seating capacity, a front entrance with a flat-floor. Novel features for 1960 were its independent air-suspension on the front axle and all-round disc brakes. Cardiff, although keen on Guys, was obviously not going to take a chance with this revolutionary model.

TAKING STOCK 1: A SUMMARY OF THE CARDIFF FLEET IN 1960

FLEET NO.	REGISTRATION	CHASSIS TYPE	BODYWORK	YEAR NEW
Motor buses				
65 to 67	CKG 407-9	Guy Arab II	Park Royal	1943
71/73/74/75	CKG 516/8-20	"	"	1943/44
78 to 80/82	CKG 582-4/6	Bristol K6A	"	1944/45
83/85 to 89	CKG 650/2-6	"	"	1945/46
92 to 94	CKG 668-70	"	Duple	"
95 to 100	CUH 371-6	AEC Regent II	Air Dispatch	1948
101 to 104	CUH 377-80	"	East Lancs	1947
105 to 113	DKG 829-37	"	Air Dispatch	1948
114 to 133	DUH 301-20	Bristol KW6G	Bruce	1948/49
23	GDF 58	Crossley DD42/3	Scottish Commercial	1947
24	GDG 456	"	"	"
25	EBO 103	Crossley DD42/5	"	1948
42 to 46, 51	EBO 896-901	Crossley DD42/7	Alexander	1949
52 to 56	EBO 7, 10, 6, 5, 8	Daimler CVD6	Longwell Green (a)	1948/49
57 to 61	EBO 3,1,9,4,2	"	" (a)	"
1 to 20	EUH 733-52	AEC Regent III	Bruce/ East Lancs	1950
134 to 138	GKG 51-5	Leyland PSU1/15	East Lancs	1952
26 to 40	GUH 931-45	Guy Arab IV	D.J. Davies	1953
301 to 315	LBO 511-25	Daimler CVG6	East Lancs	1956/57
316 to 330	MUH 316-30	Guy Arab IV	"	"
331 to 342	OBO 331-42	Daimler CVG6	"	1957
343 to 354	OUH 343-54	Guy Arab IV	"	1958
143 to 146	NKG 143-46	Leyland PSUC1/1	Longwell Green	1957
355 to 360	SKG 355-60	Daimler CSG6	East Lancs	1959
361 to 366	TUH 361-6	AEC Bridgemaster	Park Royal	1960
(a) 52 to 61 had received these Longwell Green 8ft-wide bodies in 1957/58.				
Trolleybuses				
201 to 210	CKG 191-200	AEC 664T	NCME	1941-3
211 to 220	DBO 471-80	B.U.T. 9641T	East Lancs	1948
221 to 230	DUH 716-25	"	"	"
238 to 242	EBO 891-5	"	" (saloon)	1949
243	KBO 961	"	" "	1955
245 to 247	EBO 902-4	"	East Lancs	1950
248	EBO 905	"	Bruce	1949
249 and 250	EBO 906/7	"	East Lancs	1950
251 to 264	EBO 908-21	"	Bruce	1949/50
265 to 274	FBO 85-94	"	"	1950
275 to 287	KBO 948-60	"	East Lancs	1955

Cardiff's Municipal Buses

In 1961 the ten war time AEC trolleybuses (201 to 210) were due for replacement and consideration was given to taking up the outstanding order for six, and then giving four of the AECs a major overhaul. However time had moved on, and B.U.T. were no longer prepared to supply trolleybus chassis for the home market. Sunbeam offered a two-axle 30ft chassis which East Lancs indicated it was prepared to body for Cardiff. This dilemma in part led to the decision to abandon the trolleybus network in favour of motor bus operation. The final decision came on 6 November 1961, and was seen by some as a big mistake, as so much money had been spent on developing the system in the early post-war years. However, a rundown was the national trend amongst local authority undertakings, and many systems were closed down completely in the 1960s.

Return of the Titans

The Leyland Titan PD2 was first introduced by Leyland Motors in 1947, as a development of the 1945 PD1 model. It was initially available as a 26ft chassis with 7ft 6in and 8ft width options, and as a 27ft chassis from 1950. It went on to become one of the most successful front-engine bus chassis of all time until production finally ceased in 1969. It was initially produced with an exposed radiator and traditional bonnet. However a full-width bonnet arrangement known as the "tin front" was introduced as an option in the early 1950s, and in 1960 a stylish glass-fibre bonnet assembly known as the "St. Helens bonnet" appeared, the name coming from specifications originally required by St Helens Corporation.

In September 1960, 15 double-deckers were ordered for delivery by the end of 1961 and five of these would be Cardiff's first new Leyland double-deckers since 1936. They materialised as 367 to 371 (XUH 367-71), PD2A/30 models, with 64-seat bodywork supplied by Metro-Cammell-Weymann to their Orion design. The Orion was introduced in the 1950s to meet the increased demand by some operators for lightweight bodies. One of the Orion's distinctive features was the deep lower saloon windows which contrasted with very shallow windows on the top deck. The Cardiff examples were of the "heavy weight" version and of five-bay construction, with the narrow and tapered front roof dome, which from certain angles made the bus look like a 7ft 6in-wide vehicle. Numbers 367 to 371 were fitted with the Leyland 0.600 9.8-litre diesel of 125bhp and featured a Leyland four-speed synchromesh gearbox. This gearbox in reality was a crash-box on first and second with synchromesh only on third and fourth gears. It is worth noting that vacuum-assisted brakes were still being specified by Cardiff Corporation in 1961. These Titans had an overall height of 14ft 6in and an unladen weight of 7tons 11cwt.

367 makes its way along Wood Street while working the special service to Llandough hospital. These were hardly the most attractive buses in the fleet at the time, and the fibreglass St. Helens style bonnet gives the bus a somewhat unhappy look.

(Glyn Bowen courtesy Chris Taylor CTPG)

Trolleybus Replacement, Rear Engines and One-Man Operation

These Leylands did introduce some novel features though, which were to become standard on subsequent batches of new buses. A translucent roof panel was fitted to the upper saloon which greatly improved the atmosphere on the top deck. Numbers 367 and 370 had fluorescent interior lighting in place of tungsten bulbs at an extra cost of £90 per bus. They were the first buses to be delivered without a rear destination box, its place taken by a small route number aperture. The Corporation's platform staff were said to dislike the Metro-Cammell bodied PD2As as they had a narrower gangway on the top deck compared with other buses, which was a nuisance when collecting fares at busy times. It is worth mentioning that one of the Metro-Cammell examples, 370, received some damage to its front roof dome quite late on in its life, and as a result the bodyshop at Roath depot manufactured a "one-off" front dome made mainly from aluminium. This looked distinctly odd, and had a more squared-up appearance. By today's standards the 367 to 371 had a relatively short life with Cardiff Corporation, being withdrawn in January 1972 and immediately sold. Three of them (367/8 and 371) saw some further service.

Return of the Regents

The remaining ten double-deckers ordered for 1961 were the first examples of popular AEC Regent V to join the fleet, and along with the five Leyland Titans (see above) replaced 11 motor buses. They were chosen upon the recommendation of the General Manager J F Siddall, and were bodied by East Lancs. Introduced in 1954, the AEC Regent V reflected a move towards reducing the weight of a double-decker by combining a light to medium weight chassis with a lightweight alloy body, resulting in a better fuel consumption. From the outset both a lightweight and heavyweight chassis were made available. The Regent V was launched with a new-look front and the grille was distinctive and easily recognisable. A 30ft version was introduced in 1956 and the model was revised in late 1958 when AEC introduced the AV590 9.65-litre engine and deleted the 7ft 6in wide option. Air-braked models were available in both 27 and 30ft lengths with either epicyclic (2D2RA), or synchromesh transmission (2D3RA). However the vacuum-braked model was only available as a 27ft chassis with synchromesh gearbox (2D3RV).

The ten Regent Vs for 1961 were numbered 372 to 381 and allocated registrations XUH 372-81. The first example to arrive at Cardiff was 381 on 15 November followed by 374/6 and 379 by the end of the month. The others were delivered in the December and all entered service before the end of the year.

Vacuum-braked AEC Regent V 381 is seen on Firs Avenue, Pentrebane on 17 April 1968, as it makes its way around the housing estate. It is carrying the post-1964 livery. The site to the right of the bus is where the Jug and Bottle public house was later erected.

(*Mike Street*)

These buses had AEC chassis code 2D3RV and featured the AEC AV590 9.65-litre engine of 128 bhp, coupled to an AEC 4-speed synchromesh gearbox while the brakes were vacuum (triple servo). The cost of each vehicle was £2583-12s-0d for each chassis and £2841-0s-0d for the body. From a driver's point of view they were very popular vehicles. Gear changing was easy and they had a really good top speed. They were however very noisy in the cab and lower saloon, and also on tick-over compared with a Gardner-engined Guy for example. Apparently 379 was the first bus in the Cardiff fleet to be delivered with "Formica" backed seats. All subsequent batches of vehicles had this as standard.

Cardiff's AEC Regent Vs were to be found on most city services and were particularly notable for their appearances on the route 30 to Newport in the mid to late 1960s. A number of Regent Vs were involved in major accidents. On 10 May 1962 while on Rumney Hill, 373 collided with a fruit lorry. In another incident that year, whilst returning from Whitchurch on a 23 turn, 374 was hooked up on the jib of a crane at Gabalfa, and was quite badly damaged. Number 378 had a confrontation with Fairoak Road railway bridge on 17 March 1965, and was rebuilt in the Corporation's workshops, losing its translucent centre roof panel in this process, and also gaining a 3-piece roof dome.

Buses withdrawn during 1961 were the last of the Guy Arab utilities 65, 67, 71 and 74 dating from 1943/44 and a few more of the Bristol K6A utilities. All three of the high-bridge layout Crossley DD42s (23 to 25) were also taken out of service. The first to go was 24 in February, followed by 23 in July and finally 25 in November. The first pair went straight for scrap, but 25 was sold to Stan Davies of Cardiff for use as a workers' bus on the Llanwern steel works construction contract, from April 1962 until about July.

The Passenger Transport Year Book for 1961 stated that Cardiff Corporation Transport Department operated 79 trolleybuses and 185 motor buses (of which just nine were saloons). The motor bus chassis comprised 46 Guys, 45 AECs, 43 Daimlers, 33 Bristols, 9 Leylands and 9 Crossleys. East Lancs was by far the most numerous body builder represented.

A further ten AEC Regent Vs with East Lancs bodywork were ordered for 1962, once again recommended by the General Manager. These buses appeared in November 1962, but were different in that they had Westinghouse air brakes, and were the first batch of buses to have fluorescent lighting throughout. They were delivered as 382 to 391 (382-91 BUH), and were the first buses in the fleet to have the new reversed registrations. The AEC chassis code 2D3RA reflected their air brakes and these buses were 1cwt heavier than their vacuum-braked cousins at 7tons 14cwt. They cost £2530-17s-8d each per chassis and £2952-0s-0d per body. The rear profile of their bodies was more upright than on 372 to 381 and all featured Formica-backed seats. Also worthy of note is that 383 and 385 had Beclawat "Doreas" hopper-style opening side windows, as opposed to the normal Beclawat "slamslide" type. These were the only two built like this and retained this feature throughout their lives.

388 is one of the 1962 delivery of AEC Regent Vs and shows the more upright rear profile of its East Lancs body and the small route number blind.
(Glyn Bowen courtesy Chris Taylor collection CTPG)

Number 389 was another Regent V to be de-roofed, and upon rebuild, this too lost its translucent roof panels in this process. Some members of this batch of Regent Vs lasted a little longer in the Cardiff fleet as they were earmarked for use as service vehicles. Normal withdrawals commenced in 1974 with 382/3 and 387 to 389 being taken off fleet strength. The entire batch had been withdrawn from passenger service by the end of 1975, with 384/88/9 and 391 going for scrap. Numbers 382/3 and 390 became trainers followed by 385 at a later date. 382/3 and 385 were repainted into the orange and white livery for this role. 387 became a rest room for use in the bus station between 1974 and June 1977 and was painted in plain unrelieved orange.

Trolleybus rundown begins

On 1 July 1962 single-deck trolleybus service 16 to Pier Head via Bute Street was renumbered 14. Then on 24 November 1962 the first trolleybus routes to be abandoned in favour of motor buses, were the 2 (Pengam to St. Mary Street) and the less frequent extended service 8 journeys (Pengam to Victoria Park). Pending delivery of new Leyland double-deckers 402 to 407, Daimler CVG6s from the 301 to 315 batch were used temporarily. This allowed the withdrawal AEC trolleybus 208 in September followed by similar 205 in October and 201/3/9 10 in December. 203 was subsequently sold to the Reading Trolleybus Society in May 1963 for preservation. Meanwhile a number of trolleybus drivers were now being re-trained to drive motor buses. By the end of the year only one wartime utility double-decker survived, Bristol K6A 93 (CKG 669). The first of the AEC Regent IIs to be taken out of service were 99 (CUH 375) and 113 (DKG 837), both going for scrap.

A second order for Leyland Titan PD2s was placed for delivery in 1963, and this time called for ten vehicles, again with PD2A/27 chassis and costing £2314-10s each. They were mechanically identical to 367 to 371, but on this occasion were bodied by East Lancashire Coachbuilders to an overall height of 14ft 5in. The new Titans were delivered in January and February 1963 as 392 to 401 (392-410 BUH), and they were generally considered to be much more attractive buses than the earlier PD2As. They were also significant in being the last new buses delivered to Cardiff Corporation with vacuum brakes. Seating was for 65 passengers, two more than was requested when ordered, and the unladen weight was recorded as 7tons 17cwt. They were delivered in crimson lake and cream with black lining, and over the years this livery was modified by eliminating the black lining reducing the amount of cream used. Being normal height vehicles they were put to work on most of the city's main routes, and remained so throughout their time with Cardiff. This batch were known to have regularly worked to Newport on the jointly run service 30, occasionally on the 41 (later 20) to Merthyr Tydfil and also, from the mid 1960s, on the 36 to Tredegar.

393 in original condition with black lining is about to work the 34 to Caldy Road on the Gabalfa estate. It is parked adjacent the ornamental gardens at the Friary in Cathays Park in which we can also see a statue of the 3rd Marquis of Bute.

(John Jones collection)

The East Lancs-bodied Titans had relatively short lives with Cardiff too, and 393 was the first example to be withdrawn in late 1973. The remaining members of the batch (391/2 and 394 to 401) were all taken out of service by April 1974, 392 having spent a short period as an office in Central bus station. Despite their survival into the orange and white era from 1972, none of them received these colours. The entire batch of ten buses was sold to a Barnsley dealer, and only one example (396) saw any further service.

As early as November 1963, Daimler CVG6 305 received crimson lake painted mudguards followed soon after by AEC Regent IIIs 13 and 14, this practice eventually being adopted as standard.

Longer motor buses

In mid-1956 the law changed allowing 30ft double-deckers to be built on two axles, and soon after Leyland Motors unveiled the 30ft Titan PD3 chassis. It was basically a stretched PD2 with 18ft 6 inch wheelbase. The PD3 had a slightly different rear axle, and brake modifications were undertaken to compensate for the extra weight. How Cardiff came to acquire their PD3s is not straightforward. As far back as 1951 the undertaking still had an outstanding order for 20 B.U.T. trolleybus chassis. When the extension to Ely was given the go ahead, the option on 14 of these was taken up.

This still left six vehicles outstanding, which by 1961 Cardiff was to renegotiate as new motor bus chassis. Six Leyland PD3A/1 chassis were ordered to replace trolleybuses on the Pengam routes 2 and 8. They were delivered as 402 to 407 (402-7 CKG) and had 70-seat East Lancs bodies, and were the first 30ft double-deckers for the fleet. The total cost of each vehicle was £5709-10s-9d. They also featured the Leyland 4-speed synchromesh gearbox, and were fitted with air brakes. They had an unladen weight of 8ton 4cwt and their East Lancs bodies had an overall height of 14ft 6½in.

Leyland PD3A/1 number 405 waits out of service at the bus station on 1 February 1969. Note the emergency exit incorporating a smaller window behind the driver's cab; a second lower deck exit being a legal requirement on 30ft long double-deckers.

(John Jones)

In appearance 402 to 407 had very similar lines to PD2As 392 to 401, again with five-bay bodies but incorporating longer bays. Being 30-feet long, there was an extra row of seats in the lower saloon, but strangely the upper deck had only one extra seat. One other addition to this length of vehicle was the requirement for an offside emergency exit to be located in the lower saloon. This took the form of a hinged opening window pane, and was the one located immediately behind the driver's cab. In service the PD3As were quite noisy especially in the lower saloon, however when ticking over the Leyland 0.600 could hardly be heard. Cardiff drivers generally preferred the Leyland PD2A as steering on the PD3As was regarded as very heavy. Numbers 402 to 407 were registered on 1 April 1963 and allocated to Roath Depot, from where they were put to work on the number 2 service running from Pengam to St. Mary Street.

In early 1968 the PD3As were replaced at Roath by new Park Royal-bodied Daimler Fleetlines from the 490 to 505 batch. They moved to Sloper Road depot for intended use on Llanrumney routes, and were also recorded as appearing on Rhiwbina, Gabalfa and Pentrebane services. In their later days they became more familiar on contract work and schools services. All ended their Cardiff days carrying the final livery version of crimson lake and minimal cream. All six buses were withdrawn due to mechanical faults, with 406 the first to go in April 1975 and 403 being the last two months later. 407 was initially due to go to Derby Corporation for use as a driver trainer, but the deal fell through. Interestingly, the entire batch was eventually sold in December 1975, passing directly to Swansea-based operator Morris Bros. They were all repainted into Morris's smart two-tone blue and white livery and put to work on schools and contract services in that area lasting until 1980.

The last AEC double-deckers for the Cardiff fleet were delivered during 1963/64, but this was not the end of the long relationship with this manufacturer. Approval for a third and final batch of 12 Regent Vs with East Lancs bodywork was given in October 1962 which brought the Regent V fleet up to 32 vehicles. The cost for each chassis was given as £2542-16s-0d, while the bodies came in at £2990-0s-0d each. These buses arrived between November 1963 and January 1964 as 408 to 419 (408-19 DBO). The final six vehicles in the batch (414 to 419) had 63-seat bodies completed by Neepsend Coachbuilders, a subsidiary of Cravens Ltd, Sheffield, with whom East Lancs had set up a working relationship in 1963. The result of this was the opening of a coach building plant at Neepsend in Sheffield. Production began in 1964 and bodies were built using East Lancs drawings and frames supplied by their factory in Blackburn. Apart from a few minor paint finish differences the appearance of the last six were identical to the rest of the batch, but the build quality was not so good on the Neepsend examples. They were the last vehicles delivered to the Cardiff fleet with single aperture front destination displays.

AEC Regent V 414 (414 DBO), a Neepsend-bodied example, waits in Newport's Dock Street bus station for a run back to Cardiff in June 1970. Having had its first repaint, it is now wearing the livery that was introduced in 1963, featuring crimson mudguards.

(Cliff Essex)

Mechanically 408 to 419 were identical to 382 to 391 of 1962, and were also the first buses in the fleet to be fitted with plastic ceilings in both saloons, and also plastic interior panels below the windows and down to seat rail level. Also of note is that they were the first double-deckers delivered without black lining to separate the crimson and cream. The fleet livery had been modified early on in 1963, but these 12 buses managed to be delivered with a cream band below the upper deck windows and also black front mudguards. Surprisingly this was ignored by management and they continued in this fashion until their first repaints.

408 to 419 were to receive the orange and white livery between June and December 1975, as they were to be retained longer than originally planned. All were rebuilt between October 1975 and April 1976 with a modified destination layout with the addition of a separate route number box. Following this modification the driver gained control of the blinds from his cab which saved the conductor a job on the upper deck. In its final year 419 was lent to Roath depot for a while to help out, and is believed to be the only Regent V to work out of Roath. 408 to 419 achieved 16 years' service with Cardiff, and the entire batch was withdrawn in the first half of 1979. Numbers 410 and 411 had the honour of being the last examples to go in the June when half-cab operation came to an end in the city. Number 408 was bought for preservation by the Cardiff Regent V Group, and today in preservation it is the sole surviving example of the 32 AEC Regent Vs to operate with the undertaking.

Demonstration buses on loan in 1963 included 7552 MX, an AEC Renown demonstrator from AEC (ACV Sales Ltd) in a blue and cream livery. This had a forward-entrance Park Royal body and was used on local services 23, 24, 43 and 47 in the city, as well as on the Tredegar route during February. This bus is thought to be significant as the only forward-entrance half-cab ever operated by the undertaking. Looking to the future, a 78-seat Alexander-bodied Leyland Atlantean double-decker SGD 669, appeared between 22 June and 2 July 1963. This yellow and off-white coloured bus was provided courtesy of Leyland Motors and was used on services 23, 24 and 47.

Prohibition notices

Following an inspection by the Ministry of Transport in the early autumn of 1963, prohibition notices were issued on a large number of vehicles, many of which had to be repaired by outside contractors. Out of a total of 202 motor buses, at one stage 42 were off the road. Hired from Merthyr Tydfil Corporation between 14 September and 5 October at the rate of £8 per day, were three Leyland PD2/12 double-deckers, 85 to 87 (HB 8800-2) with Park Royal 61-seat bodies dating from 1956, to help ease the vehicle shortage. Number 85 was put to work on the 51 service (Central bus station to Cyncoed via Lake Road West) while number 87 was on the 52 service (Central bus station to Cyncoed via Birchgrove), both being hourly services. Curiously number 86 was allocated to the 41 service to Merthyr, so it effectively went home every day. Two other Merthyr buses were briefly substituted in September, Leyland PD2s 72 and 73 (HB 8336/7). In addition Western Welsh took over the Penarth routes from 16 September until 13 October free of charge but kept all the takings.

Notable withdrawals by the end of 1963 included Bristol K6A 93 (CKG 669), the very last utility-type bus in normal service, and 42 (EBO 896) the first of the low-bridge Alexander-bodied Crossley DD42s. Trolleybus 206 received accident damage in February 1962 and was withdrawn, its place being taken by reinstated 201 the following month. Following accident damage Leyland Royal Tiger saloons 135 and 136 were repaired 1963 by C.V. (Sales) Ltd in Cardiff. Number 136 went on to receive flashing indicators in 1964.

On 11 January 1964 the former trolleybus service 2 from Pengam to St. Mary Street was extended through to Pier Head (via Bute Street), which enabled the withdrawal of service 14 and the single-deck trolleybuses (238 to 243) that operated it. Latterly some of these had seen the odd journey out onto other services including runs to Gabalfa. Five new 30ft Guy Arab V double-deckers were purchased to cope with this extension. The undertaking reported that it had 11 trolleybus routes left in operation:

1, 3, 4, 5, 5A, 5B, 6, 8, 9, 10A and 10B. It was also reported the following month that there were 52 motor bus routes operating, plus a further four un-numbered works services.

Trolleybus Replacement, Rear Engines and One-Man Operation

A RETURN TO GUYS

From 1964 the first 54 Guy Arab V double-deckers was delivered. In 1960 Guy Motors went bankrupt following difficulties with overseas orders, and the business subsequently passed to Jaguar Cars Ltd. Under new control the Guy Motors concern at Wolverhampton was given one last chance to try to recover some of its earlier reputation. The Arab IV was officially discontinued in 1960 but the last examples did not finally enter service until 1962, when a new double-deck chassis was developed. Christened the Arab V, this was the last conventional front-engine chassis introduced to the British market.

It was basically an Arab IV but with a reduced height frame. This allowed a front entrance requiring only two steps. The Gardner 6LW or 6LX was offered and air brakes were standard. It was available with either a Guy constant-mesh gearbox or a direct-acting epicyclic gearbox.

Guy Arab V 421 has not long been delivered to Cardiff Corporation and is posed for the photographer on Rover Way, Tremorfa. Note the revised destination display and the black mudguards which were painted thus in error. 421 was a 30ft bus for trolleybus replacement.

(Glyn Bowen courtesy Chris Taylor collection CTPG)

Apparently attracted by the lower chassis frame height and the low price, Cardiff Corporation ordered 17 Guy Arab V chassis in October 1963 for delivery in 1964/65. Five were 30ft at £2640-15s each, and the remainder 27ft at £2516-15s each. All 17 had Guy constant-mesh 4-speed gearboxes and were bodied by East Lancs with open platform rear platforms. Fleet numbers 420 to 424 and registrations ABO 420-4B were allocated to the 30ft buses which entered service in July 1964. The 70-seat bodies on 420 to 424 were built in Sheffield and were generally referred to as Neepsend, the completed vehicle having an unladen weight of 8tons 3cwt and overall height of 14ft 5in. One notable change was the introduction of a two piece destination box, controlled from the driver's cab. The route number blind was now separate from the destination blind and allowed more flexibility when setting destinations.

A whole host of buses were taken out of service by the end of 1964 including the last of the AEC Regent IIs (100/5/6/8/9), the first of the Bristol KW6Gs (128), the first of the re-bodied Daimler CVD6s (57 and 53), another Crossley (51) and all of the single-deck trolleybuses 238 to 243. 243 (KBO 961) of 1955 were subsequently sold for £17-10s to the National Trolleybus Association in May 1965 for a future in preservation. Royal Tigers 134 to 136 were taken out of service in 1966 and sold. 135 (GKG 52) was exported to Eire in December 1966 for further service, travelling it is believed via Scotland. The two remaining examples 137 and 138 continued with Cardiff until 1968. Number 137 was converted for one man operation in November 1966. This involved the fitting of power-operated doors, but it is not known if it ever ran as a one man vehicle. Upon withdrawal 138 became a driver training bus for a while. Both eventually passed to a dealer in Dublin and 138 was acquired by a Cork operator in 1970.

Delivery of shorter Guys, again with Neepsend-built bodies, commenced in December 1964 and continued into 1965, with the batch being numbered 425 to 436. The timing of this meant that the registrations were a little messy:

FLEET NUMBER	REGISTRATION	TO SERVICE
431, 433 and 434	ABO 431/3/4B	December 1964
426 and 435	ABO 426/35C	January 1965
425 and 432	ABO 425/32C	February 1965
427 to 429	ABO 427-9C	March 1965
430 and 436	ABO 430/6C	April 1965

One of the shorter Neepsend-bodied Guy Arab Vs was 425 which is seen on a service 26 on Heol Uchaf in Rhiwbina, and approaching the shops at the junction with Heol Llanishen Fach. Note the lack of fleet name on the offside of the bus.
(Glyn Bowen courtesy Chris Taylor collection CTPG)

These buses were the first 27ft examples of the Arab V produced by Guy Motors, and Cardiff was the only fleet to take Arab Vs of this length. Number 426 was delivered as ABO 426B but re-registered upon entry into service. All apart from 430 were fitted with Gardner 6LW 8.4-litre engines of 112bhp. Number 430 was experimentally fitted with a Ruston 6YDA Mark II 6-cylinder air-cooled engine from new and at an extra cost of £55. However this engine suffered a camshaft failure and the bus was in store by 27 July 1966. In November 1966 it received a reconditioned Gardner 6LW from Bristol KW6G 131 (DUH 318). Number 430 was then fitted with cab heaters in February 1968.

In October 1964 the title of the undertaking became City of Cardiff Transport. When delivered the Arab Vs 420 to 436 were in yet another variation of the standard fleet livery. They had no cream band below the upper deck windows and were without any black lining. Numbers 420 and 421 were delivered with black mudguards by mistake, the remainder had crimson. The old style fleet name Cardiff Corporation Transport below the coat of arms on the lower panels only featured on the nearside of the bus.

EARLY AUTOMATIC

An interesting bus inspected by Cardiff on 28 January 1965 was Leyland PD3A/3 RCS 380. This bus had a 67-seat low-bridge Alexander body and was on loan from Leyland Motors, although it was actually owned by Western S.M.T. (1682). The reason for its visit was to demonstrate its Voith Diwabus 200S gearbox, which was an automatic transmission based around a torque converter.

TROLLEYBUS RUNDOWN CONTINUES

The year1965 witnessed the withdrawal of another group of trolleybus services. The Victoria Park routes 5A and 5B finished on 22 July, while the 5 finished two days later. Meanwhile changes to the traffic system in the centre of Cardiff were getting under way in the latter half of the year which saw Queen Street becoming one-way only in a westbound direction. This had an impact on the trolleybus network effecting services 1, 3, 4, 8 and 9, which had to be re-routed for eastbound workings. New overhead wiring was consequently erected for the first time along Kingsway and Cathays Park Road through to Dumfries Place, resulting in trolleybuses passing (at a distance), the pleasant setting of the City Hall and National Museum of Wales.

On 16 December 1965, and at very short notice, a weight restriction was placed on the elderly Wood Street river bridge which immediately affected service 6 and 9, as trolleybuses would now be too heavy to pass over this structure. The Wood Street to Pier Head sections of these routes, would have to be operated by motor buses. Plans to abandon trolleybus routes 1 and 3 were consequently put on hold.

Three motor bus services of note to cease on 30 May 1965 were:

15	Central Bus Station	to	St. Georges-super-Ely
29	Kingsway	to	Capel Gwilym (Thornhill Travellers Rest))
30A	Greyfriars Road	to	Castleton and Marshfield

Of these the 15 and 29 did not operate on Sundays. The 29 was replaced by a new through service to Caerphilly jointly run with Caerphilly Urban District Council.

The year 1965 saw the withdrawal of a further pair of Daimler CVD6 (58 and 60) together with ten Bristol KW6Gs, and all but one of the remaining Crossley DD42s leaving just 46 (EBO 900) in service. Trolleybuses took a further hit with the last of the wartime AECs (201/2/4/7) condemned in June, along with the first B.U.T. double-deckers, 245/6 and 260/1/8.

ONE-LEGGERS

The final order for front-engine half-cab double-deckers saw a further 37 Guy Arab Vs enter service in 1966. These comprised 15 30ft chassis (as trolleybus replacements), with the remainder being the 27ft models. Unlike the 1964/65 deliveries which had manual transmission, the 1966 buses had Wilson direct-acting epicyclic 4-speed semi-automatic gearboxes incorporating a fluid flywheel, and were the first semi-automatic buses in the fleet.

The body contract also marked a change of direction as it was awarded to Walter Alexander of Falkirk, thus bringing to an end the long relationship with East Lancs. The buses continued to feature open-platforms, and the style of body was based on a design dating from 1955. The cost of each bus was £2796 (chassis) and £3265 (bodywork) for the 30ft examples, and £2694 (chassis) and £3145 (body) for the shorter buses. It is believed that 473 was the last open-platform double-decker completed by coachbuilder Alexander. The longer 70-seaters were delivered as 437 to 451 (EUH 437-51D), and entered service in January and February 1966.

These were followed by 452 to 473 (EUH 452-73D), the 65-seaters which entered service between March and May. These were good-looking buses and they offered a relatively smooth acceleration and were very comfortable to ride on as a passenger. With their column-mounted gear shifts and two-pedal control, they earned the nickname "one-leggers" from drivers. It was reported that many of the Arab Vs suffered from a mysterious steering wobble when underway. Such was the concern amongst drivers that the unions became involved and the South Wales Echo ran a story on the matter. Despite cooperation from the manufacturer, it was never completely resolved. Numbers 437 to 473 introduced a new livery variation with the new City of Cardiff Transport fleet name appearing in gold leaf on the cream band beneath the lower saloon windows. They also re-introduced cream below the windscreen, but the cream above the lower saloon was dispensed with. Number 465 at some stage believed to be late 1973 received a modified front roof dome with smaller windows and no opening vents. This was probably as a result of an accident. The first example of the Alexander-bodied Arab Vs to be withdrawn was 451 in October 1977, the last one in passenger service was 465, retired in June 1979.

Trolleybus routes 6 and 9 were converted to motor bus operation in December 1965 due to structural issues with Wood Street bridge. Number 443 is a new 30ft Guy Arab V and is crossing Clarence Road Bridge. Note the overhead is still in place.
(Glyn Bowen courtesy Chris Taylor collection CTPG)

On 16 April 1966 the remaining sections of trolleybus routes 6 (Llandaff Fields to Wood Street) and 9 (Gabalfa to Wood Street) were withdrawn and the routes became motor bus operated throughout. Trolleybus operation through to Llandaff Fields finally came to an end on 17 September 1966 when service 4 (Roath Park to Llandaff Fields) ceased altogether. The replacement motor bus service did not however serve Roath Park, and was routed via Penylan Hill to reach the edge of the new Llanedeyrn housing estate. The above conversions were made possible by the introduction of the new Guy Arab Vs (437 to 451).

In 1966 consideration was given to the purchase of one-man-operated single-deck buses, and on 15 May Cardiff borrowed an AEC Reliance saloon FTX 228C from Aberdare U.D.C. to conduct a two-week trial with such a vehicle. Its place at Aberdare, for the duration of the two-week trial, was taken by Cardiff Tiger Cub 143.

Trolleybus Replacement, Rear Engines and One-Man Operation

By the end of 1966 there were just 41 double-deck trolleybuses remaining in service serving routes 1 (Gabalfa to St. Mary Street), 3 (Roath Park to St. Mary Street), 8 (Royal Oak to Victoria Park) and the two Ely routes (10A and 10B) from Havelock Street to Green Farm Road.

To conclude 1966, the following buses were withdrawn from service: 46, the last Crossley which was subsequently sold for preservation, re-bodied Daimlers 52/4/5/9 and 61, and further Bristol KW6Gs, leaving just five in service out of the original batch of 20. Ten double-deck trolleybuses were also taken out of stock, reflecting the continued rundown of the system.

THE FLEETLINES ARE COMING

In response to the Atlantean rear-engine double-deck model from Leyland Motors, Daimler quietly developed their own version in the late 1950s. This was to appear in 1960 at the Motor Show, christened the Fleetline. With a vertical engine mounted transversely at the rear, the chassis had a 16ft 3in wheelbase and also featured conventional leaf springs and air brakes. The most noticeable feature was the drop-centre rear axle. This was of great significance as it enabled the bodybuilder to create a full length centre-gangway on both decks, and yet all within an overall height of 13ft 4in. In effect it was the first true low-floor rear-engined double-deck chassis. The three prototypes featured a Daimler engine which was to be made available as an option. All early production models had the Gardner 6LX power unit which gave 150bhp and good torque characteristics, while a few featured the smaller 6LW power unit, which also had an excellent reputation. Another important feature was the very compact concentric-drive gearbox. This gave a very neat transmission layout, and allowed room for the installation of the essentially bulky Gardner 6LX engine.

Numerically Cardiff's first rear-engine double-decker, 474 (JKG 474F) is seen when new at Ely on the long cross-city service to Llanrumney.

(Glyn Bowen courtesy Chris Taylor CTPG)

In January 1966 Cardiff Corporation Transport announced that 32 double-deckers with maximum seating capacity and a front entrance with doors, would be required for 1967/68. This resulted in an order in April for 32 Fleetlines with Gardner 6LX engines at a cost of £115,376-18s-6d. The body order being split equally between two suppliers. Metro-Cammell-Weymann (MCW) would supply 16 vehicles in 1967 and Park Royal would complete the order with 16 in 1968 at an additional cost of £68,400 and £66,240 respectively.

From 22 August 1967 until 4 September, prior to the delivery of the new buses, Manchester Corporation Transport Daimler Fleetline 4747 (FNE 747D) was borrowed in a deal arranged by Daimler, for the purpose of driver familiarisation. Due to the late delivery of new vehicles, AEC Regent IIIs 6, 7 and 18 were recertified in June 1967, while 18 also received a repaint. Number 6 and a few others also worked from Roath garage towards the end of their lives. The first of Cardiff's Fleetlines were delivered as 474 to 489 in November and December 1967, and were allocated registrations JKG 474-89F. Their MCW bodies were similar in appearance to Fleetlines that had been purchased by the municipal fleets at Manchester and Birmingham. All 16 entered service in December 1967, and were to be found as crew vehicles on routes like the 27 Llanishen (Templeton Avenue) and 19 (Michaelston Road, Ely, to Mountpleasant Avenue via Castle Street). They also enjoyed runs to Tredegar on route 36, Merthyr Tydfil on route 20 and Newport on the 30.

The balance of the order arrived in January and February 1968 from Park Royal Vehicles in London. They had modern distinctive-looking 75-seat bodies that followed the "Sheffield" design which that municipal fleet had specified from 1964. They had fleet numbers 490 to 505 with matching registrations JKG 490-505F.

Park Royal-bodied Daimler Fleetline 491 and its proud crew pose for the camera at the new terminus of the 8 in Dorchester Avenue, Penylan, when fairly new. This was the extension to the former trolleybus service from the Royal Oak.
(Glyn Bowen courtesy Chris Taylor CTPG)

All 32 Fleetlines had an overall length of just under 31 feet, and an overall height of 14ft, or 14ft 1in for the Park Royal batch. Numbers 490 to 505 were initially allocated to Roath depot, replacing trolleybuses and a regular turn was route 2, which ran from the Pier Head via Newport Road to Pengam.

Passenger complaints about upper deck conditions in warmer weather may have initiated the trial fitting of opening alloy-framed ventilators to the two front upper windows of 489 in April 1972 followed by 502 in May. All 32 buses remained as crew-operated vehicles until June 1972 when 497, 499 and 502 were modified to make them suitable for one-man operation, which included installing a periscope arrangement in the cab. The rear route number blind and nearside destination aperture fell out of use at this point and was later panelled over in most cases. The remaining 29 buses had been converted for one-man operation by 1974. When scheduled repaints became due from 1970, a number of these Fleetlines received the revised crimson lake and cream livery which incorporated less cream and used a smaller fleet name with a conventional typeface. Other special liveries followed for the MCW-bodied batch, but it is of interest to note that none of the Park Royal batch (490 to 505) carried anything other than fleet livery. The MCW batch (with the exception of 485) were withdrawn between

Trolleybus Replacement, Rear Engines and One-Man Operation

August 1979 and March 1980 and 15 of them passed directly to National Welsh for further service. The Park Royal batch was withdrawn between 1980 and 1982 with most being cannibalised for spares. Two became driver training buses and three sold for further service, while 497 passed to a preservationist.

1967 witnessed inroads into the much-admired batch of 20 AEC Regent IIIs of 1950, with 1-4, 8 to 17/9 being taken out of service leaving just five examples running; while the first Guy Arab IVs to be withdrawn were 28, 30 and 35 in 1967. 35 became a driver training bus in March 1968 followed by 27 and 34 in January 1969. All but one of the Bristol KW6Gs (131) had now also gone from passenger stock. Surprisingly, just three trolleybuses were withdrawn.

REAR-ENGINE SALOONS FOR ONE-MAN OPERATION

In 1967 with the planned introduction of one-man operation to a number of services, Cardiff was in the market for a quantity of suitable single-deckers and a number of makes including the very popular Bristol RE, were considered. Eventually an order was placed in December 1966 for 20 AEC Swifts with two-door Alexander W-type 36ft bodies for delivery in the summer of 1968 at a cost of £6778 per bus. At the time, this was the largest order ever placed by Cardiff for single deck buses, and at this stage no agreement had been reached with the unions for one-man operation. The AEC Swift was introduced in 1965, and featured a horizontal longitudinally-mounted engine at the rear. Cardiff's Swifts were MP2R models and were delivered as 506 to 525 (MBO 506-25F) with 47-seat dual-door bodywork. These were the first 36ft motor buses in the fleet and had spacious, uncluttered interiors, despite having a centre exit door. The overall style and finish of the Alexander W body was unique to Cardiff. They boasted translucent roof panels and the body incorporated forced ventilation, while a large full height luggage rack was fitted just forward of the centre exit. The front entrance was fitted with two fully-glazed glider doors, while the centre exit was wider and incorporated a pair of two-piece folding doors. A long bench-type seat was installed over each of the front wheel arches, while a low driving position was specified, which unfortunately resulted in a poor view of the centre-exit from the cab. The buses were fitted with radios from new and it was originally intended to put them straight into service as one-man vehicles, but this did not happen. As crew-operated buses they were put to work on a variety of services, and they were not converted to one-man operation until February 1970. Initially they were allocated to both Roath and Sloper Road, but later the whole batch was concentrated at the latter.

AEC Swift 507 is seen on Llanrumney Avenue and working the short-lived Commutabus Limited Stop service 44. This service was introduced in June 1969 and operated by Roath depot.
(Glyn Bowen)

Delivered in standard crimson lake and cream, the Swifts were the last new deliveries with traditional gold lettering for fleet numbers and fleet name. When they became due for a repaint around 1971 onwards, a number of them received minimal cream relief, resulting in a completely crimson front and rear. In 1972, AEC Swift 524 was the bus selected to carry the experimental tangerine orange and white livery, this being the new colour scheme eventually adopted by the transport department, and it is believed that all but four of the batch (506, 514, 518 and 520) were destined to receive the orange and white livery.

In 1967/68 extensive road improvements throughout the city created a number of major problems for the remaining trolleybus system, and only served to highlight the drawbacks of trolleybus operation. In many cases the re-alignment of the overhead proved to be very costly, and as a result of changes in the Royal Oak area of Newport Road, service 8 was converted to motor bus operation on 17 February 1968. New Daimler Fleetlines took their place, and the service was extended to Dorchester Avenue, Penylan. Road improvements in the Monument area of the city centre would also mean expensive modifications to the overhead, but in the event this did not occur as trolleybus operation of services 1 and 3 ceased on 27 April. And so now, only the two routes to Ely (10A and 10B) remained, plus the section along Newport Road to the garage at Roath.

Just 14 trolleybuses remained available for service although this later dropped to a dozen and motor buses were now to be found helping out on the Ely services. By November 1968 Cardiff Corporation was responsible for operating 61 motor bus and just two trolleybus services as well as two advertised works services from the General Station to East Moors steel works (Lewis Road and East Tyndall Street) and the hospital service from Fitzallen Road to Llandough. From 1968 inspectors were issued with two-way radios to help improve communications out on the streets.

The writing was on the wall for the four Leyland Tiger Cubs (143 to 146) after 1968 when Cardiff received its 20 AEC Swifts. The Swifts began to appear on the Penarth area routes and the Tiger Cubs spent increasingly long periods parked up on the forecourt of Sloper Road depot, occasionally being sent out on relief services. Number 145 was withdrawn in 1969 and donated its engine to 146. The other three continued until withdrawal in 1970, and all were sold for scrap. Eight of the D.J. Davies-bodied Guy Arab IVs were taken out of service in 1968, leaving just four in service. Other types eliminated in 1969 were the last Bristol KW6G, 131 (DUH 318), the last AEC Regent IIIs (6, 7 and 18), and the two remaining Leyland Royal Tigers (137 and 138). It was not a good year for the trolleybuses as 19 were condemned.

Memorable services 2: Cardiff to Tredegar

On 13 May 1929 a joint service between Cardiff and Caerphilly was commenced by the Cardiff Corporation Transport (C.C.T.) and Caerphilly Urban District Council (C.U.D.C.) undertakings. In the C.C.T. timetable it was given as route number 36. On 1 December 1930 an extension to Markham was operated by C.U.D.C., but during 1931 C.C.T. together with the West Monmouthshire Omnibus Board, joined C.U.D.C. on the full route to Markham. Cardiff initially used a Dennis E, Bristol B or one of the Albion PM28s on this service. Cardiff withdrew from the service upon the outbreak of war in September 1939, but resumed once again on 31 August 1947 using double-deckers for the first time. On 29 February 1948, the joint service was extended to Tredegar. For this run which took 1hr 48min in each direction and ran seven days a week, Cardiff initially used the Leyland PD1 they had on hire from Hants and Sussex. From 1949, examples of the six Alexander-bodied Crossley DD42 double-deckers (42 to 46, 51) were the new order on the 36. The arrival of the AEC Bridgemasters (361 to 366) in 1960, afforded passengers the luxury of saloon heaters and platform doors which must have made this journey quite acceptable in the cold weather. From 1967 the Tredegar service changed over to Daimler Fleetlines from 474 to 489 batch. The Fleetlines being lower than normal anyway could now safely negotiate the full route 36 to Tredegar, while later examples 551 to 585 were associated with the route for many years.

Metro-Cammell-Weymann-bodied Fleetline 480 climbs Market Street in Caerphilly heading for the bus station on its 33-mile run from Tredegar to Cardiff on 6 September 1971.

(John Jones)

On 1 April 1974 C.U.D.C. became part of the newly-formed Rhymney Valley District Council fleet while West Mon Omnibus Board became part of Islwyn Borough Council. The joint arrangement continued as before. Cardiff's ECW-bodied Bristol VRTs (586 to 605) also put in appearances on the 36 from 1974 until the early 1980s. By May 1986 the service had been renumbered 26, while a new limited stop service numbered X26 commenced between Cardiff and Blackwood and operated jointly by Cardiff and Islwyn Borough Transport (IBT). By this time Cardiff was using a fleet of new low-height Leyland Olympians with coach-type seating. Following the collapse of the Rhymney Valley operation in 1989, National Welsh became the third operator on the Tredegar service. On 26 May 2001 Cardiff Bus withdrew from service 26 and all other interests it had in the Caerphilly and Rhymney Valley areas. The service was later curtailed to Blackwood and, as IBT ended its operations in 2010, is now solely operated by Stagecoach South Wales.

Difficult times and the passing of the Cardiff trolleybus

As 1969 dawned the undertaking was still experiencing a severe shortage of platform staff, which led to many services being cancelled, and its reputation being called into question in the local press. One notable event in April 1969 involved another bridge with structural issues, this time over the River Ely at the eastern end of Cowbridge Road West. Fortunately this time, the weight restriction imposed exempted service buses, and so the trolleybus routes 10A and 10B were not subject to major disruption. However Bailey bridges were installed, pending the construction of a new bridge, and the necessary new section of overhead wiring was brought into use on 29 June 1969.

74-seat double-deckers capable of one-man operation were sought to replace the final trolleybuses, and a total of 25 Daimler Fleetline chassis were ordered for delivery in August 1969 at a cost of £3858 each. It was originally intended that they would replace the last trolleybuses as well as Daimler CVG6s 301 to 315. Duple won the tender for the bodies which would be supplied to Cardiff by their subsidiary coachbuilder Willowbrook of Loughborough, a first for the undertaking. The bodies would be five-bay construction, of dual-door layout and have a centrally situated forward-ascending staircase. Allocated fleet numbers 526 to 550 and registrations PKG

526-50H, these attractive buses had two-piece flat windscreens and each doorway had a pair of fully-glazed glider doors. The lower saloon incorporated bench seats over the front wheels and back-to-back seating over the rear wheel arches. Being intended for one-man-operation, periscopes were fitted in the driver's cab, while two-way radios were fitted from new. Despite having a second door, Willowbrook still managed to fit 30 seats on the lower deck and the completed vehicle had an unladen weight of 9 tons 1cwt. Another first was the fitting of white-backed reflective registration plates on the front of the buses. From July 1969 the undertaking looked to simplify its crimson lake and cream livery even further by reducing the amount of cream. On double-deckers this was achieved by eliminating the cream below and above the lower deck windows though, fortunately, this new batch of buses retained the cream above. Fleet names and numbers now appeared on vehicles in plain white letters.

The final day for trolleybus operation in Cardiff was set for 27 September, but delays to the delivery of the new Daimler Fleetlines saw this date pass. However, by October seven of the Fleetlines had arrived and entered service on the Ely routes alongside the remaining trolleybuses. Fleetlines 526 to 541 had all arrived in the autumn of 1969, and the remainder (except 550) followed in early 1970. A new date for the end of trolleybus operation was set for 11 January 1970, but due to an industrial dispute at Roath depot, the system ceased on 3 December 1969 with trolleybus 286 operating the last normal duty. A "Last Trolleybus Week" was organised for early in the New Year and 262 which had just been sold to local enthusiasts was hired back for the week and decorated with coloured lights. The last day of trolleybus operation was on Sunday 11 January 1970, when 262 brought things to a close. It departed Victoria Park at 16.00 and worked to Roath depot, after which the power was switched off. The last trolleybus had run on the streets of Cardiff.

At this point the Ely services 10A and 10B were revised and given new numbers 14 and 15. The six trolleybuses on active fleet strength at the end were 215/8/20 (DBO 475/8/80), 227 (DUH 722) and 277/82/6 (KBO 950/5/9). Cardiff had the distinction of being the last operator of 3-axle trolleybuses in the United Kingdom. As previously mentioned, 262 passed to enthusiasts in 1968 prior to the closure of the system while 215 passed to the National Museum of Wales in 1970 for eventual display at the Welsh Industrial and Maritime Museum. Of those that were sold to scrap dealer Bill Way at Cardiff East Dock, 253, 267 and 278 were still present in their yard in 1978, while 218, 220 and 227 were still there in the early 1980s.

Willowbrook-bodied Daimler Fleetline 530 is waiting at the Gabalfa terminus of service 1, just off Whitchurch Road. It is standing in what was the former trolleybus turning point and is quite clearly marked as a Pay-As-You-Enter vehicle.
(Tom Powell)

Trolleybus Replacement, Rear Engines and One-Man Operation

The last of the trolleybus replacement Fleetlines 550, was delivered in grey primer and entered service in May 1970, painted in an overall advertisement livery for Silexine Paints. This very colourful livery depicted silhouettes of scenes around Cardiff city centre, and was one of the first overall advert buses to appear in the UK.

In its very colourful advertising livery for Silexine Paints, Fleetline 550 waits in Greyfriars Road on 26 May 1970 before heading out to Pantmawr. It is being inspected by a young lad who will hopefully recognise some of the Cardiff landmarks painted on the bus. In this livery 550 was unpopular with CCTs coach painters, should there be a need to replace damaged panels.

(John Wiltshire)

All 25 new Fleetlines entered service as crew-operated vehicles, with 526 to 535 allocated to Roath depot and 536 to 550 to Sloper Road. The Roath allocation was initially used on services 10A and 10B, as well as being regular performers on services 6, 9 and 34. 536 to 550 were to be found on various crew-operated turns around Cardiff as well as the service 20 to Merthyr Tydfil. The Willowbrook-bodied Fleetlines were subject to quite a few special liveries during the 1970s (see table at back of book). It is known that 537 suffered fire damage in March 1974 but was repaired. After withdrawal in early 1982 it became a temporary office in the Central bus station and was once again damaged by fire. The first member of this batch to be withdrawn was 544 in October 1980 and all had gone by September 1982.

As the complete rundown of the trolleybus system drew to a close a further 12 examples were withdrawn by the end of 1969 leaving just six survivors. In 1970 the three Guy Arab IV trainers (27, 34 & 35) received a modified livery with the whole area between the decks repainted cream, and crimson lake applied above and below, in order to differentiate them from normal service buses. All three were withdrawn by February 1972 when they were replaced on training duties by East Lancs-bodied Arab IVs. The three remaining Leyland Tiger Cubs were withdrawn and sold for scrap during 1970 while the first of the 1956/57 Daimler CVG6s 308/11/4/5 and 341 were also withdrawn.

GUH 932 was one of three Guy Arabs IVs to receive this distinctive livery for their role as driver training buses.
(Glyn Bowen courtesy CTPG)

With the trolleybus system consigned to history, attention turned to the urgent need to convert more services to one-man operation. This began on 1 March 1970 using the AEC Swifts on routes 40A/40B - Heath, 29 - Caerphilly via Thornhill, 33 - Radyr and Morganstown, 54 - Llanedeyrn and the 44 - Llanrumney Commutabus.

In February 1971 three Guy Arab IVs, 326 to 328 were lent to Aberdare Urban District Council. The final working on service 32 to Hensol Castle took place on 27 March 1971 and the honour fell to AEC Bridgemaster 364. And so ended another era as this service passed to local independent Prance Coaches. From 6 June 1971 most of the Fleetlines from the 526 to 550 batch were converted to one-man operation for use on routes 1, 6, 9, 22 and 23. In 1973 the Sloper Road allocation (536 to 550) was moved to Roath, by which time 526 to 531 had transferred to Sloper Road. At this time, the Heath Hospital routes were revised, and became services 7, 8, and 9 continuing to serving Heath Hospital, Roath, Butetown and Grangetown. The Willowbrook-bodied Fleetlines then began a long a long association with these services and 532 to 550 were rarely seen in other parts of the City until about 1977. In May 1977 526 to 531 were transferred back to Roath depot.

Decimalisation

On 15 February 1971, the pound sterling was decimalised and the whole country switched from using pounds, shillings and pence to a new system of pounds and pence where there would be 100 pence to the pound. All businesses would have to adjust, and for Cardiff's bus fleet that meant a lot of publicity and the introduction of a new fare structure and newly printed tickets.

New Bus Grant

The 25% new bus grant was introduced with the Transport Act of 1968 and came into effect from the autumn of that year. It is interesting to note that it was introduced by the Labour government at that time, and its main aim was to do away with conductor jobs. Not too long before this Act, double-deckers without conductors were illegal. To qualify for the grant, buses had to be built to very specific dimensions and configurations, and this spelt the end for the traditional front-engine double-deck designs. Possibly even more curious politically, was that from November 1971, the Bus Grant was increased to 50% by the then Conservative government and continued as such until 31 August 1980. To conclude the Bus Grant was then reduced as follows:

    40% from 1 September 1980

    30% from 1 April 1981

    20% from 1 April 1982

    10% from 1 April 1983

    nil from 1 April 1984

The last new Daimlers

In May 1969, it was decided that 15 double-deckers would be required for delivery in 1970/71. In November tenders for Bristol VRT chassis at a cost of £4255-14s-0d each and MCW bodies at £5726-10s-0d each were accepted. However by the end of 1969, the general manager was informed that the MCW tender had been for 15 bodies on Daimler Fleetline chassis, as MCW had no body design available for mounting on a VRT chassis. To produce such a design would increase the individual body price by £595 and delay delivery until late 1971, or even early 1972. No other bodybuilders were able to oblige, so Daimler was approached with a view to supplying Fleetline chassis within the time laid down. They would be required to have Leyland 0680 engines, and if this was accepted, then the chassis could be delivered to MCW by March/April 1971. An order for 15 MCW-bodied Fleetlines was approved, and a second order for a further 20 similar buses for 1971/72 delivery was approved on 13 April 1970. The exact specification of the bodies had been drawn up some time earlier and included the provision of front entrance/centre exit. However with increasing experience of this layout it was decided that a combined front entrance/exit was preferable. It was noted this change would save the CCT an estimated £2,300 on 35 vehicles.

MCW-bodied Fleetline 552 is seen leaving Caerphilly bus station, as it continues its journey to Tredegar on service 36. Just visible on the upper deck is the translucent roof panel. Number 552 was the first of this batch to be withdrawn after barely 9 years' service.

(*Author's collection*)

Once again, delivery dates were missed and ten older vehicles (including 323/5 and 328) had to be recertified in 1970/71 at a cost of £82 each to cover for this. The first buses started to arrive during December 1971, with delivery of all 35 buses being completed in January 1972. Fleet numbers allocated were 551 to 585 with matching registrations WUH551-85K. Unlike earlier Fleetlines, these buses had Daimler chassis code CRL6-30 which reflected their Leyland 0680 engines, while their MCW bodies had seating for 74 and an overall height of 14ft 2in. They were modern-looking buses with an upright and box-like profile to a standard MCW design. The Leyland engine gave them a completely different sound, and they were quite noisy compared to a Gardner-engined Fleetline.

They were very lively performers in service. However, there were reported to be reliability problems early on with engine auxiliaries and engine mountings.

These were the last vehicles ordered by the General Manager Mr Singleton before he retired, and the last buses delivered in the traditional crimson lake and cream livery, thus ending over 70 years use of these basic colours. They were also the last buses to feature the "bird's eye maple" Formica interior panels and seat backs. These were destined to be Cardiff's last Daimlers and the only double-deckers to feature the Leyland 0680 engine. They were the first buses in the fleet with power-assisted steering and the first rear-engine buses to feature inward-facing seats over the rear wheel arches. This batch retained the rear route number box and side destination box, the last buses delivered to Cardiff with these features. Finally, they were the last buses to have a translucent roof panel in the upper deck ceiling.

Once in service all 35 were allocated to Sloper Road, undertaking most duties from that depot. Out of the City they were to be found working to Newport on the 30 and to Tredegar on the 36. It was on the latter route that nearly-new 565 came to grief on Nantgarw Hill on 28 February 1972 when the driver collapsed at the wheel and the bus toppled over onto its offside. Following repair it returned to service repainted in the new experimental orange and white livery. In September 1972, after an accident, 585 was repainted to celebrate Cardiff's recent twinning with Stuttgart in West Germany. It visited that city in July 1973. The first example to be taken out of service was 552 in 1980, with the remainder coming off between 1982 and 1984, except for 576 which soldiered on into 1985.

A BIG CLEAR OUT FOLLOWS

This massive influx of new buses in 1971/72 brought about the demise of 63 older vehicles. In March 1971 AEC Bridgemaster 362 was withdrawn with a fractured underframe, and was broken up by the Corporation for spares to keep the others going. The remaining five (361, 363 to 366) were ousted by early 1972 and were fortunate enough to see further service, probably due to the fact that they had platform doors and heaters, which made them an attractive and safe vehicle for duties such as school or works contracts.

The fleet also bid farewell to the Daimler CSG6s (355 to 360), Metro-Cammell-bodied Leyland PD2As (367 to 371) and the last of the Daimler CVG6s. Also, all but three of the Guy Arab IVs departed, leaving just 323/5/8 in passenger service, the trio that were recertified in 1970. The bulk of the Daimlers and Guys ended up in Barnsley scrapyards, whilst a few made it to Bill Way's yard at Cardiff's East Dock. They had no future as complete buses, their only real value was their Gardner engines. Meanwhile, Guy Arab IVs 319, 324, 327 and 345 became driver trainers in early 1972, and in this role they lost all of their upper and most of their lower-deck seats. 319 was then loaned to Cardiff City Council in March 1972 and used as an exhibition vehicle, branded the "Magic Bus". It received a mainly brown and orange livery later changed to a multi coloured blue based livery by 1974. The six Daimler CSG6s 355 to 360 had relatively low mileages when sold to Paul Sykes (dealer) of Barnsley, and two of them were to survive a little longer. SKG 357 was used in conjunction with a children's TV programme called "Hope and Keens Crazy Bus" which was screened around 1972/73. The television series ended and, by 1974 the bus had become a caravan with Gerry Cottle's Circus. It visited Cardiff with the circus in 1975 and 1976 and it ended up in one of the Barnsley scrapyards by 1978. Meanwhile SKG 360 found further use in Sheffield with the Atlas School of Motoring, but it was back with a Barnsley dealer by December 1972. Three of the Metro-Cammell-bodied PD2A Titans (367/8 and 371) saw further service with 368 and 371 returning to the South Wales area. 368 survived long enough, latterly as a training bus; to be saved for preservation in 1992.

AEC Regent Vs 372 to 376 were delicensed in April 1972, but the first three were then recertified and returned to service by March 1973. Number 376 on the other hand was initially cannibalised, before being recertified and returned to service at the same time, having also received a partial repaint.

CHAPTER SIX

THE COLOURFUL SEVENTIES: DIVERSITY AND VEHICLE SHORTAGES

Although the undertaking had many modern vehicles, the overall visual impression the public would be presented with on a day-to-day basis was of a rather shabby fleet which, coupled to reliability issues, meant there would have to be big changes. A new general manager David R. Smith, previously traffic manager at Leicester City Transport, was appointed in 1971. Those big changes would soon follow.

Cream is off the menu. 520 (MBO 520F) is a particularly scruffy AEC Swift and a good example of the final application of crimson lake and cream. It is seen at the Heath Hospital on City Circle duties in the spring of 1975, and was repainted into orange and white by July. Note the prominent rear route number display now painted out.

(*Andrew Wiltshire*)

Looking for a bright new image

From about 1969, Sloper Road paint shop which could at this time accommodate two buses side by side, seemed content to outshop vehicles with the minimal amount of cream, as we can see in the photograph above. Roath depot paint shop did however buck the trend turning out Leyland PD3As (402 to 407) and AEC Regent Vs (408 to 419) with cream above the lower saloon windows. Some of Roath's last repaints in crimson lake and cream included Guy Arab Vs 426/7/32 and 447, which additionally received extra cream above and adjacent to the bonnet area which did look good. 427 had the distinction of being the last bus of all outshopped in crimson lake and cream. However the Cardiff fleet really needed a new image and a new brand, and livery experiments began in early 1972. Three buses were selected for a repaint into experimental base colours. These emerged as Guy Arab V 461 (aquamarine), Daimler Fleetline 488 (dark orange) and AEC Swift 524 (tangerine/light orange).

AEC Swift 524 was chosen to trial the light orange colour scheme. It is seen on 27 July 1972 in the bus station about to depart for Snowden Road, Ely. Note the Cardiff buses fleet name.

(*John Wiltshire*)

All three entered service during March 1972, and carried a white identification band with the lettering 'Cardiff buses' in black on both sides, and the City's coat of arms in gold on a black disc. The coat of arms also appeared in black on a white disc on the front of double-deckers above the destination aperture. The three buses were put to work across the city and the travelling public were encouraged to comment. Willowbrook-bodied Fleetline 550 lost its Silexine Paints overall advert livery by July 1972, and became the second vehicle to carry the experimental "aquamarine blue" livery as part of the livery trials, thus representing a more modern bus than Guy Arab 461.

In July 1972 MCW-bodied Daimler Fleetline 476 gained an overall advert livery to the order of Barclaycard. Further overall advert liveries were introduced from 1973 onwards which would generate some useful revenue as well as brightening up the streets of Cardiff. Some special livery adaptations were unveiled to promote a number of causes. For more details see the table in Appendix 1.

The driver and conductor smile for the camera as Fleetline 476 proudly shows off its distinctive Barclaycard overall advert livery on 29 July 1972. It is working to the Pentrebane estate via Llandaff village on the 32D. Note the repositioned registration plate.

(John Wiltshire)

MCW-bodied Fleetline 556 of 1971 in a smart advert livery for Hill House Insurance Brokers Ltd is viewed from Gabalfa flyover on 2 July 1973, while working a 25 from Rhiwbina into the city centre. These hand-painted liveries were most eye-catching.

(John Wiltshire)

The Colourful Seventies: Diversity and Vehicle Shortages

By August 1972, it had been decided that the new fleet livery would be the light orange (described as tangerine) with a white band. The Cardiff buses fleet name that appeared on 461, 488, 524, 550 and 565 was substituted for City of Cardiff appearing on the nearside, while the Welsh translation Dinas Caerdydd was carried on the offside of the bus. No time was wasted in making a start on repaints, and the table below shows the progress made during the first 12 months:

	GUY ARAB V	AEC SWIFT	DAIMLER FLEETLINE
August 1972			491 494
September	436 469		484 486 585 (twin city Stuttgart version)
October	443 451	507 523	492 548
November	453		490 528 547
December	437 448		529 530 535
By end of 1972		510 522	493 526 (twin city Nantes version) 527 531
January 1973	463		
February	466		475 479
March	455 468		477
April	473	519 521 525	
May	467	508	541 550 (ex aquamarine)
June		513	480 (British Rail)
July	446 454		536

The orange did look good when the vehicle was freshly turned out, but unfortunately was not very durable. It soon began to look grubby with ingrained road grime and also discoloured after a few months. The dark orange may have been a better choice.

As 1972 drew to a close, progress was such that the undertaking was running 57 regular services plus two timetabled works services, 13 of which were operated by one-man buses. During 1973, in addition to a number of overall advert and special liveries, a bus was decorated for use as a campaign vehicle. The vehicle selected was Fleetline 488 which wore the dark orange experimental livery. In May it received a matt black waistband with silver foil lettering to promote the campaign that was trying to prevent the closure of the East Moors steelworks in Cardiff. Similarly Fleetline 480 upon repaint into orange received a white waistband with red and blue stripes. This was to promote the proposed relocation of British Railways' Western Region headquarters to Brunel House in Cardiff. As such it spent a short time in June 1973 fitted out as an exhibition bus visiting London Paddington, Reading and Bristol, before being placed in normal service in July. In an unusual move, Guy Arab V 444 (EUH 444D), newly repainted into orange and white, was loaned to Gelligaer Urban District Council from 23 September to 13 October. It was one of several buses hired to cover a shortage of vehicles.

On 14 March 1973 a brand new head office for the City of Cardiff Transport Department was opened in Wood Street at a cost of £353,000. It was built on the site of the converted former Victorian school which the Transport Department had occupied since 1950. A Leyland National demonstrator FRM 499K that was on loan at the time was present for the opening ceremony. To coincide with major service revisions, 13 new one-man operated services were introduced throughout the city on 10 June 1973. The City Circle was a new concept linking the city centre and a number of suburbs in both the east and west of the city to the Heath Hospital complex. Numbered 1 (clockwise) and 2 (anti-clockwise), it was initially operated by the AEC Swifts, and due to a number of low bridges, it was always operated by saloons. Although revised on a number of occasions, the City Circle was still running in 2016. Initially linked in with the City Circle were the services 3 and 4. Other new services included number 7 (Llandaff Fields to Heath Hospital); 8 (Grangetown to Heath Hospital) and 9 (Butetown - St. Mary Street - Splott) all of which utilised one-man operated double-deckers.

Fleetline 486 freshly outshopped in the new light orange livery, but yet to receive its coat of arms emblems, makes a good contrast with similar 488 which wears the experimental dark orange. They stand alongside Swift 506 which was one of the last recipients of the crimson lake and cream colour scheme.

(John Wiltshire)

Another change to take place during 1973 was the revision of destination displays. From June all displays would now show the district served instead of individual roads on the route. For buses that did not have a separate route number blind, the route numbers were displayed in the front nearside lower saloon bulkhead window. This took the form of individual cards that were dropped into a metal frame that was fixed to the glass. It was crude, but it did the job.

Swift departure

By 1973, it was becoming obvious that all was not well with Cardiff's batch of 20 AEC Swifts, then barely five years old. For example in June 1972 11 were off the road awaiting attention. Reliability in service was unacceptable and this was aggravated by the poor availability of spare parts. The somewhat drastic decision to withdraw and dispose of all 20, once suitable replacement buses could be obtained, was taken in May 1973, when the General Manager recommended that tenders be issued for the supply of ten single-deckers for delivery in 1973/74. In July 1973 it was reported that British Leyland were offering a prototype Leyland National for delivery before 31 March 1974, which would be fitted with a new improved heating and ventilation system, and it was decided to buy this bus for £11887 less 50% grant. On 23 August 1973, an order was placed for ten two-door 10.3m Leyland Nationals and these would also have ZF 2-speed gearboxes. The requirement for fully automatic transmission added £782 to the cost of each bus. A further ten 10.3m Leyland Nationals were subsequently ordered for 1975/76.

The Colourful Seventies: Diversity and Vehicle Shortages

Enter the midi-bus

During 1973 it was announced that some small buses would be purchased to operate a new series of weekdays only, off-peak routes serving areas where normal length buses could not operate. These services would be County Council supported and would commence from April 1974. For this venture a trio of Seddon Pennine IV-236 midi-buses were ordered in July 1973. They arrived in December 1973 and were the first new buses to be delivered in the orange and white livery. As 101 to 103 (RNY 101-3M) they started a new numbering scheme. Bodywork was by Seddon's in-house coachbuilder Pennine and they featured 25 comfortable high-backed seats. The Seddon Pennine IV-236 was a small midi-bus version of the front-engine Pennine IV coach chassis, and it too featured the Perkins 4-cylinder diesel. The chassis was 20ft 11in long, 7ft 6in wide and wheelbase of only 9ft 6in. They featured steep entrance steps and a small platform with a raised cover over the engine, and an open driver's cab layout. Despite the comfortable seating, they were rather cramped and noisy vehicles from a passenger's perspective.

Having been in service for just over a week, Seddon midi-bus 103 heads south along Lake Road East on 10 April 1974. It is passing Roath Park Lake and heading into town having picked up a few passengers in Cyncoed. Its Perkins engine would have a very distinctive exhaust note.

(John Wiltshire)

The Seddons eventually entered service in April 1974 covering the following routes:

101	Central Bus Station	Heath (via Crwys Road)
102	Central Bus Station	Heath (via Maindy Road)
103	Central Bus Station	Grangetown
104	Central Bus Station	Gabalfa circular
105	-	Gabalfa Local service
106	Central Bus Station	Cyncoed
107	Central Bus Station	Pentwyn

These services would later be revised on a number of occasions.

Cardiff's Municipal Buses

Cardiff gets its first Bristol VRTs

The VRL chassis, with its longitudinal rear engine, did not qualify for the New Bus Grant, so Bristol Commercial Vehicles hastily set about producing a chassis with a Gardner engine mounted transversely at the rear in similar fashion to the Fleetline. No prototype was built and the VRT went straight from the drawing board into production and, as a consequence, early examples were plagued with reliability issues. In 1970, Bristol updated the chassis, rectifying many of the faults found in the original model and resulting in the much more successful Series 2 model.

As mentioned in Chapter 5, Cardiff had unsuccessfully tried to obtain Bristol VRTs for delivery in 1970/71 but had to settle for more Daimler Fleetlines. However in May 1971 the Transport Department ordered 20 VRTs with low-height 74-seat ECW bodies for delivery by early 1974, and they were very similar to the standard vehicles specified by the National Bus Company at this time. Power steering was originally specified but this was later cancelled, and the total cost of the order was approximately £103,000 (20 chassis) and £124,000 (20 bodies). The first two examples (586 and 587) arrived in early December 1973, with 587 soon running out of Sloper Road on driver familiarisation. The batch was numbered 586 to 605 (PKG 586-605M) and during January the remaining 18 were all delivered and placed in store at Roath depot until a number of faults had been rectified. They had a wheelbase of 16ft 2in, an overall height of 13ft 8in and featured the Gardner 6LX engine of 150bhp. As delivered, they had CAV 4-speed semi-automatic gearboxes, but it was decided to convert all 20 to fully-automatic transmission with electro-pneumatic control. 588 and 589 were the first to be converted and used for staff training, though it was several months before the programme was complete. It is generally accepted that the "in house" conversion did not live up to expectations. With most faults corrected, the entire batch of 20 entered service from 1 April 1974 with 586 to 595 initially at Sloper Road, and the remainder at Roath. The new Bristols were quite attractive buses and featured a number of firsts. They were the first new double-deckers delivered in orange and white, the first rear engine buses in the fleet with a forward-mounted radiator and the first with a spring-operated parking brake. They were also the first rear-engine double-deckers to have the engine compartment completely enclosed, and to feature a single-line destination display and three-track route number display.

Brand new Bristol VRT 592 is captured on Newport Road on 5 April 1974 inbound from Tremorfa. It is heading towards Queen Street in the city centre with a Victoria Park bound service 5.

(John Wiltshire)

The new VRTs could be found on most double-deck routes around the city, but were rarely seen on the 30 to Newport. They did however have a spell on the 36 to Tredegar, until complaints from drivers saw K-reg Daimler Fleetlines return. Being of low height construction, headroom in both saloons was restricted and the drivers cab was reputed to be rather cramped too. However the cabs were generally well laid out, and the brakes were regarded as excellent, and a top speed of between 42 and 45mph could be expected. It is thought the one member of this batch, believed to be 597, was loaned to Northampton Transport for about two days in May 1974. The first casualty was 596, withdrawn in 1983 as the result of accident damage sustained inside Sloper Road garage, while the final five in service, 601 to 605, lasted until 1989. In 2015 just one example survives, 587, which is now safely in the hands of preservationists.

In 1974 City of Cardiff Transport set out their future plans for a large number of new double-deckers to complete the conversion of all services to one-man operation by the end of the decade. The following would be required:

| 26 in 1976/77 | 34 in 1977/78 | 23 in 1978/79 | 31 in 1979/80 |

In the autumn of 1974 the Council Trading Services Committee inspected two double-deck vehicles in relation to the above. The MCW Metropolitan double-decker NVP 533M was inspected in September, while on 11 October, Motor Show exhibit RCN 165N, a Series-3 Bristol VRT with dual-door ECW bodywork was given the once over.

From October 1974 Cardiff simplified its fare structure by creating four zones across the city with five fare stages. Also introduced at this time was the Multiride Ticket for weekly or monthly travel, which would soon become very popular with the travelling public. It would be valid on all routes except the out of town services, 29 (Caerphilly), 30 (Newport), 36 (Tredegar) and 70/71 (Lower Penarth). The undertaking also experimented with a secondary method of fare collection aimed at speeding up boarding times. The T.I.M. Videmat self-service system was already in use in a few other towns including Sheffield, and in 1973 Cardiff decided to trial it on route 24 by installing it on a number of one-man operated double-deckers. In March 1974 Videmat machines were fitted in Willowbrook-bodied Fleetlines 528, 532 to 535 and 537 to 550, plus a number of the new ECW-bodied VRTs. It was basically a large ticket-issuing machine that was situated on the right hand side of the entrance and just ahead of the wheel-arch. After dropping the exact fare into a hopper and pressing a large plastic button, the machine issued a ticket showing an image of the coins tendered. The driver was still able to issue tickets from his Almex machine.

By early 1974 the three remaining Guy Arab IVs 323, 325 and 328 were generally regarded as spare buses, restricted to peak-time duties when required. However 325 did manage a run to Tredegar in 1973. In addition, 325 and 328 had their cab bulkhead windows modified in May 1972 with a removable section for use when on driver training duties. They were withdrawn in early 1974. The first examples of the ten AEC Regent Vs (372 to 381) to be withdrawn were 373/377 and 379, which were taken off in 1973, as was East Lancs-bodied Leyland PD2A number 393. The remaining 1961-vintage Regent Vs were taken out of service in early 1974, and all ten were promptly sold for scrap by May that year. Other buses withdrawn during 1974, having been displaced by the new Bristol VRTs, were air-braked AEC Regent Vs 382/383/387 to 389 of 1962, and the remaining Leyland PD2As 392/394 to 401, which were the last vacuum-braked buses in passenger service. The three vacuum-braked Guy Arab IV training buses 324/327 and 345 remained active, but were replaced by Regent Vs. Incidentally, at this time 345 was the last vehicle owned that carried the older version of crimson lake and cream with the fleet name in gold lettering below the lower saloon windows.

Leyland Nationals

The new Leyland National also arrived in April 1974, as 201 (RUH 201M), and had an unladen weight of 8680kg. The Transport Department was quoted as saying "The Leyland National heralds a new era in bus travel. Travelling in a Leyland National is a new experience…..…..Cardiff buses are leading the way." The first batch of ten appeared in October/November 1974 as 202 to 211 and carried fairly meaningless registrations GBO 137-146N, as it was no longer possible to reserve matching registrations. They differed from 201 in having the new smaller roof pod, and also featured anti-roll bars, both of which were to become standard.

202 to 208 joined 201 at Sloper Road from 1 November 1974, whereas 209 to 211 were at Roath depot. All eleven were 10351/2R models with a front entrance and centre exit, and 40 seats.

The final batch of Leyland Nationals arrived in May/June 1975 as 212 to 221 (JBO 352-4N, JBO 345-51N) and were outwardly identical to the previous ten with small roof pods, but had standard Leyland G2 5-speed fully automatic gearboxes. This featured driver-operated gear hold on 2nd, 3rd and 4th gears and gave a much smoother ride than 201 to 211. All were based at Sloper Road from new, and by the time they entered service, the withdrawal and disposal of a number of AEC Swifts was well under way.

217 is seen on Museum Avenue on 28 June 1976 working the short-lived 99 Centrelink service. This view is enhanced by the lack of parked cars outside the main university building which is behind the bus.
(*John Wiltshire*)

The Leyland Nationals were well received by drivers and regarded as superior vehicles to the Swifts as they were fully-automatic, featured power steering, air suspension and were of course shorter, so would be easier to manoeuvre. The ZF gearboxes were however more unreliable than the G2. The duties for these buses confined them to the lighter-loaded routes around Cardiff. They were regular performers on the City Circle (1 and 2) throughout their lives with Cardiff and also worked to Lower Penarth. Other regular turns were the 39 and 39A from St. Mary St to Manor Way and Ely Bridge respectively, as well as the number 3 and 4 from St. Mary Street to Rhydypenau Cross Roads (3 via Heath Hospital and 4 via Lake Road East). Normal withdrawals commenced in 1984 with the last examples remaining in the Cardiff fleet until 1989. A few would see further service.

With the new Leyland Nationals in service, twelve AEC Swifts were officially withdrawn in April/May 1975 (506/8/9, 511/3/4, 516 to 518, 521/3/5), although several of them including 506 and 514 had been off the road for some time prior to that, including 506 and 514 which were still in crimson and cream livery. 514 had gradually been cannibalised for spares while 525 was inspected by Chesterfield Transport with a view to acquisition, but to no avail. To avoid a chronic vehicle shortage it was decided to retain five, later eight, of the Swifts, and those selected were 507, 510/2/5/9, 520/2/4. They were recertified between May and July 1975, with the intention of giving them a further two years' service. Other buses withdrawn in 1975 were the last of the 1962 AEC Regent Vs (384 to 386, 390/1) and the entire batch of six Leyland PD3As (402 to 407). The last bus in normal service in the old livery was Daimler Fleetline 533 (PKG 533H) which eventually gained orange and white fleet livery during December 1975.

The improved VRT

The Series 3 Bristol VRT was subject to much research and development work and a prototype chassis was completed in November 1973. Launched in 1975, it was originally offered with a choice of three engines, Gardner 6LX, 6LXB engine and Leyland 501, though the 6LX was later dropped. The engine compartment was fully enclosed with no ventilation grills. Both semi and full-automatic transmission options were also available. The Series 3 was the final and most successful version of the chassis, remaining in production until 1981.

The Colourful Seventies: Diversity and Vehicle Shortages

In February 1975 tenders were received from Bristol Commercial Vehicles and Walter Alexander for the supply of 26 chassis at £12,125 each and 26 bodies at £8,970 each with delivery required before 31 March 1976. At this point both were given the option to supply a further 88 vehicles. The tender for 26 was soon approved but, in October, British Leyland (BCV) announced that they were increasing the price of the 26 chassis from £548,470 to £601,596. A proposal for 34 similar vehicles for 1977/78 was soon confirmed with both suppliers, with delivery required by 31 December 1977, as it was originally thought that the 50% New Bus Grant scheme would end then. An order for a further 23 similar buses for 1978/79 was later confirmed.

In January 1976 three 27ft Guys (452 to 454) were moved to Roath to enable Leyland Nationals 209 to 211 to transfer to Sloper Road. Service 99 commenced on 2 February 1976 and, branded as "Centrelink", was an attempt to provide a frequent service for both commuters and shoppers, linking the two main railway stations via the Civic Centre. It ran every six minutes (Monday-Friday 07.30-10.30 and 15.00-18.30) travelling from Central station via Kingsway, Corbett Road, Museum Avenue and on to Queen Street station, and then retracing route. It had a 2p flat fare and was sponsored by South Glamorgan County Council, and usually operated by a number of Leyland Nationals. The service was not a success and finished on 16 July.

In March 1976 there was a brief vehicle shortage due to chassis problems with some Daimler Fleetlines from the 551 to 585 batch which needed urgent rectification. There was also a need to provide suitable vehicles to enable further services to be converted to one-man operation. As a result half-cab double-deckers were allocated to the Tredegar service to free up more modern vehicles. For a period this resulted in the 27ft Alexander-bodied Guy Arabs (452 to 473) being regular performers on the 36 in place of Daimler Fleetlines which did not go down too well with crews, despite being semi-automatic. However, further variety was added as manual gearbox AEC Regent Vs from the 408 to 419 batch also put in appearances as did Neepsend-bodied, manual gearbox Guy Arab Vs, 430 and 436. Also, a number of buses were brought in on short-term hire from Borough of Newport Transport. All were officially hired from 1 March 1976, but were not all present at the same time. The vehicles are detailed below and retained their Newport fleet numbers as shown:

101 to 104, 107	JDW 301-4/7F	Bristol RESL6L	ECW	B42F	1967
89	MDW 389G	Leyland PDR1A/1	Alexander	H43/31F	1969
98, 100	PDW 98/100H	"	"	"	1970

These buses returned to Newport for servicing, often as a one way trip on the 30. The Bristol REs were used on a variety of routes, but the Atlanteans were confined to the Tredegar service. All had returned by the end of the month.

Open-top bus tours, more midi-buses and a coach

To cater for a growing interest in the leisure market, City of Cardiff Transport applied for and was granted an Excursion and Tours licence in 1976. Initially two Guy Arab V half-cabs were converted to open-top for use on seven new tours within the City boundary. 30ft Guy Arab Vs 422 and 424, were selected for conversion to open-top configuration, but in the event "shorter" Guy 434 which had sustained roof damage replaced 422 in the conversion programme. They appeared in a white livery with orange bands and their first engagement was at the Lord Mayor's Parade on 26 June 1976. The programme of tours detailed left, commenced on 4 July 1976 with the season ending on 30 September; the start point being Kingsway but also picking up at Central Station.

91	City Tour
92	Llandaff Cathedral and St. Fagans
93	St. Fagans and Castell Coch
94	Cefn Onn and Caerphilly Mountain
95	Roath Park mystery tour
96	Evening Tour
97	Roman Tour

All were 2½ hours duration except the 96 which was just 1¼ hours. At seven journeys per week, the 91 was the most frequent while the 97 only operated three journeys in the season. An adult paid 50p to ride on the top deck, but only 40p in the lower saloon. The tours were then developed further in 1977/78.

On 27 August 1977 open-top Guy 434 heads down Kingsway towards Central Station at the start of the Cardiff Tour (now renumbered 97). Despite the sunny weather a few passengers have chosen to remain on the lower deck.

(John Wiltshire)

Only three new buses were acquired in 1976. Two additional buses were now required for the midi-bus services and, as the Seddon Pennine IV-236 was no longer being built, a pair of Bristol LHS6L chassis with 125bhp Leyland 401 engines and 5-speed manual gearboxes were ordered in April 1975. The two LHSs were delivered in May 1976 as 104 and 105 (LUH 104/5P), and entered service on 7 June. The 7ft 6in-wide ECW bodies were 24-feet long and featured orange and black moquette high-back seating for 27 passengers. Number 104 was fitted with an experimental remote-control "flap-style" destination and route indicator, which was later removed. Being of underfloor-engine layout, the entrance platform area was far more satisfactory from both a driver and passenger perspective compared with the Seddons.

An immaculate 105 pauses opposite the National Museum of Wales alongside Gorsedd Gardens on the evening of Monday 28 June 1976, while working the 99 Centrelink service. These were more attractive buses than the three earlier Seddons, but were still quite noisy.

(John Wiltshire)

A brand new coach was ordered for delivery by July 1976, and was a 36-foot long Leyland Leopard PSU3C/4R with a Duple Dominant body. It had a Leyland 0680 engine and a pneumocyclic gearbox. Completed to Bus Grant specification, this specified that it be used in service as well as for private hire work. This fine new vehicle was delivered on 18 August 1976 as fleet number 1 (NWO 901R) and had seating for 51 and an unladen weight of 9043kg. It lasted with Cardiff until May 1989 when it was withdrawn and eventually passed to an operator at Balregan in the Irish Republic.

The Colourful Seventies: Diversity and Vehicle Shortages

Towards the end of its service in Cardiff, the first coach 1 (NWO 901R) waits at the Heol Llanishen Fach terminus of service X22 on 10 December 1987 and will shortly depart for St. Mary Street in the City Centre. The appearance of this coach changed very little in its thirteen years with the fleet.

(Andrew Wiltshire)

The first of the large number of new double-deckers on order in 1976 were due for delivery by the end of this year. However severe delays at the body-builder meant that delivery of the first 26 new buses had to be put back by many months and, in November 1976, Alexander announced that they would be unable to meet delivery dates for this batch of Bristol VRTs. The order was then reassigned to Willowbrook International of Loughborough, at a cost of £13,890 each.

Taking stock 2: A summary of the Cardiff fleet in September 1976

FLEET NO.	REGISTRATION	CHASSIS TYPE	BODYWORK	YEAR NEW
1	NWO 901R	Leyland PSU3C/4R	Duple Dominant	1976
101 to 103	RNY 101-3M	Seddon Pennine IV	Pennine	1973
104 and 105	LUH 104/5P	Bristol LHS6L	ECW	1976
201	RUH 201M	Leyland National	10351/2R	1974
202 to 211	GBO 137-46M	"	"	"
212 to 221	JBO 352-4/45-51N	"	"	1975
408 to 413	408-13 DBO	AEC Regent V	East Lancs	1963
414 to 419	414-9 DBO	"	Neepsend	1963/64
420 to 424	ABO 420-4B	Guy Arab V	"	1964
431/33/34	ABO 431/3/4B	"	"	"
425 to 428	ABO 425-28C	"	"	1965
430/32/35/36	ABO 430/2/5/6C	"	"	"
437 to 451	EUH 437-51D	"	Alexander	1965/66
452 to 473	EUH 452-73D	"	"	1966
474 to 489	JKG 474-89F	Daimler CRG6LX	Metro-Cammell	1967
490-505	JKG 490-505F	"	Park Royal	1968
507/10/12/15	MBO 507/10/2/5F	AEC Swift MP2R	Alexander	"
519/20/22/24	MBO 519/20/2/4F	"	"	"
526 to 550	PKG 526-50H	Daimler CRG6LX	Willowbrook	1969/70
551 to 585	WUH 551-85K	" CRL6-30	Metro-Cammell	1971/72
586 to 605	PKG 586-605M	Bristol VRTSL6G	ECW	1973/74

Note that Guy Arab V 424 and 434 are open-toppers.

The first normal withdrawals of Guy Arab Vs occurred in June 1976 when 429 was taken off with a major engine defect. It last ran in service on 20 May and was later stripped for spares. This was followed by 431 in November and 433 in December, and all three were sold for scrap. By the summer of 1977 425 to 428/30/2/5 had gone too, leaving just 436 and open-topper 434. The 30ft examples 420 to 423 remained in normal service.

In March 1977 the midi-bus fleet strength was once again boosted by the addition of a sixth vehicle, Eastbourne Borough Council's solitary Seddon Pennine IV-236 MJK 94L. Like the original Cardiff trio (101 to 103), it was fitted with 25 high-backed seats, but was slightly older being new in March 1973. It was collected from Eastbourne on 3 April and upon arrival in Cardiff, given fleet number 106. It entered service on 2 May, and was notably the first second-hand bus acquired by Cardiff since the Crossleys in 1947. It differed from 101 to 103 by having luggage racks, a rear boot, single rear wheels and different destination layout.

Former Eastbourne Seddon 106 passes the Prudential building on Kingsway (now the Hilton Hotel) in August 1977. It has worked the 16.25 from Michaelston y Fedw, a small rural village out to the east of Cardiff. Note the blue-coloured seating of Eastbourne origin.

(John Jones)

A VERY INTERESTING PERIOD

By the early summer of 1977, the delays caused by the late delivery of the new double-deckers inevitably led to severe vehicle shortages, as the Certificates of Fitness (CoF) of older buses due for replacement were about to expire. The Transport Department had two options, the first being the costly recertification of half-cab double-deckers, which it really wanted to dispose of, as they were not capable of one-man operation. The preferred alternative was to hire-in vehicles, most of which would be suitable for one-man operation (omo). This would allow the omo conversion programme to move forward. A variety of vehicles were therefore hired until late autumn 1977, when the new Bristol VRTs finally started to arrive. The vehicles on loan from Southend stood out from the others as they were immaculate both inside and out. The PD3s were interesting as they had manual gearboxes and re-introduced vacuum-braked vehicles onto the streets of Cardiff once again. The buses loaned from Plymouth and Tyne and Wear could best be described as well-used, but they were most welcome at this difficult time.

The Colourful Seventies: Diversity and Vehicle Shortages

Vehicles hired in during this period were:

\multicolumn{6}{c}{**FROM CITY OF OXFORD M.S. 28 JULY 1977.**}
\multicolumn{6}{c}{Based at Roath for omo services for one month.}
Fleet no.	Registration	Chassis	Body	Seating	Year new
910/10/12	5284/48/50 HA	Daimler CRG 6LX	Alexander	H44/33F	1963
915/7	5278/71 HA	"	"	"	"
\multicolumn{6}{l}{Re-seated to H43/33F before entering service. All five were new to Midland Road.}
\multicolumn{6}{l}{They worked service 55/56 (daytime) and 57/58 (evenings). Off loan 25 August 1977}

FROM SOUTHEND TRANSPORT 31 JULY 1977.					
Based at Sloper Road on indefinite loan.					
333-335	CJN 433-5C	Leyland PD3/6	Massey	H38/32R	1965
338-341/4	CJN 438-41/4C	"	"	"	"
361, 362	WJN 361/2J	Daimler CRL6-33	NCME	H49/31D	1971
The Leyland PD3s worked services 14/17 and 19, and 338 to 341 were returned by late September. The others returned by 8 October.					
361/2 were modified to 76-seaters before entering service and worked services 4/5/6/61 and 62. They were returned by mid-November 1977.					

FROM CITY OF PORTSMOUTH 31 JULY 1977.					
Based at Roath for omo work on indefinite loan.					
238, 239	BBK 238/9B	Leyland PDR1/1	Metro-Cammell	H44/33F	1964
They worked service 55/56 (daytime) and 57/58 (evenings). Off loan 3 December 1977.					

FROM TYNE AND WEAR PTE ARRIVED BETWEEN 21 AND 29 SEPTEMBER 1977.					
All at Sloper Road for omo work on indefinite loan.					
116/19/24	16/9/24 JVK	Leyland PDR1/1	Weymann	H44/34F	1963
130, 141	30/41 JVK	"	Alexander	"	1964
174	ETN 74C	"	"	"	1965
189, 197	ETN 89/97C	"	"	"	"
203	ETN 103C	"	"	"	"
211	KBB 111D	"	Metro-Cammell	"	1966
Re-seated to H42/34F before entering service. They worked services 75 to 80					

FROM PLYMOUTH CT ARRIVED 27 TO 28 SEPTEMBER 1977.					
Based at Roath for omo work on indefinite loan.					
149/54	WJY 749/54	Leyland PDR1/1	Metro-Cammell	H44/33F	1962
156/57	WJY 756/7	"	"	"	"
Re-seated to H42/33F before entering service. They worked service 55/56 (daytime) and 57/58 (evenings).					

Cardiff's Municipal Buses

FROM SOUTHEND TRANSPORT ARRIVED 29 TO 30 SEPTEMBER 1977 FOR ONE MONTH. Based at Sloper Road and immediately replaced 338-41, and later 333-5/44 by 8 October 1977.					
363 to 366	WJN 363-6J	Daimler CRL6-33	NCME	H49/31D	1971
They were modified to 76-seaters before entering service and worked services 4/5/6/61 and 62. 363 and 364 were returned by mid-November 1977. 365 and 366 were returned by early December 1977.					

FROM BOURNEMOUTH TRANSPORT ARRIVED 5 NOVEMBER 1977 FOR ABOUT 5 WEEKS. Based at Soper Road for omo services.					
220 to 223	ORU 220-3G	Leyland PDR1A/1	Alexander	H43/31F	1969
Cardiff initially inspected Bournemouth Daimler Fleetline 180 in early November 1977, with a view to taking 180/1/8/97 on loan.					
They worked services 22/24 and 25. They were returned on 17 December 1977.					

An additional vehicle taken on loan for about ten days in October was Rhymney Valley Leyland Atlantean 21 (HHB 48N) in place of Cardiff overall advert Fleetline 578, which went to Rhymney Valley to publicise the undertaking's Multiride ticket.

Number 445 was a 30ft Guy Arab V and is seen in 1977, followed along Greyfriars Road by a hired Southend Daimler Fleetline and behind that Cardiff Fleetline 502.

(John Jones)

The Colourful Seventies: Diversity and Vehicle Shortages

Cardiff during the summer of 1977 was certainly a place to visit if you wanted to see a variety of buses and liveries and this continued to be the case well into 1978.

WJY 157 was one of four Leyland Atlanteans to arrive on loan from Plymouth City Transport. It is seen on 10 October 1977 leaving Wellfield Road on a working of the 56 from Pentwyn to Fairwater.

(John Wiltshire)

On 10 August 1977, City of Portsmouth Leyland Atlantean BBK 239B stops at the north end of Park Place in the Cathays Park area on a run into town from Pentwyn via Birchgrove, on service 55.

(John Wiltshire)

The six Fleetlines received from Southend were 33ft long low-height vehicles and were finished to a high standard. On 26 November 1977 WJN 365J heads down Kingsway into the city centre. The blind has already been reset for its return journey to the Trowbridge estate in the eastern suburbs of the city.

(Andrew Wiltshire)

The last vehicles to arrive on hire and adding a further splash of colour were four Alexander-bodied Atlanteans from Bournemouth Transport. ORU 220G passes the Mormon Church on Heol Llanishen Fach, Rhiwbina on 15 November 1977. It will turn left into Heol-y-Deri and head into the city centre.

(John Wiltshire)

New buses at last

Eventually, in November 1977 the first of the new Bristol VRTs were delivered and, by the end of December, all 26 arrived, though some did not enter service until early in 1978. They commenced a new fleet number series for Bristol double-deckers being numbered 301 to 326 and were originally intended to be registered PTX 301-26R but, due to their late arrival, became SWO 301-26S. With seating for 74, and rather dated four-piece folding entrance doors, they had curved windscreens and a fairly plain radiator grille featuring a Willowbrook badge. It is worth noting that this batch of buses introduced larger size fleet numbers, which was soon adopted for all subsequent repaints.

This view of 308 in the bus station on 10 April 1978, is a good illustration of the first batch of Series-3 Bristol VRTs. The Willowbrook bodies had a very basic standard of finish to them and were to give some structural problems after a few years service.

(John Wiltshire)

These were the first buses in the fleet to feature the Gardner 6LXB 10.45-litre engine with an output of 180bhp @1850rpm. The transmission was a 5-speed Self Changing Gears (SCG) gearbox and all were delivered as semi-automatic. Upon arrival at Cardiff they were then fitted with CAV511 automatic transmission controllers by CAV staff rendering them fully-automatic. The chassis had a wheelbase of 16ft 2in, the body an overall height of 14ft 6in, while the complete bus had an unladen weight of 9573kg. Initially 301 to 319 were based at Roath depot, while 320 to 326 were at Sloper Road depot. Later in their lives they had to be extensively rebuilt in the region of the lower deck and in particular the frames and panels needed to be strengthened between the wheel arches.

In April 1977 Guy Arabs 425 and 430 became driver training buses whilst 427 joined them in August that year. The withdrawal of the Alexander-bodied Guy Arab Vs started in October 1977 with 451, which had been out of use at Roath for some time. It was rapidly followed by others, some of which had also been off the road for a while, providing spares. Also withdrawn in 1977 were the last Swifts in service (507, 510/2/5/9, 520/2/4).

On 1 December 1977, 12 of the Leyland Atlanteans which had been on hire for a number of weeks were acquired including the four from Plymouth, which were purchased for £5000. Of the ten hired from Tyne & Wear PTE, only eight were purchased initially, as ETN 74/103C had short Certificates of Fitness. Their planned return to Tyneside and replacement by Alexander-bodied 1/10 JVK did not happen, and they joined the Cardiff fleet later in December as set out in the table. The ten Tyne and Wear Atlanteans were obtained for £19,500 and were allocated fleet numbers in the gap left by the AEC Swifts, Swift training vehicle 508 had therefore to be renumbered T522. These second-hand buses were the first Leyland Atlanteans owned by Cardiff and during 1978 were gradually repainted into orange and white fleet livery. Number 509 was the first repaint and the first to receive the new larger fleet numbers as featured on the new VRTs 301 to 326. As a result of these used acquisitions, the final batch of Bristol VRTs on order was reduced in number.

506-9	WJY 749/54/6/7	Leyland PDR1/1	Metro-Cammell	H44/31F	1962
510-2	16/9/24 JVK	"	Weymann	"	1963
513/4	30/41 JVK	"	Alexander	"	1964
515/6	ETN 89/97C	"	Weymann	"	1965
517	KBB 111D	"	Metro-Cammell	"	1966
518	ETN 74C	"	Alexander	"	1965
519	ETN 103C	"	Weymann	"	"

Note from the table the revised permanent seating layout carried out by Cardiff.

The Colourful Seventies: Diversity and Vehicle Shortages

Weymann-bodied Atlantean 516 (ETN 97C) was a former Tyne and Wear PTE example and had been new to Newcastle City Transport. It is seen at the Pier Head terminus in Bute Street in September 1978, smartly turned out in Cardiff's colours.

(John Wiltshire)

By 1977 Cardiff was running 71 regular services, 65 of which were now one-man operated. Included in this total were 9 midi-bus services and additionally there were the open-top bus tours.

Planning for the next decade

In late 1977 it was announced that trials of new generation of double-deckers would take place in order to establish what types would need to be ordered to meet Cardiff's needs for the 1980s. These would be the rear-engine Dennis Dominator, Leyland Titan B15, MCW Metrobus and front-engine Volvo Ailsa B55. It was initially decided to order one of each for the comparative trial. It was announced in early January 1978 that a single East Lancs-bodied Dennis Dominator had been ordered for evaluation, with delivery due in October 1978. The cost of the chassis was £21,927 and the body was £15,980. A Leyland Titan and a MCW Metrobus were also ordered, though delivery dates could not be guaranteed. Cardiff was still seeking to evaluate a Volvo Ailsa, and a deal was arranged with Volvo and Scottish municipal operator Tayside Regional Transport at Dundee for a long-term loan. They would supply an Ailsa for about 6 months, and in exchange, one of Cardiff's new VRTs (326) would go to Dundee. The Ailsa arrived on loan in July 1978 from Tayside and stayed until early November, being used on many routes across Cardiff. It was Tayside 247 (SSN 247S) and upon arrival in Cardiff was allocated fleet number 54. It had an Alexander 75-seat dual-door body and had been new in January 1978.

It was decided that a second coach would be required for the 1978 season, and a new Leyland Leopard was duly ordered. However as the new vehicle would not be ready in time, Leyland Leopard PSU3B/4R LVK 406L of 1973 with a distinctive Willowbrook 51-seat body was hired from Tyne and Wear PTE for 11 months in April 1978. It was given fleet number 3 after being repainted into full Cardiff white and orange coach livery. In exchange Cardiff sent Bristol VRT 600 (PKG 600M) to the PTE at Newcastle, where it received full yellow and white PTE livery.

Alexander-bodied Volvo Ailsa 54 (SSN 247S) on loan from Tayside negotiates the roundabout in Llanishen village on 27 May 1978. It is working the 78 Llanishen (Templeton Avenue) via Lake Road West service and will return to the City Centre via Caerphilly Road. Behind the bus is St. Isan church which has its origins in the 15th Century.
(John Wiltshire)

Tyne and Wear Leyland Leopard LVK 406L had a Willowbrook 002 body and was on loan to Cardiff as number 3 for the 1978 season. It is seen, along with coach number 1, adjacent to the Central bus station on 14 September 1978.
(Andrew Wiltshire)

The Colourful Seventies: Diversity and Vehicle Shortages

VEHICLE ALLOCATIONS FOR 1 MAY 1978		
	Double-deckers	Single-deckers
Roath	419-423, 444-446/50, 456-459/64/5/70/71	101-106
	498-505, 506-509, 526-550, 301-305	
Sloper Road	408-418, 424/34, 474-497	1, 3(loan), 201-21
	510-519, 551-605, 306-26	

Note that 600 was actually away on loan at this time.

In the spring of 1978 the order for a total of 88 Bristol VRTs was reduced to 86 as the 1978/79 order was reduced from 23 to 21. The reason for this was that Cardiff had ordered in their place a Leyland Leopard coach and a new Leyland Titan double-decker for evaluation. The Titan order was reported to be worth in the region of £39,000. The next batch of VRTs had Alexander bodies as originally planned and were allocated fleet numbers 327 to 360. They were now due in the summer of 1978, and two of them were convertible open-toppers at an extra cost of £1600 per bus.

The National Eisteddfod was held at Llanedeyrn, Cardiff, between 7 and 12 August 1978 and a special service numbered 51 was operated between Llandaff Fields and Pentwyn via the City Centre and Newport Road. In order to cope with a need for extra vehicles, a number of buses were hired from Taff-Ely Borough Council including AEC Reliance 11 (GTG 93L) and Leyland Nationals 18, 19 (HUH407/8N) and 22 (MBO 22P) as well as some Leyland Nationals from National Welsh. Meanwhile the new coach materialised in August numbered 2 (WTG 902T) and entered service on 20 September alongside number 1. It was a Leyland Leopard PSU3E/4R model with attractive 51-seat Plaxton Supreme III Express bodywork to Bus Grant specification. This coach had an electric gear change, and when new rather surprisingly did not have power steering. Following complaints from drivers, this was subsequently fitted. Number 2 remained in the fleet until May 1989, when it was sold to local coach operator Cyril Evans of Senghenydd, and eventually passed into preservation.

Plaxton-bodied Leyland Leopard coach number 2 spent a fair amount of time on stage carriage work and is seen in Penarth working service 307 to Cyncoed in March 1986.

(Paul Dudley)

121

The first Dennis for many years

British Leyland's domination of the double-deck bus market in the UK, coupled to labour disputes at various plants and their poor "after sales" service, prompted manufacturers like MCW and Volvo to introduce their own double-deck models. Dennis Motors from Guildford had given up bus building in 1967 to concentrate on fire engines and refuse collection vehicles, and they had been part of the Hestair Group since 1972. With the planned withdrawal by Leyland of the Fleetline model, they spotted a market for a rear-engine double-decker chassis offering a Gardner power unit and a bodybuilder of the customer's choice. The prototype chassis was rolled out in 1977 and christened the Dominator. In early September 1978 Cardiff received their Dennis Dominator for evaluation, numbered 51 (WTX 51T), and it was put to work straight away. The Dominator featured a Gardner 6LXB engine coupled to a Voith D851 3-speed fully automatic gearbox. The wheelbase was 16ft 3in and the suspension was conventional leaf springs. The body was a standard East Lancs single-door product seating 74, with the characteristic peaked roof dome at both the front and rear. There was no Dennis badge on the front radiator grille, while the livery was standard City of Cardiff orange with a white band.

Dennis Dominator 51 continued in service long after it was considered unsuitable for future orders. In about 1984 it is seen turning right out of High Street into Duke Street on its way to Pentwyn via Albany Road.

(John Jones collection)

In service Cardiff's Dominator was certainly a lively performer and initially it gave very little trouble, though this was to change in later years when it spent much time out of service. It was regarded as a poorly engineered vehicle, the steering was difficult on tight corners, there were throttle issues and the brakes were unpredictable. The Voith D851 3-speed transmission incorporated a built-in retarder which did all the braking until the road speed was down to about 10mph, at which point the foot brake took over. The transition between retarder and brake was very jerky and made for uncomfortable stopping. The Dennis Dominator, was not chosen for future orders and 51 was to remain unique in the Cardiff fleet for nearly eight years.

Alexander-bodied VRTs

The first examples of the second batch of Bristol VRTs with their intended Alexander bodywork also arrived around this time and entered service in October 1978 as 327 to 336. Delivery of the remainder of this batch (337 to 360) followed and was completed in February 1979 with the arrival of 358 and the two convertible open-toppers 359 and 360. They were allocated registrations WTG 327-60T, and like the Willowbrook-bodied batch (301 to 326), they were Bristol VRT/SL3/6LXB models. Their Alexander bodies had seating for 75 and the completed vehicle had an unladen weight of 9150kg.

A fairly new Alexander-bodied Bristol VRT 328 is seen in Newport on 28 October 1978, about to return to Cardiff on a 30 working. Note the short-lived opening vents in the upper deck front windows. Behind the bus are the ruins of the 14th Century Newport Castle, the Clarence Place Bridge crossing the River Usk, and in the distance the main South Wales railway line.

(John Jones)

These buses had two-piece glider doors and a large very distinctive black radiator moulding featuring a standard Bristol VR badge. The Alexander body (designated AL) was of aluminium frame construction and based on a design introduced in 1970. They featured well pronounced fibreglass peaked domes at front and rear, and all were fitted with opening vents in the upper front windows when delivered. These gave trouble very early on, letting in water which dripped into the destination box and cab area. They were subsequently removed in September/October 1979 and replaced by plain glazing. As a result all subsequent deliveries featured plain glass.

The intention was that 359 and 360 would only be used as open-toppers in the June to August period. Their first duties as such were to the 1979 Epsom Derby for three days in early June. As time went on, 359 and 360 were usually de-roofed during the spring, the roof sections being suspended from roof girders in Roath garage for the season. In their place a shallow windscreen and handrails would be bolted to the upper deck perimeter.

The last Ultimate ticket machines remained in use until April 1978 after which, only Almex machines were employed. Routes 57 and 58 were converted to one man operation with effect from 4 June. Withdrawals for 1978 included the last of the 30ft Alexander-bodied Guys from the batch 437 to 451, and also many of the shorter examples too. Between 1978 and 1980 six of the Alexander-bodied Guys, 446/450/464 and 470 to 472, were in use as permanent driver trainers. The first of the second-hand Atlanteans 507 (WJY754) was also taken out of service after receiving accident damage. The Leyland Leopard coach 3 (LVK406L), on loan from Tyne and Wear PTE had been plagued with engine faults during its stay with Cardiff but, despite this, it did not return north until March 1979. Cardiff's VRT 600 came home and was then repainted before carrying out a courtesy visit to French twin city Nantes. Two further Leyland Leopard coaches were ordered in spring of 1979.

In May 1979, the order for the MCW Metrobus, to have been numbered 52, was cancelled and, instead, a Metrobus and a Leyland Titan were taken on demonstration loan to evaluate against the Dennis Dominator 51 and Volvo Ailsa 54. The MCW Metrobus was TOJ 592S which took fleet number 52 and arrived in late March, and was only used on routes 14 and 61. From British Leyland came Titan FHG 592S, which gained fleet number 55, a single-door model with a Gardner engine. It arrived in early February and spent a few weeks on loan to Newport in March/April, before returning to Cardiff, staying until the end of July.

In its very distinctive livery, the single-door Leyland Titan demonstrator 55 (FHG 592S) is caught on Kingsway, Cardiff, on Sunday 4 March 1979 with a handful of passengers inbound from Pantmawr. This was a very impressive bus to travel on.
(Andrew Wiltshire)

The delivery of the new Titan intended to become 53 (WTX 53T) became even more unlikely as production at the Park Royal plant in London was in crisis due to problems with the workforce. The Titan order was never cancelled but the Park Royal works was ultimately closed down, and production moved to Workington in Cumbria in 1981. A second Volvo Ailsa, a Mark II, model was borrowed from Volvo Bus from 29 June until 10 July 1979. This was registered WTS 275T and destined for Tayside Regional Transport, and saw a little service during its stay at Cardiff.

A further batch of 21 VRTs 361 to 381 (WTG 361-81T), started to enter service during July 1979. As mentioned previously, this batch had been originally ordered as 23 buses, but was reduced when Leopard number 2 and a Titan had been ordered. They were identical in most respects to the previous batch but were delivered with plain glass upper deck front windows. One minor difference was a slightly lower positioned destination aperture, a modification requested by drivers after experience with 327 to 360.

All 97 Series-3 VRTs were delivered in standard orange and white but many carried adverts and other special liveries. In July 1980 343 was painted in the old Cardiff tramway livery of maroon and cream with a grey roof and gold lining, to celebrate 75 years of Cardiff receiving City status and 25 years as a Capital. It regained orange in March 1983 shortly before both the convertible open-toppers 359 and 360 received a similar colour scheme, but with maroon roof areas. There were at least sixteen other overall adverts over the years details of which can be found in the table at the back of this book. In addition to overall adverts, two other advertising layouts were used on many of these buses. The most numerous was the "rear end advert" which occupied the full height of the bus. The other was the "broadside advert" which occupied the area between decks all around the bus.

The last Guy Arab Vs in normal service were 420/22/23 and 465 which soldiered on to June 1979. Also taken out of service at this time were AEC Regent Vs 410 and 411, and this event marked the end of normal half-cab operation in Cardiff. This was a significant event in the history of the undertaking, the previous such event being the end of trolleybus operation in early 1970.

Number 423 and 465 were then used on an enthusiast's farewell tour on 30 June 1979. Shortly after this two dozen withdrawn Cardiff Buses were advertised to appear in an auction held by British Car Auctions (BCA). These included 13 AEC Regent Vs, 10 Guy Arab Vs and a solitary former Plymouth Leyland Atlantean that was not in a serviceable condition. One of the Regent Vs was 408, which ultimately passed into preservation.

As early as 1977 British Leyland was looking at producing a separate chassis based on the Titan B15 model, as many customers including the National Bus Company would have a requirement for a low-height vehicle, an option that was unavailable with the integrally-constructed Titan. This development took much of the Titan technology and developed it into a separate chassis form designated Leyland B45, capable of being bodied by an outside coachbuilder.

Alexander-bodied Guy Arab V 465 of 1966 was the last example of this combination in service. It is seen posed at the St. Fagan's terminus on 30 June 1979, the day of the farewell tour. Note the CCT-fabricated upper front window arrangement fitted in 1973.

(Mike Street)

Following the evaluation of various types of double-deckers, on 6 July 1979 an order was placed by Cardiff for 72 new buses as follows:

YEARS	QUANTITY	CHASSIS	BODYWORK
1981/82	18	Volvo B55-10	NCME
1982/83	9	"	"
"	9	Leyland B45	East Lancs
1983/84	9	Volvo B55-10	NCME
"	9	Leyland B45	East Lancs
1984/85	18	"	"

After nearly 40 years, it is interesting to see that Northern Counties (NCME) has once again featured as a supplier of bodywork to Cardiff.

To conclude our look at 1979, a very interesting cross-section of vehicle types was withdrawn during the year, including the very last AECs in the fleet, Regent Vs 408 to 419 and Swift trainer T522 (MBO 508F), together with the last Guy Arab Vs in normal service 420 to 423 and 462/4/5, 470 to 472. Also taken out of service were the remaining second-hand Leyland Atlanteans 506/8/9 (formerly Plymouth), and 510 to 519 (formerly Tyne and Wear PTE), together with the first of the 1967 Daimler Fleetlines to be withdrawn 475 to 480, 482 to 484 and 489. To add to this, similar Fleetline 485 was decapitated by a crane on 6 November 1979 while working service 76, and subsequently placed in store pending a decision on its future. During November a total of 15 Fleetlines were advertised as being for sale for £45,000, a figure which was later revised to £40,000.

CHAPTER SEVEN

COMPETITION, DEREGULATION AND SMALL BUSES

In early 1980 the outstanding order for Alexander-bodied Bristol VRTs was duly delivered and entered service from March onwards. This order was originally for 31 vehicles but was later reduced to 16 after the purchase of the 14 second-hand Leyland Atlanteans in late 1977. They took fleet numbers 382 to 397 and registrations CTX 382-97V.

None of the 97 Series-3 Bristol VRTs were particularly lively or comfortable buses to ride on, being very noisy in the lower saloon. They featured brown vinyl seats on both decks and a fibreglass bench at the rear on the upper deck and all featured inward-facing seats over the rear wheel arches. They were deployed on all the major City routes, a duty which they performed for many years. Having an overall height in the region of 14ft 6inches, they could not be used on some out of town services such as the Tredegar service.

In 1986, 364 was experimentally re-seated from 75 to 73, when the rear seats on top deck were replaced by an inward facing row of three. This may have been an attempt to reduce the anti-social behaviour often found on this part of a double-decker at night. These were the days before CCTV on buses.

As a result of the rebuild and modernisation of the Sloper Road garage, on 21 April 1980 the Roath garage closed as an operational depot and became solely a workshop facility. The last Guy Arab V driver training buses 464 and 472 were withdrawn from these duties in May 1980. The two Leyland Leopards ordered in spring of 1979 were delivered in late August 1980, and entered service in September, taking the coach fleet to four vehicles.

Duple-bodied Leyland Leopard 4 (GTG 634W) stands outside the National Museum of Wales, on 26 June 1981. It is similar in many ways to the first coach 1 (NWO 901R), but the Dominant II body has a re-styled front end.

(John Wiltshire)

The new Leopards were numbered 3 and 4 (GTG 633/4W) and were PSU3E/4R models. They marked a return to Duple bodywork being 53-seat Dominant II models and the pair represented an investment of £70,680. It is worth noting here that they were to have been registered CUH 3/4V.

Open-top Guy 424 was withdrawn in March 1980, being replaced by MCW-bodied Daimler Fleetline 485. Before sale, 424 lost its top-deck handrails which were used in the conversion of 485. The remaining 1967 delivery of Daimler Fleetlines (474/81/486 to 488), were withdrawn and passed to National Welsh for further service. A number of other Fleetlines were withdrawn in 1980. These were the first of the 1968 Park Royal-bodied batch (492/4/5, 500/1/4), the first dual-door Willowbrook-bodied batch (531/44) and finally the first K-registration MCW-bodied example, 552 of 1971.

It was also announced that Cardiff's Central Bus Station would be completely rebuilt from January 1981 until February 1982. The first stage commenced on 4 January 1981, which resulted in some services being diverted to new temporary termini. On 6 April 1981 City of Cardiff Transport was to experience its first competition since 1927. On that date CK Coaches (Cardiff) Ltd commenced operating on a number of services in the city using second-hand double-deckers. The vehicles were crew-operated and lower fares were charged which prompted a "fares war". To confuse matters, CK also used an orange and white livery. A route serving the heavily-populated Llanrumney area seemed a logical choice for CK to launch its inaugural service, but the lightly-used service to Cyncoed did seem an odd choice for a second route. A third route to Llanedeyrn commenced at a later date, but CK Coaches got into difficulties in early 1982 and temporarily ceased trading on 22 February. Gloucestershire independent Swanbrook of Staverton stepped in on 1 March, having acquired an interest in CK. Operations recommenced using some Swanbrook vehicles, only to cease permanently on 31 March.

The first Olympian

The proposed production of the Leyland B45 chassis was announced in 1980 and the model was christened the Olympian. It incorporated many Titan B15 features, but being a separate chassis could be bodied to the customers' requirements. The standard engine was the Gardner 6LXB with Leyland hydracyclic transmission. Initially production was undertaken at the BCV works at Brislington in Bristol. Olympian production began in 1981 and soon became very popular. As the Leyland Titan ordered by Cardiff in 1978 was never cancelled, it materialised as a B45 Olympian chassis. This was bodied by East Lancs as a 74-seater in the autumn of 1981, and was delivered to Cardiff in December. It was the first East Lancs-bodied Olympian to be built, and featured a new style of body.

This is Olympian 501 when fairly new on 23 January 1982. Note the one-off livery and the original style of front radiator grille which was later rebuilt in line with later examples.

(Andrew Wiltshire)

It was numbered 501 (LBO 501X) starting a new number series specifically for the Leyland Olympians. The livery was orange with a narrow white band and black relief around the windows. The fleet name and coat of arms was in black above the wheel arches. The bus was designated an ONLXB/IR by Leyland but in fact had a 6LXC2 engine of 195bhp when built. The gearbox was a five-speed Leyland G2 Hydracyclic and the chassis featured a drop-centre rear axle and had air suspension throughout. The body featured orange/gold/black moquette seating on the lower saloon with brown vinyl on the top deck and the bus was fitted with a tachograph. Number 501 only ever wore its unique version of the fleet livery, latterly without the black areas, but also received two broadside advertisement liveries. It is believed that the initial cost of each Olympian chassis was in the region of £25,000, but no doubt this increased with subsequent orders. In December 1980 the final order for 18 Olympians was reduced to 17 vehicles and at some stage after this it was split into a batch of nine for 1984/85, followed by one of eight for 1985/86 delivery.

In October 1979 Fleetline 557 was experimentally fitted with a farebox and tested on several routes using an exact fare system, with no change given. The fare was dropped into a hopper and visually checked by the driver before being released into the cash vault. Being emptied at the depot at the end of each day meant that drivers no longer handled cash. From 1981 this system branded Fastfare by CCT, was gradually introduced across the city using Almex ticket machines and Control Systems fareboxes. In April 1980 the goal of achieving 100% one-man operation of normal services was reached. With the conversion of the Ely service 16 to Pay-As-You-Enter, this saw the elimination of conductor operation apart from the open-top services. The conversion to Fast Fare across the network was completed by 1983. Meanwhile the active life of Leyland National 210 was brought to a premature end on 26 August 1981 when it caught fire on Leckwith Hill and was completely gutted. Ironically, this was the bus that received a major rebuild when fairly new in May 1975 following an accident. It was duly withdrawn and removed to Roath depot pending disposal, being scrapped by July 1982. Only three other buses were withdrawn during 1981, and comprised three Daimler Fleetlines 505, 540 and 542.

Return of the front-engine double-decker

During early 1982 delivery of the first batch of front-engined Volvo Ailsas B55-10 MkIII double-deckers took place, with 403 arriving on 1 March, and the remainder by 29 March. However, the first did not enter service until 30 April, though most were in use within a week. They too commenced a new fleet number series being 401 to 418 with matching registrations NDW 401-18X. Cardiff's Volvo Ailsas were fitted with a Volvo TD70H engine of 201bhp that was coupled to a Voith D851 three-speed gearbox with built-in retarder. Suspension was leaf-spring, and the vehicles had an overall height of 14ft 6in and unladen weight of 9462kg. Their Northern Counties bodies had a seating layout of H39/35F. When ordered the chassis were quoted as £21,410 each which later increased to £24,961, and the bodies came in at £20,118 each.

On 25 March 1982, newly-delivered Ailsa 404 stands alongside 401 on the forecourt at Sloper Road. Neither have entered service and interestingly 404 shows Lavernock on its destination blind, a place it would almost certainly have never visited during its long service with Cardiff.

(Andrew Wiltshire)

Competition, Deregulation and Small Buses

The new Volvo Ailsas settled down to service on most major double-deck routes within the city. They were very different machines from anything purchased by Cardiff before, and quite unlike the Bristol VRTs and Olympian (501) of recent years. The internal layout of the bus was noticeably different and they were quite noisy in the lower saloon. The lack of air suspension was very apparent, but they were quite lively buses given their small engine. The cabs were small, noisy and access was via a hinged offside door. In the summer months the driver's compartment was rather hot, partially overcome at an early stage by the fitting of electric fans mounted on top of the engine cover. The passenger entrance door was a one-piece forward-folding arrangement. This allowed a more open area forward of the front nearside wheel-arch and helped reduce the platform congestion caused by the presence of the engine adjacent to the front entrance.

Cardiff was now starting to experience excessive brake-lining wear with the Series-3 Bristol VRTs, and a solution was sought. A four-speed gearbox manufactured by Maxwell was ordered, which featured transmission braking, and in June 1982 it was fitted to VRT 390. A further six were later ordered, three being fitted to 391/3/5 in 1983/4. In 1985 16 examples were similarly fitted, while the years 1986/87 saw a further 19 equipped as well. In service the gearbox was not particularly reliable, and it is thought that some of the buses converted actually reverted to their original gearboxes at some stage.

In March 1982 open-top Guy 434 (ABO 434B) and Daimler Fleetline 485 (JKG 485F) were renumbered to 34 and 85 respectively. During the last quarter of 1982 Leyland Nationals 212 and 218 spent periods on hire to Taff-Ely Borough Council who were experiencing a vehicle shortage. Also, the final 22 Gardner-powered Daimler Fleetlines (except open-top 485) were taken out of service. These were 491, 496 to 499, 503 (Park Royal-bodied), 527 to 530, 532 to 536, 538/41/45, 547 to 550 (Willowbrook-bodied) along with four of the Leyland-powered MCW-bodied examples of 1971/72.

Willowbrook-bodied Fleetline 548 waits at the terminus at the junction of Bwlch Road and Fairways Crescent, Fairwater on a damp 26 May 1981. The bus will then set off on the cross-city route 56 to Pentwyn. 548, like many of this batch, has with time, received a plain lower front panel in place of the ornate Willowbrook grp moulding.

(John Jones)

The year 1983 saw delivery of a further nine Volvo Ailsas plus the first examples of the order for 36 Leyland Olympians. The second batch of Ailsas was originally quoted as being due in October 1982 but in reality started to appear from 22 December, when 419 and 422 were delivered. All nine were identical in every respect to the first batch and were numbered 419 to 427 (RKG 419-27Y).

Now ten years old, Ailsa 425 picks up at the much photographed Victoria Park bus layby while working a service 18 from Ely on 13 March 1993. Prior to 1970, this was the location for many trolleybus photographs. The substantial bus shelter has failed to survive though, and has been replaced with a much smaller affair.
(John Jones)

The first nine of the main order for Olympians (502 to 510) was originally due for delivery in August 1982, but this was later put back to early 1983. Prior to this a demonstrator was taken on loan from Leyland in the form of Roe-bodied UWW 11X. It was used on the Tredegar service on 16/17 February, and was a bus eventually destined for service with West Yorkshire PTE. The first Olympians to arrive were 502/4/7/10 which were delivered in an experimental livery which included black window surrounds. 503 differed slightly from the other eight as it had moquette covered seats on the top deck and it was the intention to make this bus available for private hire work. The others had brown vinyl seats on the top deck with hard "vandal proof" seats to the rear. In addition 502 to 505 were fitted with tachographs. Registrations would be RBO 502-10Y and the seating capacity was the same as 501 at 74.

East Lancs-bodied Olympian 503 is still quite new when seen at University Hall, Cyncoed, on 9 April 1983. It was providing transport for the 1983 PSV Circle AGM held in Cardiff, and would soon depart for a visit to the premises of municipal operator Newport Transport.
(Andrew Wiltshire)

Competition, Deregulation and Small Buses

USED BRISTOLS

In August 1983, four interesting second-hand buses were acquired from London Country Bus Services, who had actually withdrawn them in 1981. They were Bristol LHS6L models new in 1974/75 and like 104 and 105 they too had Leyland 401 engines and 5-speed manual gearboxes. Their 7ft 6in ECW bodies were however longer and accommodated 35 bus-type seats. They were given fleet numbers 107 to 110 (GPD 299,306/15/7N) and following several modifications 107 and 109 were the first into service with Cardiff in December. 108 and 110 finally entered service in May 1984 and bolstered the existing midi-bus fleet and allow the withdrawal of two of the Seddons for use as spares donors. Number 109 was fitted with a towing bracket in September 1984.

109 stands in Lawrenny Avenue on 3 July 1984. At one time this Monday to Fridays only service had two morning runs, but by May 1986 was reduced to just one. The former London Country LHSs were instantly recognisable by their off-white window rubbers and two-piece destination aperture.

(Paul Dudley)

ECW-bodied Bristol VRT number 588 went on loan to National Welsh at their Barry depot from 31 May until 13 June 1983. This was for evaluation with a view to a possible sale of some of these buses to National Welsh, but nothing came of this trial. The last Guy Arab in the fleet, open-top 34 (ABO 434B), carried on in service until the end of 1982, and was officially withdrawn in January 1983. Daimler Fleetline open-topper 85 along with VRTs 359 and 360 were repainted into a maroon and cream tramways livery in February 1983 in preparation for the forthcoming season. Other withdrawals for 1983 comprised further K-reg Fleetlines and the first of the Series-2 Bristol VRTs, 596 (PKG 596M), which had sustained accident damage.

With its lid off, VRT 359 in Cardiff Corporation Tramways livery is seen at the Welsh Hawking Centre on Five Mile Lane near Barry on 19 June 1983.

(Andrew Wiltshire)

In late 1983 a number of changes had been made to the final Leyland Olympian order which would have become fleet numbers 520 to 536. Nine of these were now due in October 1984 as low-height buses fitted with tachographs, and starting a new fleet number series. The final eight were due by October 1985 as normal-height buses (520 to 527), and without tachographs. The outstanding order for nine Ailsas was delivered between 30 December 1983 and 15 February 1984. They were allocated fleet numbers 428 to 436 with registrations A428-36 VNY. 428/32/3 entered service on 9 January with 436 being last one on 16 March.

The afternoon sun catches 433 as it is seen heading along Pwllmelin Road, Llandaff towards the Pentrebane estate on 20 June 1987. Its broadside advertisement is to the order of local oil distributor Curran Oils.
(John Wiltshire)

The second batch of Olympians (511 to 519) was due from East Lancs in late 1983 and 513 duly arrived on 23 December while the last one to arrive was 517 on 3 February 1984. They were registered A511-9 VKG, and all had entered service by 4 February and, unlike 501 to 510, these were delivered without Leyland badges. All 19 Olympians could now be found on service across the city, and were also regular performers on the service 30 to Newport. The experimental livery on 502/4/7/10 was deemed not to be a success and all four received standard fleet livery between May and August 1984.

Olympian 518 is seen on Newport Road, crossing the junction with Fitzalan Place on 17 July 1993, while working the 47 from Llanrumney into the centre.
(John Jones)

Competition, Deregulation and Small Buses

In service a number of Ailsas were to receive major accident damage and in April 1987 434 was damaged by fire in an arson attack and much of the upper deck was destroyed. It is thought that it was sent back to Wigan to be rebuilt by Northern Counties, returning to service in October. All 36 Ailsas were delivered in standard orange and white fleet livery and remained so for some time to come. This was in contrast to the Bristol VRTs and the Olympians (501 to 519) which were popular candidates for special liveries. It was not until May 1986 that 433 gained a dark blue broadside advert to the order of Curran Oils. Overall adverts were not applied to the Ailsas for a good many years, until August 1996 in fact, when 434 received a yellow and black livery for Darlows Estate Agents.

A very smart and nearly new East Lancs-bodied Volvo Citybus was taken on loan from Derby City Transport in 1984 for three months. It was A129 DTO and had seating for 76. The Citybus was an underfloor-engine double-decker and was regarded by Volvo as the successor to the front-engine Ailsa. In exchange Cardiff sent Bristol LHS 104 to Derby on loan from May until August 1984.

As a result of the new vehicles detailed above, a further seven MCW-bodied Fleetlines and six series-2 VRTs were withdrawn during the year. Leyland Nationals 201 and 202 were taken out of service in January 1984 and cannibalised for spares at Roath depot. They were less than ten years old. Number 214 also sustained accident damage in October 1983 and was officially withdrawn in June 1984, being scrapped by Cardiff the following month. Also officially withdrawn in 1984 were two of the Seddon midi-buses 101 and 102, which were cannibalised to keep similar 103 and 106 in service. The latter part of the year saw the start of a programme to modify Leyland Nationals 212/3, 215 to 221 to single-door layout. 218 was dealt with in November by initially closing off the centre door-way. This was later rebuilt in a more permanent fashion, along with the others, using parts from withdrawn 201/2/14. All were re-seated to 44 as single-door buses between December 1984 and July 1985.

DOUBLE-DECK COACHES

The nine low-height Leyland Olympians mentioned previously arrived between December 1984 and March 1985. They featured a new livery with a lot more white, and entered service as 551 to 559 (B551-9 ATX). They had standard East Lancs bus body shells (as per 501 to 519), but to an overall height of 14ft 1in. High-backed dual-purpose seats were fitted which were finished in brown and orange moquette, in effect making them double-deck coaches. The upper deck allowed seating for 43, but the lower saloon catered for just 27. The original plan was to use them on services 28, 29, 30, 32 and 36 as well as private hire, and initially this batch tended not to stray from the duties for which they were originally intended. They were soon being promoted as being available for advertised tours to Penscynor Wildlife Park and Dan yr Ogof Showcaves.

555 picks up in Cardiff Road, Caerphilly, near the Castle, while bound for Tredegar on 13 July 1990. It carries the revised livery applied to the vehicles that returned from hire to Southend Transport. Note the chrome wheel trim.

(John Jones)

By 1985 Cardiff was advertising open-top tours to destinations such as Creigiau Pottery, Tredegar House and Dyffryn Gardens while the coach tours included the Royal Mint at Llantrisant, Big Pit at Blaenavon and the Brecon Beacons. Convertible open-top Bristol VRT 360 was loaned to Merthyr Tydfil Transport for testing on 24 June 1985. Following this, sister bus 359, was used on a Merthyr Borough Tour for five days from 1 to 5 July.

The coach fleet was set to benefit from a smart new pair of Leyland coaches in 1985, obtained from dealer Kirby Bus and Coach. These were the first underfloor-engine Tigers for Cardiff, and featured Duple Caribbean II bodies, and introduced a new coach livery of white with brown and orange bands. They were numbered 5 and 6 (B905/6 DHB) and were Leyland TRCTL11/3R models with an overall length of 11.97m. The coaches arrived in May and June respectively, sporting Leyland TL11 engines and ZF 6-speed manual gearboxes. They were completed as 53-seaters, but were both converted to 51 seaters (with a toilet) after delivery.

Just two buses were taken out of service in 1985, Daimler Fleetlines 576 (last of the type) and Bristol VRT 592. In a surprise move series-2 VRTs 594 and 598 were treated to full repaints late in 1985.

An arms-length company

The 1980s were a period of great change for the Cardiff undertaking. The Transport Act was passed in 1985 and deregulation was on its way. The removal of government legislation and laws in a particular market, often known as removing barriers to competition, meant an operational transfer from public bodies - regulated - to private companies - deregulated.

Full deregulation of the British bus industry outside of London on 26 October 1986, saw the Cardiff fleet become an arms-length company in which Cardiff Council retained ownership. Arms-length effectively meant that both the Council and the Cardiff Fleet were now independent and on an equal footing. Such transactions is known as an "arm's-length transaction". The fleet would no longer receive Council subsidies and would be run on a commercial basis.

There followed the mass introduction of minibuses on many services as Cardiff followed the trend across the entire bus industry at the time. The first signs that the double-decker was falling out of favour came in at the end of the decade when the big bus returned, but in the form of single-deckers. New residential areas had been established in the 1970s including Pentwyn and Danescourt and during the 1980s St. Mellons, and Thornhill.

By the end of the decade Cardiff Bay joined them, which meant more new services. In April 1986, in anticipation of deregulation, two buses (Ailsa 427 and Olympian 513) received the new fleet name "Cardiff Bus" on the nearside, with "Bysiau Caerdydd" on the offside, and there was no coat of arms. In May 1986, both convertible open-toppers 359 and 360 lost their special tramways livery.

The Wood Street offices, occupied since 1973, were vacated in July 1986, as the transport department moved to a new purpose-built office at the Sloper Road garage at Leckwith. The last item of rationalisation was the closure of the Roath garage workshops in September 1986, with all engineering services now concentrated at Sloper Road depot. The historic former tram shed at Roath was subsequently demolished during June and July 1987.

Prior to deregulation, the balance of the order for Leyland Olympians was delivered. Yet another change of plan saw this final batch of Olympians also emerge as additional low-height buses. As a result they took fleet numbers 560 to 567 with registrations C560-7 GWO. 567 arrived in January 1986 delivered in all over white as the basis for an overall advert livery. The other seven arrived by the end of March and carried the same livery as the first batch. They entered service alongside 551 to 559, and from 17 March 1986, the low-height Olympians also started to appear on the new services 307/308 (Cyncoed to Penarth). The lower saloon of these buses was capable of being fitted with tables, which in theory would result in a lower seating capacity. It is thought that this adaptation was never implemented though.

Competition, Deregulation and Small Buses

Too many buses

By the summer of 1986 it was apparent that around six of the low-height Olympians were actually surplus to operational requirements. Rather than sell these buses which were just over a year old, they were sent on loan to Southend Transport. Here they were deployed on the limited-stop express service X1, running from Southend into London primarily for the benefit of commuters. The buses chosen to travel to Essex were 553 to 555 and 557 to 559, with the first example leaving in September. At Southend they were painted in a smart yellow and blue livery and received fleet numbers 363 to 365 and 367 to 369. They also rather surprisingly acquired extra embellishments such as chrome wheel trims. By coincidence 363 to 365 were the fleet numbers of three of the Southend Fleetlines that were loaned to Cardiff nine years earlier. The Olympians remained in East Anglia for between 12 and 18 months, returning to Cardiff between March and May 1988. Before re-entering service in Cardiff, all six were repainted into a revised low-height double-decker livery using slightly more orange, and all retained their chrome wheel trims for a while at least.

Small buses are the way forward

The minibus revolution had started in certain parts of the United Kingdom during 1985. It was set to spread rapidly across the nation with large fleets of van-derived vehicles being pressed into service in many fleets, and often replacing larger buses. The overall aim was to reduce costs in the industry by using small cheap vehicles and introducing lower rates of pay and to extend bus services along roads unsuitable for big buses. On the positive side frequencies were sometimes increased on busy routes making the service more attractive to the public. The passenger experience in these small and uncomfortable vehicles often left a lot to be desired though. Just prior to deregulation Cardiff placed in service a pair of Mercedes minibuses based on the L608D van with minibus conversion carried out by PMT. They were numbered 111 and 112 (D111/2 LTG) and were 20-seaters.

With effect from 26 October 1986 the title of the fleet changed to City of Cardiff Transport Services Ltd, and the slogan "Pick an orange" was adopted. Also, a new company Cardiff Minibus Ltd came into being, and registered by this new operating company. Both Mercedes carried Cardiff Minibus / Minibysiau Caerdydd fleet names and Pick an Orange branding, while Seddon midi-bus 103 also gained Cardiff Minibus / Minibysiau Caerdydd fleet names at this time.

On 26 June 1987 Mercedes L608D 112 is seen loading in Penarth town centre and about to undertake a run on local service P1 to St. Cyres. The Cardiff Minibus fleet name in both English and Welsh is prominent plus the Pick an Orange slogan.

(Andrew Wiltshire)

The following vehicles passed to Cardiff City Transport Services Ltd on 26 October 1986

DOUBLE-DECKERS				
Fleet numbers	Chassis type	Body	Year	Comments
85	Daimler Fleetline	MCW (open –top)	1967	withdrawn
591/4/5, 597-9	Bristol VRT	ECW	1973/74	all six were withdrawn
601-605	"	"	"	
301-326	"	Willowbrook	1977	
327-358	"	Alexander	1978/79	
359, 360	"	"	1979	Conv. open-top
361-381	"	"	"	
382-397	"	"	1980	
401-418	Volvo Ailsa	NCME	1982	
419-427	"	"	1983	
428-436	"	"	1984	
501	Leyland Olympian	East Lancs	1981	
502-510	"	"	1983	
511-519	"	"	1984	
551-559	"	"	1985	Coach seating
560-567	"	"	1986	"
SINGLE-DECKERS				
203-209,211	Leyland National	dual-door	1974	206-9/11 were withdrawn
212/3, 215-221	"	single-door	1975	
MIDIBUSES				
103, 106	Seddon Pennine	Pennine	1973	106 acquired 1977
104, 105	Bristol LHS	ECW	1976	
107-110	"	"	1974/5	Acquired 1983
111, 112	Mercedes L608D	PMT	1986	
COACHES				
1	Leyland Leopard	Duple	1976	
2	"	Plaxton	1978	
3, 4	"	Duple	1980	
5, 6	Leyland Tiger	"	1985	

During 1986 the very last Daimler Fleetlines in the Cardiff fleet were withdrawn and sold. These were open-topper 85 (JKG 485F) and training vehicles 068/070 (WUH 568/70K). A further six of the ECW-bodied VRTs were taken off fleet strength along with five Leyland Nationals from the first batch of ten with 2-speed ZF gearboxes. A notable withdrawal and sale was that of Dennis Dominator 51 (WTX 51T), which passed to a dealer in Weymouth, and spent its final years working for an independent operator in Somerset.

Enter the Metrorider

A number of manufacturers were now developing purpose-built minibuses and midi-buses which were intended to be more attractive to larger operators than van conversions. MCW developed its Metrorider midi-bus which was launched in 1986. It was of integral construction and available with an overall length of either 7 or 8.4m. A choice of either Cummins or Perkins engines coupled to an Allison fully-automatic transmission or a ZF manual gearbox. It had a stylish body and large two-piece windscreen, while the interior was well laid out compared to the many van-derived vehicles on the market. Cardiff Bus took delivery of 22 in 1987, 7m models with the Cummins B-Series 5.9-litre engine of 115bhp, driving through an Allison fully-automatic gearbox. These vehicles were numbered in the midi-bus series, but started from 120. The first ten arrived as 120 to 129 (E120-9 RDW) and were followed by 130 to 141 (E130-41 SNY). All were MF150 models and 23-seaters, and 127 to 132 benefitted from high back dual-purpose seats.

MCW Metrorider 128 of 1987 is seen on Nantgarw Road, Caerphilly, on 17 March 1990. The destination blind tells us that it is returning to Cardiff via the Heath Hospital site on service 71, which originated in Penyrheol.

(John Jones)

Numbers 120 to 129 were launched into service during September 1987 and wore a new livery of white with a brown skirt separated by a deep orange band. The lower edge of the white carried narrow gold and orange bands and the branding Cardiff Clipper Bus. 130 to 141 entered service from 17 January 1988.

The two 1980 Leyland Leopard coaches 3 and 4 were overhauled in April and May 1987 respectively and received Leyland TL11 engines in place of their Leyland 0680 units. They were both out-shopped in the new coach livery as carried by Tigers 5 and 6. Number 3 was eventually withdrawn and sold in 1989 while 4 lingered on until May 1994.

The following small buses were taken on loan in 1987.

FLEET NO:	REGISTRATION	CHASSIS	BODY	SEATING	YEAR
From Yorkshire Rider (1905/22) May to June 1987					
153, 154	D505/22 NDA	Freight Rover Sherpa	Carlyle	B19F	1986
From Nottingham CT (125/6) June 1987 until July 1987 (153) and November 1987 (154)					
153, 154	D125/6 URC	Dodge S56	Reebur	B25F	1987
From National Welsh (MD397) July 1987 until October 1987					
153	KWO 568X	Bristol LHS6L	ECW	DP27F	1981
From South Yorkshire Transport Ltd June until October 1987 for driver training					
	C62/3 LHL	Ford Transit	Carlyle	DP20F	1986
From MCW Ltd, Birmingham September until October 1987 and used in service					
	D483 NOX	MCW Metrorider	MCW	DP23F	1986
From Stevensons of Uttoxeter Ltd (179/80) October until December 1987 for driver training					
179	D179 CRE	Freight Rover Sherpa	PMT	B20F	1987
180	D180 CRE	"	"	C20F	"

No buses were actually withdrawn from service in 1987, although a number of ECW-bodied Bristol VRTs that had been withdrawn in 1986, and which had passed to the arms-length company at deregulation, were sold for scrap in this year.

Harsh winter sunshine makes this a great study of an MCW Metrorider. Number 150, one of the six diverted from SUT Ltd, lays over outside the Welsh Industrial and Maritime Museum in Bute Street on 28 December 1988.

(John Wiltshire)

The Return of the Big Bus

An early casualty was 607 which went out of control after pulling away from its stand in Cardiff's Central Bus Station on 6 September 1990 and embedding itself in a shop front in the adjacent Marland House. It had been in service less than a month and received severe front end damage. It was duly sent back to Alexander at Falkirk, and did not return to service in Cardiff until 2 November. During 1990, further inroads were made into the Willowbrook-bodied VRTs in 1990 with ten examples being taken out of service.

From February 1991 the coat of arms was replaced by the City's new red dragon emblem which was duly applied to most buses. In June 1991 two former Ministry of Defence (MoD) Bedford NJM2BZ0s were acquired for the training fleet. They had Marshall 37-seat bodies and dated from July 1978, being specifically required for their manual gearbox configuration. Allocated fleet numbers 046 and 047 (Q346/7NTM) they had previously been with the Royal Air Force and registered 47AO68 and 47AO73 respectively. In July four more Optare Metroriders 172 to 175 (H172-5 RBO) joined the fleet, and were more or less identical to the previous batch 168 to 171.

THE LAST LEYLANDS

The Leyland Lynx was revised in late 1990 to appear as the Lynx II. The Lynx II was longer as it had a protruding grille and front dash panel, and featured full DiPTAC specification fittings throughout the passenger area. A new gearbox was specified for this model and the front suspension had also been revised. A demonstrator from VL Bus at Warwick carrying registration number H48 NDU was inspected before Cardiff placed an order for a dozen Lynx II models for delivery late 1991 in a deal worth £900,000. The batch was numbered 260 to 271 (J260-71 UDW), and 260 was a former Volvo demonstration vehicle H49 NDU. They all had Cummins engines, a ZF 4-speed gearbox and were 49-seaters with a stepped saloon floor. Number 260 initially entered service as J260 UDW, but being new in June 1991, the DVLA made sure that it reverted to its original plate of H49 NDU fairly promptly. All twelve had arrived by the end of October 1991, and entered service the following month. As the Bristol VRTs were gradually phased out, the Lynx began to appear on many busy services across the city.

An announcement by Volvo Bus in December 1991 made it clear that the Lynx model would be discontinued, and that production at the Workington plant would cease in 1992. These were therefore the last Lynx and the last Leylands for Cardiff Bus.

The former demonstration Leyland Lynx II number 260, picks up in Whitchurch village on 4 November 1991 having not long entered service. Note the route number characters are smaller than those normally specified by Cardiff Bus.
(Andrew Wiltshire)

Cardiff's Municipal Buses

During 1991 Cardiff Bus was awarded the contract for a special service from Cardiff city centre to the forthcoming National Garden Festival at Ebbw Vale. For this service to be numbered 900, three new Scania N113DRB double-deckers were ordered. These were also bodied by Alexander, but this time, to Cardiff's own specification.

Withdrawn this year were the last three Willowbrook-bodied VRTs, 310 and 318, with the last being 319 in November. 319 then joined the service bus fleet in December as an office and rest room, and was usually based in the Central Bus Station. Also withdrawn in 1991 were the two Sherpa minibuses 066/067, which were sold for use as internal transport at the forthcoming National Garden Festival at Ebbw Vale.

Pastures new

The year 1992 saw Cardiff Bus expand its operations in Barry and the Vale of Glamorgan to compete with National Welsh. A new network of services commenced on 24 February, whilst an enquiry and sales office opened at Kings Square, Barry, in December 1992. As the network grew rapidly in size the demand for buses was high, and so additional vehicles had to be obtained. In February a batch of ten Dodge S56 minibuses with Reebur 23-seat bodies, dating from 1986, were acquired from Plymouth City Transport in February. Cardiff Bus soon repainted them into a new white livery with orange roof and brown skirt with fleet names in orange. Fleet numbers allocated were 101 to 110, while their registrations were D138/58, 160/1/2/4/5, 177/8 and 181 LTA, and had been Plymouth 38 etc.

Former Plymouth Dodge 105 (D162 LTA) approaches Kingsway from Greyfriars Road on service 5 from Queen Street (Capitol) on 31 July 1992. It is heading to Grangetown (Paget Street) via Wood Street and Clare Road. The service 5 consisted of five runs in the evening rush hour Mondays to Friday only.

(Andrew Wiltshire)

These Dodges were put to work over the entire network and could be seen in Barry or the Caerphilly areas. In addition to the used vehicles from Plymouth, a dozen similar Dodge S56/ Reebur minibuses were obtained on loan from West Midlands Travel in February 1992 and entered service alongside 101 to 110. They had just 19 seats and were new in October 1986. They remained in their owners colours which were either cream and blue or silver and blue, and were given Cardiff fleet numbers 701 to 712. They were returned to West Midlands during July and August 1992.

The Return of the Big Bus

To help with the demand for extra vehicles a number of small buses were taken on loan.

FLEET NO	REGISTRATION	CHASSIS	BODY	SEATING	YEAR
From GM Buses Ltd and inspected in January/February 1992					
	D536 MJA	Fiat 49.10	Robin Hood	B21F	1987
From West Midlands Travel Ltd, Birmingham mostly from February until August 1992					
701 to 704	D565-8 NDA	Dodge S56	Reebur	B19F	1986
705 to 708	D571-3/5 NDA	"	"	"	"
709 to 712	D576/9/82/1 NDA	"	"	"	"

Scania saloons

Scania sold very few saloons in the UK after production of the MCW Metro-Scania ceased in 1974, but this changed with the introduction of the Scania N113 model. In 1991 Plaxton introduced the Verde body which was designed specifically to be mounted on rear-engine single-deck chassis. It was based on an alloy frame using some of the technology used in the Plaxton Pointer body. It was a boxy-style body with a distinctive "barrel-curved" front end design, deep roofline and glass-fibre skirt. It soon appeared on the Scania N113CRB and Cardiff inspected a demonstrator. They subsequently purchased 14 similar buses in February 1992 from Scania dealer Stuart Johnson. Fleet numbers allocated were 272 to 279 and 281 to 286 (J272-9/81-6 UWO), which allowed for the fact that a matching registration for 280 would not be available. All were finished in Leyland Lynx-style white with a brown roof and orange skirt, and Cardiff Bus fleet names between the wheel arches, as well as on the front of the vehicle below the windscreen. The 51-seat bodies to full DiPTAC specification featured deep windows with rubber-mounted gaskets, and there was a radiator mounted ahead of the rear axle on both offside and nearside. They were powered by a 6-cylinder Scania DSC11 unit driving through a Voith D863 fully-automatic gearbox. They had an overall length of 11.4m and an unladen weight of 9607kg.

Number 275 follows the road into Duke Street from Kingsway, Cardiff, late in the afternoon on 26 August 1994. In the background at the entrance to Queen Street is the statue of Aneurin Bevan, who as Health Minister was instrumental in establishing the National Health Service.

(John Jones)

The three new double-deckers arrived in May 1992 as 608 to 610 (J608-10 VDW). Based on the Scania N113DRB chassis their Alexander bodies they had seating for 78 passengers. A smaller destination box and revised front dash panel were obvious changes from the earlier batch 601 to 607, as was the application of a narrower white waistband. The trio were put to work on the service linking 900 Cardiff with the National Garden Festival at Ebbw Vale, before taking up normal duties in the main fleet from early October 1992. In June 1992 the two convertible open toppers 359/60 were given a revised livery incorporating large areas of white, very similar to the colours carried by open-toppers 424 and 434.

Scania 608 is seen in Park Place on 27 April 1996 having just returned from Newport on a 30 service.
(John Jones)

The last MR01 model Optare Metroriders with the narrow body joined the Cardiff Bus fleet as 176 to 187 in the summer of 1992. 176 to 182 entered service in July 1992 with registrations J176-82 WAX while 183 to 187 followed in August with the new year prefix as K183-7 YDW.

Optare Metrorider 177 is seen on the Hayes, Cardiff, on 18 July 1992, an area which was fully pedestrianised by 2009. In the distance looms St. Davids Hall. Number 177 is heading for Barry with the hourly P8 and operating via Penarth Centre, Sully and Cadoxton.
(John Jones)

The Return of the Big Bus

The remnants of former National Bus Company subsidiary National Welsh, now based only at Barry depot, ceased operating on 7 August 1992, and Cardiff Bus assumed responsibility for most services in the Barry area. Some thought was given to opening an outstation for vehicles here, but this idea was not pursued. Just three buses were withdrawn in 1992, when Alexander-bodied Bristol VRTs 357/8 and 378, the first examples with this body to go, retired in November.

A SERIOUS COMPETITOR

On 24 September 1993 Cardiff Bus experienced the start of some serious competition from a new operator, Cardiff Bluebird. This operation was owned by Tellings Golden Miller who had acquired Cardiff-based independent Globeheath Ltd in January 1991. Operating from a base in Penarth Road, Cardiff, they continued to expand their services throughout the City, using a mixture of elderly double-deckers, mostly from the 1970s, and smaller more modern vehicles such as Dodges and Metroriders. They were operating to Ely and St. Mellons by the end of the year, and went on to introduce services to Llanrumney, Penylan, Pentwyn, Pentrebane and Penarth - some of which were linked as cross-town services.

There were no new vehicles for Cardiff Bus in 1993, but Alexander-bodied VRTs 363 and 372, together with five of the former Plymouth Dodge minibuses (101, 106 to 108, 110) were withdrawn. The remaining Dodges had been taken out of service by January 1994. Optare revised the Metrorider model and in 1994 Cardiff took the first of many to this new style designated MR15, and fitted with Telma retarders. The body, while still 8.4m long, was of a much more angular appearance, and it was wider too, at 2.38m. Deliveries of new 31-seat Optare Metrorider MR15s commenced with 188 to 197 (L188-97 DDW) which entered service in the January. These were then followed with a new fleet number series starting from 101. 101 to 106 (L101-6 GBO) entered service during July 1994, followed by 107 to 109 (M107-9 JHB) in October and 110, 112 to 116 (M110/2-6 KBO) during November. There was no 111 as a matching registration could not be issued. It should be noted that 101 to 103 and 107 to 109 were DP31F with high-backed seats and 101 onwards carried the revised "Clipper at your service" slogan. The new style of Metrorider continued to utilise the Cummins B-series engine coupled to an Allison automatic gearbox. In addition to the 31 seats, there was a standing capacity of 13 and most had an unladen weight in the region of 5320kg, although those with DP-type seating were around the 5520kg mark. The date of 24 February 1994 marked the start of increased activity in the Caerphilly area with the introduction of town services by Cardiff Bus. With effect from 14 August, Cardiff Bus and Rhondda Buses (Caerphilly Busways) introduced return ticket inter-availability on some of the Caerphilly area routes, while timetables became coordinated.

Optare 110 is now looking a little scruffy as it picks up passengers in Whitchurch on 26 April 2002. It is working the Whitchurch Circle service 38 which was a Monday to Saturday off-peak circular service.

(Andrew Wiltshire)

A further delivery of Scania N113CRB saloons was planned for 1994 and numbered just seven buses. Their engines were to Euro1 emission specification. The original intention was for these to receive similar Plaxton Verde bodies to the 1992 batch, but in the event, bodywork was supplied by Alexander to their new Strider design with seating for 50. When they arrived they took fleet numbers 287 to 293 (L287-93 ETG) and were delivered between 11 and 21 April 1994, entering service in May. The Alexander Strider was a much plainer body with a deep curved windscreen, shallow roofline and no separate skirt. Unlike the previous batch, the nearside radiator was located behind the rear axle.

Alexander Strider-bodied Scania 291 departs from Blackwood bus station and heads for Cardiff on 14 September 1999.
(John Jones)

Duties for all 21 Scania N113 saloons were varied. Early on, both batches were regular performers on the Heath Hospital services 8 and 9, and also took turns on the Newport service (30) as well as Llanishen and Rhiwbina routes. Another area where they were regularly seen was in the Vale of Glamorgan on working such as the 353 to Barry via Wenvoe, X91 from Cardiff to Llantwit Major, and later the X96 to Kings Square, Barry. The Plaxton Verde examples spent their later Cardiff Bus days working the 57 and 58 to Pentwyn/Pontprennau, and also the Llanrumney services 49 and 50.

Finally a used Scania coach dating from 1988 was purchased in May 1994 to enable the withdrawal of the last Leyland Leopard coach number 4. It was new to Bland, Stamford as E701 NNH, and was obtained from Midland Fox (Foxhound) of Leicester (252) which had reregistered it 972 SYD. It was a K113CRB model with Jonckheere 51-seat bodywork which included a toilet. It became number 2 in the Cardiff Bus fleet. In conjunction with Crosville Wales, Cardiff Bluebird introduced an express service between Cardiff and Aberystwyth. Possibly in response to this, and on 19 June 1994, Cardiff Bus launched a similar daily express coach service 801 "The Cambrian Express". This departed from Cardiff at 09.00 and arrived at Aberystwyth at 13.05 running via Swansea, Carmarthen, Lampeter and Aberaeron. It then returned from Aberystwyth at 14.00, and an open-ended return ticket could be obtained for £10. This ambitious venture occupied one of Cardiff Bus's coaches, but appears to have ceased running by November 1994.

Leyland Tiger number 6 pauses at Aberaeron in 1994 while working the short-lived Cambrian Express.
(David Donati)

Withdrawals from service in 1994 were a further ten VRTs which included the first of the V-registration batch to go (383/5/7, 390 and 397). Also the last Leyland Leopard coach number 4 and both the Mercedes L608D minibuses (111 and 112) were withdrawn. However perhaps the most surprising vehicles to come out of service were of the first MCW Metroriders (120 to 128, 130, 133 to 137) of 1987. Of these, 120 to 128 passed to GM Buses North for service in the Greater Manchester area. In 1995 delivery of Optare Metroriders continued with 117 to 124 in January and 125 to 133 in February, all carrying matching registrations in the M117-33 KBO series.

Bristol VRT 371 heads along Pencisely Road, Cardiff, crossing the junction with Ely Road bound for Pentrebane on 14 April 1994. The bus has come from the Trowbridge estate via the city centre on the 61. These buses were a familiar sight on the streets of Cardiff for many years.

(John Jones)

To make way for new deliveries, MCW Metroriders 129, 131/2 were renumbered 029, 031/2 in February 1995, while the following month 139, 141/2/4, 146 to 149 were re-numbered 039, 041/2/4. 046 to 049.

FLEET SUMMARY MARCH 1995			
Double-deckers	Single-deckers	Midi-buses	Coaches
135	62	91	4

On 15 February 1995 Cardiff Bus acquired the premises, services, contracts and goodwill of Golden Coaches, of Llandow, but no vehicles were included in the deal. Branded as Vale Busline Limited in the May, Cardiff Bus then created a nine vehicle outstation at Llandow. It initially allocated three short and three long-wheelbase MCW Metroriders along with three Leyland Lynx, the identities of which regularly changed to coincide with maintenance schedules. After less than a year Llandow operation was sold off passing to Brewers on 1 October 1995, and once again, no vehicles were involved.

The Dennis Dart arrives in town

Cardiff also received the first of many Dennis Darts in 1995. Seven were purchased which were the only step-entrance versions of this popular bus to be acquired. The Dart was a rear-engine midibus launched in 1989, and rapidly became very popular with operators large and small across the whole of the United Kingdom. It was originally available in two lengths, 8.5m and 9.8m to a common width of 2.3m. The engine deployed was the Cummins 6BT driving through an Allison AT545 automatic gearbox. It was bodied by many coachbuilders and some very distinctive body styles appeared. The most popular was probably the Pointer produced initially by Plaxton-owned Reebur and then at Scarborough by Plaxton itself. Cardiff Bus's Darts were 9.8m SDL models with air-suspension throughout, and had rather attractive Alexander Dash bodywork. They were delivered between 13 and 21 November 1995 and entered service on 3 December as 023 to 029 (N23-9 OBO). With seating for 40 plus 18 standing, they had an unladen weight of 6280kg.

Arriving from St. Mellons, Alexander Dash-bodied Dennis Dart 028 is about to pass the Hilton Hotel on Kingsway, Cardiff, on its way to the bus station on 2 September 2002. Note the route number blind positioned on the nearside of the vehicle.

(Andrew Wiltshire)

They carried a livery very similar in layout to the former Plymouth Dodges (101 to 110). For a period from November 2000, two members of this batch (028 and 029) became temporary driver training vehicles, but were back in normal service by mid-2001. Two buses 024 and 025 were involved in serious accidents, but were both repaired and returned to service. Upon repaint, all seven step-entrance Dennis Darts lost their brown skirts in favour of orange. The coach unit was closed down in October 1995 and this prompted the sale of Leyland Tigers 5 and 6 and Scanias 2 and 7. Other withdrawals included six further VRTs and eight Metroriders plus Bedford SB training bus 047.

In March 1996 the last Optare Metroriders were delivered to Cardiff Bus and comprised ten examples which were placed in service in April as 134 to 143 (N134-43 PTG). They were virtually identical to the previous batch from 1994/95.

136 from the final delivery of Optare Metroriders, approaches the bus station at Caerphilly in the morning sunshine on 15 March 2000.

(John Jones)

In April 1996 a proposal to replace the orange fleet livery was put forward and the public was given an opportunity to have a say. It was suggested that a reversion to the old livery of crimson lake (described as maroon at this stage) and cream be considered. However, this got no further than a telephone poll in which 430 voted against it compared to just 131 for the idea.

A dozen more Ailsas

This was the year when the double-deck fleet would benefit from some second-hand additions. 12 years after the last Volvo Ailsa was added to stock back in 1984, a further dozen of this reliable type were purchased in January 1996 from Merseybus, to help speed up the withdrawal of the Bristol VRTs. These particular Ailsas were from a total of 15 similar vehicles purchased new by Merseyside PTE between 1982 and 1984, for evaluation purposes. The batch comprised 437 to 446 (A151/2/4/6/8-63 HLV) of 1984, while 447 and 448 were DEM 821/2Y and were the two 1982 vehicles. They were ex Merseyside 0069/70/2/4/6-81/54/55 respectively, and all 12 were delivered to Cardiff in Merseybus maroon and cream. They had Alexander RV type bodies and the drivers cab featured a sliding access door. All retained their two-piece dot-matrix destination displays and received a full overhaul which included re-trimming of the upholstery and much re-panelling. The first bus 448, did not enter service until July, while the last did so in November.

Recently refurbished former Merseyside Ailsa 437 passes Cardiff Castle on its way to Llanrumney on 20 July 1996. Note the sliding cab door is open, a feature the NCME-bodied examples could not offer.

(John Jones)

All 12 Ailsas were outshopped in the revised livery featuring white lower panels first seen on Scanias 601 to 610 (see page 144). On a technical note, 448 was the odd one out as it had a Self Changing Gears (SCG) 5-speed gearbox as opposed to 3-speed Voith D851 on 437 to 447, which was also standard on Cardiff's original Ailsas 401 to 436. It is thought that the ten 1984-built Ailsas 437 to 446, had air suspension on the rear axle.

On 7 September 1996, Cardiff Bus acquired the financially-troubled Cardiff Bluebird business and promptly closed it down. The deal included around 40 vehicles, and consisted of eight Metrobus and eight Leyland Atlantean double-deckers, a Leyland Leopard saloon plus a large number of MCW Metrorider and Dodge S56 minibuses. None were operated and most were sold during September and October. A plan to use the five Rolls Royce-engined former South Yorkshire Metrobuses as training vehicles was soon abandoned, and these were sold in March 1997. MCW Metrorider F116 EKO which was not actually placed in service by Cardiff Bluebird was retained by Cardiff Bus as a source of spare parts. Withdrawn Bristol VRTs 337 to 342 and 344 to 347 were then reinstated to cover the schools contracts previously held by Cardiff Bluebird. Further Bristol VRTs were taken out of service during 1996 along with seven Metroriders and the remaining Bedford SB training vehicle 046.

CHAPTER NINE

EASY ACCESS BUSES, STANDARDISATION AND ANOTHER NEW IMAGE

199 ... ENTER THE LOW-FLOOR SALOON

With the gradual introduction of low-floor easy-access single-deck buses across the UK from 1994, it was inevitable that Cardiff Bus would eventually follow suit. Having already purchased some Dennis Darts in 1995, rather surprisingly they did not opt for the low-floor Dart SLF, but instead went for the rather stylish-looking Excel model from Optare. The Optare Excel was the first purpose-built low-floor single decker to be produced by this Leeds-based bus manufacturer. It was a full-size bus launched in 1995, constructed as a fully-integral vehicle with a very striking deep windscreen and was available in four lengths, 9.6m, 10m, 10.7m and 11.5m. Seating usually ranged from 27 up to 45, but varied to suit individual customer's requirements. The Excel soon became very popular with orders coming from both large and small operators. Ordered for delivery in 1997 were 15 11.5m L1150 model Excels featuring the Cummins 6BT 6-cylinder turbocharged engine and an Allison B300R World-series gearbox. They had improved suspension and were fitted with "greener and quieter engines". Delivered in October 1997, they took fleet numbers 201 to 215 (R201-15 DKG), marking the commencement of a new series. 204 appeared at the Motor Show held at the NEC in Birmingham in October 1997 while 201 and 202 were initially used for driver training. They were painted in a similar style to the seven Darts (023 to 029) delivered in 1995, using white with an orange roof and a brown skirt. However the Excels had branding applied on all four sides which featured the slogans "Easyrider", "Low floor bus" and "Easy Access" in addition to the fleet name Cardiff Bus / Bws Caerdydd. Delivered as 43-seaters, they were immediately re-seated to 42.

Optare Excel 213 has just crossed the River Ely on 5 May 2000 on its way to Ely on route 17, the last stamping ground for these saloons. Two months later it passed to Reading Transport.

(Andrew Wiltshire)

From 3 November 1997 they were put to work initially on services 8 (Heath Hospital to Cardiff Bay County Hall) and 9/9A (Heath Hospital to Grangetown). They were launched as the Easyrider brand, and were promoted as vehicles that offered "Easy access for all, with wide centre aisles and no steps in the first half of the saloon".

Refurbished double-deckers

In 1997 Cardiff Bus embarked on a refurbishment programme for its ageing Volvo Ailsas and Leyland Olympians. One of each type was selected for a complete mechanical and body overhaul, the Ailsa being 402 whilst the Olympian selected was 512. The Ailsa also received new side window rubbers and the window ventilators were now of the hopper-opening type. The fan in the driver's area was repositioned to the roof of the cab and both buses had dot-matrix destination blinds fitted and appeared in the revised livery as adopted for the former Merseybus Ailsas. In all 22 Ailsas from the 401 to 436 series were refurbished by the summer of 2000. The last two examples completed were 431 and 436 which retained their original destination blinds. Other Leyland Olympians refurbished were 509, 516 and 559, but in February 1998 Cardiff Bus decided that the work being carried out on the Olympians was proving to be far too costly, and it was decided to dispose of all 36 vehicles instead. In addition 552 was repainted in the revised livery but was not refurbished.

| VOLVO AILSA REFURBISHMENT PROGRAMME ||||||
Vehicle	Date	Vehicle	Date	Vehicle	Date
401	10/98	409	09/98	425	03/98
402	08/97	410	06/99	427	08/98
403	11/98	411	12/99	431	06/00
404	11/98	415	05/98	432	03/00
405	07/98	417	09/98	433	03/00
406	01/99	419	06/98	435	06/98
407	03/99	423	07/98	436	07/00
408	04/99				

| LEYLAND OLYMPIAN REFURBISHMENT PROGRAMME ||||||
Vehicle	Date	Vehicle	Date	Vehicle	Date
509	01/98	516	02/98	552	05/98 (repaint only)
512	05/97	559	09/97		

A further 13 Bristol VRTs were taken off service in 1997 leaving just 30 in regular service. Also withdrawn were MCW Metroriders including 150 to 155 of 1988, and the first of the ten long-wheelbase examples 156 to 161. A new cross city service serving Heath Hospital was launched on 4 August 1997. Numbered 100 it ran hourly from the Ely area via Fairwater, Llandaff, Whitchurch and Rhiwbina to Heath Hospital; and on to Roath, Llanedeyrn, St. Mellons, Trowbridge, Rumney and finally Llanrumney.

The year 1998 saw many significant changes at Cardiff Bus with the arrival of a new Managing Director Alan Kreppel, and the first of many low-floor Dennis Darts, as well as some interesting second-hand vehicles. Cardiff was now looking for a vehicle to form the basis of a "standardised" fleet of full-size single-deck and midibus-size vehicles, from the same family, which shared the same common parts and units. The Optare Excel was deemed not suitable, but the Dennis Dart SLF on the other hand was considered ideal.

Easy Access Buses, Standardisation and Another New Image

Newly-refurbished Leyland Olympian 512 makes its way along the causeway to Barry Island, where it will be displayed at the bus rally, being held on 1 June 1997.
(John Wiltshire)

The first of many

The first batch of Dennis Dart SLFs to arrive at Cardiff Bus consisted of 20 that entered service between November 1998 and early January 1999 as 301 to 320 (S301-20 SHB). These Darts represented an investment of £1.8 million and featured a similar livery to the Excels and were the last new vehicles in this livery. Fitted with the popular Plaxton Pointer SPD (Super Pointer Dart) body, Cardiff now adopted the Plaxton Pointer as standard for all future Dart deliveries. These buses had an overall length of 11.3m, a width of 2.4m and an unladen weight of 7795kg. The engine was a Cummins B160 5.9-litre turbo-charged unit of 160bhp driving through a 4-speed Allison fully-automatic gearbox. The seating capacity of 41 includes six tip-up seats. The completed vehicle was officially referred to as the SPD (Super Pointer Dart).

Plaxton Pointer SPD-bodied Dart SLF 315 is heading into Cardiff past the City Link retail park on 28 September 2000. It is on a service 65 from St. Mellons to Central Station.
(Andrew Wiltshire)

157

The Volvo Ailsa double-deckers were still regarded as rugged and reliable and the refurbishment programme was considered a success. With the decision now having been made to dispose of the Leyland Olympians, withdrawals began in 1998. Cardiff Bus now looked to purchase further second-hand double-deckers and eventually a batch of eight Alexander-bodied Volvo Ailsas of 1984 vintage was sourced, this time from Stagecoach Fife Scottish. They were allocated fleet numbers 449 to 456, while their registrations were A969-74/67/8 YSX respectively. They all arrived at Cardiff in Stagecoach livery and delivery, a protracted affair, commenced on 22 September 1998 with A967 YSX, and was concluded with A972 YSX in late February.

Number 451 is seen with an inbound 57 from Pontprennau in Custom House Street, Cardiff, on 14 December 2000, whilst services were on diversion due to an unsafe structure near Queen Street station.

(Andrew Wiltshire)

Number 455 was the first into service on 9 November 1998 while 452 and 454 were the last to enter service in June 1999. All were thoroughly refurbished and re-trimmed and entered service with a seating capacity of 81. Their Scottish Bus Group origins were emphasised by their distinctive pyramid-shaped destination boxes. However, these were removed and replaced by a rectangular electronic dot-matrix display, similar to that fitted to the refurbished NCME-bodied Ailsas (402 etc) from 1997 onwards.

A number of open-top tours were still operating in 1997 including Roath Park, Cosmeston Lakes, Rhondda Heritage Park, Brecon Mountain Railway, Castell Coch and Caerphilly. Also the 45-minute Cardiff Bay Tour ran seven times a day, every day in July and August which was extended to take in Penarth for the 1998 season. Unfortunately, 1998 was the last season for the two remaining open-top buses, Bristol VRTs 359 and 360. They were withdrawn at the end of the season and sold for further service. One member of the first batch of Scania saloons, 283, was involved in a collision with a lorry near Rhoose in August 1998, while working the X91 Llantwit Major service. The bus suffered major rear end damage, and was officially withdrawn in the December. It was subsequently used for spares, and was eventually sold for scrap locally.

Easy Access Buses, Standardisation and Another New Image

Four second-hand Mercedes 709D minibuses were obtained in December 1998 to operate on "low-cost" service 114 to Ely. This was in response to competition from Barry-based operator Alister's Coaches (Alister Colburn) who had started a service from Ely into Cardiff as well as one in Barry town. All four had Reebur bodies with 25 dual-purpose seats, and were purchased from Stagecoach Devon. They carried a plain white livery with Ely Value Bus branding for the duration of their three year stay with Cardiff. They took fleet numbers 010 to 013 (E830 ATT, F714 ADV, F405/8 KOD) and had all been new in 1988. Colburn eventually surrendered his licences around July 1999.

On 7 June 2000 Mercedes minibus 011 is seen leaving the Hayes on its way to Ely (Grand Avenue) on service 114 which was withdrawn a few months later. The brick building behind the bus is the Duke of Wellington public house, owned by Brains Brewery, which is still trading in 2016, in what is now a fully pedestrianised area.

(John Wiltshire)

Other vehicles withdrawn in 1998 were Bristol VRTs 348 to 351 and 356, and the first ten Leyland Olympians, 501 to 508, 511 and 513.

Setting new standards, new buses and a new livery

A number of Dart SLF midi-buses arrived in the latter half of 1999 and were the first buses to carry Burges blue and cream with an orange band, which was to be the new standard livery for the fleet and reflected Cardiff Council's corporate colour scheme. These vehicles were seen as the natural successor to the Optare Metrorider in the Cardiff fleet and had an overall length of 8.8m, width of 2.38m and an unladen weight of 6600kg. Seating capacity was for a maximum of 30, while 16 standees were permitted. They were numbered 144 to 158 (T144-50 DAX, V151-8 JKG) and their Plaxton Pointer body was known as a MPD (Mini Pointer Dart). All entered service during September/October, and 144 to 150 were route-branded for services 7/8 (Heath Hospital to Cardiff Bay). They were all later rebuilt with side and rear electronic route number displays.

Cardiff's Municipal Buses

Mini Pointer Dart (MPD) 147 on a 1 (Bay Circle) working picks up in Crwys Road on 2 September 2003. It is in the new Burges blue and cream livery in its original form, as introduced on this batch of buses. For a short period the City Circle routes 1 and 2 were renamed Bay Circle.

(Andrew Wiltshire)

In 1999 Cardiff Bus gained the University of Wales Institute Cardiff (UWIC) student transport service from local independent operator Venture Travel. This served the three campus sites at Western Avenue, Cyncoed and Colchester Avenue. For this duty two of the former Merseyside Ailsas (445/446) were repainted into UWIC blue livery and were joined by similar bus 444 by the autumn of 2000.

Two buses were on loan from Optare to cover for warranty work being undertaken:

FROM APRIL UNTIL JUNE 1999					
Fleet no:	Registration	Chassis	Body	Seating	Year
330	N330 EUG	Optare Excel L1000	Optare	B34F	1995
FROM JULY UNTIL OCTOBER 1999.					
100	T422 ADN	Optare Metrorider VN2320	Optare	B29F	1999

The last Bristols

1999 was to be the last year for the Bristol VRTs, a type which had been represented in the Cardiff fleet for the around a quarter of a century. Of the 17 examples that were on the books at the start of the year, 359 to 362/5, 367 to 370 and 374 to 377 bowed out by the end of January while 380/1/6 lasted until February. The honour of being the last VRT in service and the last Bristol in the fleet went to 391 which was withdrawn in May 1999. This marked the end of another era, which had begun with the purchase of four Bristol B saloons in 1928. Also taken out of service were the last of the normal-height Olympians (510, 514 to 519) plus 14 of the 17 low-height examples from the 551 to 567 series. The last of the MCW-built Metroriders in normal service (162 to 165) plus the first Optare examples 166 to 171 dating from 1990 were also withdrawn, but 167 was later reinstated.

Buses and satellites

In late 1999 Real Time Passenger Information was launched on services in the north of Cardiff, and with the aid of a Welsh Office grant represented an investment of £1.5 million. This system aimed to provide intending passengers with up to date kerb-side information displayed on screens in bus shelters. The buses were fitted with Delta Track GPS (Global Positioning System) which uses satellites to relay their position to a control centre, which in turn sends information to the bus stops. It was later rolled out to most parts of the city.

Disappointing performers

Early examples of the Optare Excel in service throughout the UK soon gained a poor reputation for reliability, with a number of fleets taking the opportunity to dispose of them prematurely. It was announced in early 2000 that all 15 Cardiff examples (201 to 215) of 1997, would pass to Reading Transport as they were not considered to be a very suitable vehicle by either the Managing Director or the Fleet Engineer. Three main problem areas were identified at an early stage including body structure corrosion, structural problems with gearbox mountings and heavy fuel consumption, with buses often returning figures as low as 6mpg. During their final months in service with Cardiff, the remaining Excels were to be found mainly confined to the Ely routes 17/18. The first to go were 201 to 205 which departed in May 2000, while the other ten followed in July.

Cardiff Bus replaced them with a further batch of 41-seat 11.3m Plaxton SPD-bodied Dennis Darts SLFs in the summer of 2000 which arrived as 361 to 369, 371 (W361-9/71 VHB). There was no 370 due, once again, to the difficulty obtaining matching registration numbers. These buses were put to work in July on the main Ely routes (17 and 18), and they carried the following branding "Services 17/18 Central Station-Canton-Ely every 5 minutes Mondays to Saturdays daytime". They also featured side and rear route number displays.

Plaxton Pointer SPD-bodied Dart 366 approaches St. David's Hospital on Cowbridge Road East in Canton on 18 July 2000. It is working a 17A, and the brand new bus looks very smart with route branding in place and an absence of adverts. Note the revised position for the orange band.

(Andrew Wiltshire)

Refurbishing the Leyland Lynx

By 2000, the upholstery of the four dual-purpose examples was looking very tired and in need of replacing. In the event it was decided not to proceed with any refurbishment, and consequently 237 to 240 were withdrawn in October 2000 and advertised for sale. It was then decided that the bus-seated MkI Lynx (231 to 236, 241 to 259) would be replaced in due course by new buses. The Lynx IIs (260 to 271) however received a major refurbishment. This began in July 2000 when 271 was stripped of nearly all its panels and interior and completely rebuilt. In the process it lost its fibreglass bolt-on skirt panels which were replaced by conventional plain alloy panels. The completed bus retained its original destination display but was outshopped in the new livery of Burges blue and cream as applied to all new "low-floor" vehicles. It returned to service in October and was followed by 261 in the December 2000. All 12 Lynx II were eventually refurbished.

Newly refurbished 271 is caught waiting on Heol Hir, Llanishen, on 14 November 2000. It will depart on the 81 to the City Centre via Lake Road West and Mackintosh Place. The replacement of the bolt-on fibreglass skirt gives the bus a much tidier appearance.
(Andrew Wiltshire)

Some 25 MPD-size 30-seat Darts were received during the summer to replace Metroriders. They would be more or less identical to the 1999 deliveries, except for the livery details. There were a number of gaps in the number series, but the batch comprised 159, 161 to 169, 171 and 172 (W159/61-9/71/2 EAX) which entered service in August 2000, followed in September by 173, 174, 176 to 179 and 181 to 187 (X173/4/6-9/81-7 CTG).

172 was the only W-reg MPD-size Dart to gain the later post-2006 livery and is seen on Ffordd Y Mileniwm adjacent to Morrisons superstore in Barry, on 25 May 2012.
(Andrew Wiltshire)

Overall-advert liveries were very much back in favour once again and at least four appeared during 2000. In August 443 received a mainly blue livery for George Street Furnishers. The imminent withdrawal this year of Scania double-deckers 601 to 610 (three of which were advert buses), meant Ailsas 439, 441/2 received advert liveries. In conclusion, 2000 witnessed the elimination of several notable types. In addition to the premature departure of the 15 Optare Excels, the last of the Olympians in service (553, 561 and 566), the entire collection of Scania N113 double-deckers (601 to 610) were withdrawn. Optare Metrorider 166 which had become a trainer was also withdrawn, along with previously reinstated 167. Normal Metrorider withdrawals were of 172 to 187. 2000 also witnessed the demise of the first of the unrefurbished Ailsas, 412 to 414.

Lynx departures and more Darts

The year 2001 started with the sale of the dual-purpose seated Leyland Lynx (237 to 240), the withdrawal of which took place in late 2000. All four passed to Ensignbus for resale, and were quickly snapped up by private operators. In May 2001 further 41-seat SPD-size Dennis Dart SLFs entered service, to coincide with service changes. This time a batch of 15, numbered 372 to 374, 376 to 379 and 381 to 388 (Y372-4/6-9/81-8 GAX). There was no 375 or 380 due to the lack of suitable registrations. They were mainly intended for use on the St. Mellons area routes, and most carried appropriate branding. However from new 377 and 378 were extra buses branded for the 17/18 Ely routes. Number 372 to 374/6 and 383 were also fitted with tachographs, while in the July, 372 and 373 had towing hooks fitted so that they could tow bicycle trailers on the Brecon Beacons National Park summer services.

The brand new 385 approaches Cardiff Royal Infirmary on Newport Road with an inbound X46 from St. Mellons on 22 June 2001.

(Andrew Wiltshire)

A Dart SLF was taken on loan to cover for warranty repairs:

FROM PLAXTON, SCARBOROUGH MAY 2001 UNTIL PURCHASED IN MAY 2002					
Fleet no:	Registration	Chassis	Body	Seating	Year
861	S861 VAT	Dennis Dart SLF 11.3m	Plaxton SPD	B41F	1998

It was repainted into Cardiff fleet livery and eventually received a Vultron electronic destination display in August 2001. It had an earlier style front dash panel, and featured traditional metal-framed seats.

On 26 May 2001 Cardiff Bus withdrew from the Caerphilly area routes after having a presence for around thirteen years. It also surrendered its share of the Tredegar service 26. Digital radios were introduced to the fleet which, combined with the Delta Track GPS, further enhanced the vehicle movement tracking. A start was made on repainting the first batch of Dennis Dart SLFs 301 to 320 into the Burges blue and cream livery. This was to bring them visually into line with subsequent deliveries in the new "low-floor" buses livery. This process commenced with 303 in October 2001. Meanwhile, further inroads were made into the Volvo Ailsas with 11 withdrawn as the double-deck fleet continued to dwindle in numbers, in favour of modern low-floor saloons. These included 437/8, 440/7/8. Also departing were the four Mercedes minibuses 010 to 013 after just two years, while Leyland Lynx 231 and 232, Optare Metroriders 188 to 197 and 101 to 106 were withdrawn. However, 103 to 106 were later reinstated as were Leyland Lynx 231 and 232.

The year 2002 saw the arrival of 32 Darts, comprising 12 SPDs and 20 MPDs, all featuring Vultron electronic destination displays which were much brighter. The former entered service in April 2002 as 388 to 399 (CE02 UVD/G/H/J-P/R) and were officially described as Transbus Darts with Transbus Pointer SPD bodies seating 41. They had an unladen weight of 7960kg and were fitted with Euro3 compliant engines. The smaller MPD examples were also described as Transbus models and had a revised seating capacity of 29 plus 17 standing and at 6850kg were slightly heavier than previous MPDs. They were numbered 188 to 207, but fleet numbers 200 to 207 proved to be incompatible with the radio system, and so the batch became 188 to 199, 211 to 218 (CE02 UUG/H/J-P/R-T, UUV-Z, UVA-C). These would be the last 8.8m MPDs acquired. Branding for north Cardiff services was carried by 188 to 197 and 389 to 398, with the buses serving the Thornhill, Rhiwbina and Whitchurch areas from 14 April. The bodies on all 30 buses were built at the Alexander plant at Falkirk. Number 399 was delivered in black, and was to form the basis of an overall advert livery. The former demonstration Dart on loan since May 2001 was officially taken into stock during 2002 as fleet number 861.

Number 188 is seen leaving Whitchurch village and crossing Whitchurch Brook when brand new on 24 April 2002. The 21 service will have come from Rhiwbina and Pantmawr Road and will now cross Whitchurch Common and head back into town via Birchgrove and North Road.

(Andrew Wiltshire)

Easy Access Buses, Standardisation and Another New Image

Former demonstrator 861 was to remain unique in the fleet. It is noted in the Central Bus Station on 17 July 2002. The traditional style seat frames are clearly visible towards the rear of the vehicle, as is the plain front dash panel which made this bus easy to distinguish from a distance.
(Andrew Wiltshire)

During April 2002 Cardiff Bus launched the Airbus Shuttle X91 service that served Cardiff Wales Airport at Rhoose. Initially five of the Alexander Strider-bodied Scania N113CRB saloons received a special blue livery, designed by a Cardiff School of Art and Design student. Eventually all seven of the batch carried this livery. However not all seven were required for this service at any one time, and so they also appeared on the X96 to Kings Square, Barry, as well as on city routes in Cardiff.

On 25 May 2004 Airbus-liveried Scania 293 is seen on Newport Road passing the City Link retail park, and working the short-lived X46. This was a Monday to Friday limited-stop service between St. Mellons Business Park and Cardiff Bay, although this particular working was truncated to run Hendre Road, Trowbridge Estate to Central Station.
(Andrew Wiltshire)

FLEET SUMMARY MAY 2002			
Double-deckers	Single-deckers	Midi-buses	Total
28	101	96	225
Of these, 116 were low-floor vehicles.			

A century of service

In 2002 the undertaking celebrated its centenary and a special 64-page booklet titled "All Aboard" was published by Cardiff Bus in March. There was also a bus rally held in the Civic Centre on 7 July, and a competition encouraged local school children to design an appropriate livery to mark the occasion. SDP Dart 320 was the bus chosen to receive the winning design, the work of pupils from All Saints Church in Wales School, Llanedeyrn, and Llysfaen Primary School, Lisvane. They were allowed to visit the paint shop at Sloper Road to see artist David Patterson transfer their designs onto the bus.

SPD-size Dennis Dart 320 was chosen to receive this special livery to mark the centenary of Cardiff Bus and its predecessors. The livery was designed by local school children and the winning entry is seen in the Central Bus Station on 17 July 2002.
(Andrew Wiltshire)

To conclude the celebrations, a Depot Open Day was held at Sloper Road on Saturday 7 September. An interesting selection of Cardiff Bus and former Cardiff vehicles were on display for all to inspect, and AEC Regent V 408 was used on a free shuttle service.

Privately-preserved AEC Regent V 408 has had its original destination layout restored and has been repainted by Cardiff Bus as part of the centenary celebrations. It is seen in the yard at Sloper Road depot about to depart for the Central Bus Station while engaged on the free shuttle service.
(Andrew Wiltshire)

Easy Access Buses, Standardisation and Another New Image

Dart SLF 319 completed the programme to repaint all of the batch 301 to 320 out of the orange, white and brown Easyrider colours. In 2002 Leyland Lynx 257 to 259 (G257-9 HUH) became permanent driver training buses, and each gained a new training livery of yellow and orange with black lettering.

The following bus was taken on loan:

FROM TRANSBUS IN 2002 FOR DRIVER TRAINING ONLY					
Fleet no	Registration	Chassis	Body	Seating	Year
	V257 BNV	Dennis Dart SLF 8.8m	Plaxton MPD	B29F	1999

In October 2002, 451 became the first of the former Fife Scottish Ailsas to receive an overall advert livery, for Peter Allan Estate Agents. Withdrawn during 2002 were Olympian trainers 509 and 512 which were the last of the type in the fleet, ex Merseybus Ailsas 439 and 441 to 444, Metrorider 109 and no fewer than 19 Leyland Lynx. Previously withdrawn Ailsa 423 was donated to the Winterbus Project for use as a mobile soup kitchen in Cardiff. It was maintained by Cardiff Bus and given unofficial fleet number CV1. In August 2002 Ailsa 438 was donated to the Re-start Project and converted for use as a mobile computer classroom in the Cardiff area. It was also maintained by Cardiff Bus, given unofficial fleet number CV2 and housed at Sloper Road depot alongwith 423. Finally, the seven step-entrance Darts (023 to 029) were repainted between 2002 and 2003, and lost their brown skirts in favour of orange.

Testing times again

Dennis Dart V257 BNV returned once again in January 2003, but this time was placed in service, still in overall white, but with fleet number 222 and Cardiff Bus fleet names. It was used mainly on route 92 from Cardiff city centre to Penarth, and stayed until late April. In 2003 Cardiff Bus tried out some demonstrators as they looked beyond the Dennis Dart for future vehicle requirements. The Transbus Enviro 300 demonstrator SN03 LFU was inspected in late summer 2003. Also on loan for demonstration were an Optare Solo 223 (YF02 SKU) which was used on Barry town services, and an East Lancs-bodied MAN (PN03 OWA).

SN03LFU was one of three Transbus Enviro 300 demonstrators inspected by Cardiff Bus. It is seen approaching the bus station in Wood Street on 4 September 2003, working in from Newport on service 30.

(Andrew Wiltshire)

During the late summer of 2003 the final delivery of Transbus SPD Darts took place. These buses featured the Cummins ISBe 185PS engine and had an unladen weight of 7784kg. They were numbered 501 to 508 (CA03 VRD-G/J-M) and 509 to 520 (CN53 AKY/Z, ALO/U, AKY/Z, ALO/U, AMK/O/U/V/X, ANF/P/R). Numbers 501 to 510 were specifically intended for use on the 57/58 services to Pontprennau. They featured a cream band above the saloon windows which carried branding reflecting this, while 511 to 517 just had a plain cream band. The orange band was in the normal position but in addition there was a swept up orange stripe in the region of the rear wheel arch and the Cardiff Bus website address was also displayed for the first time on a vehicle. Numbers 518 to 520 were delivered in black, purple and silver base-colours respectively, as they would become overall advert buses in September and October.

A batch of 12 intermediate length 10.1m Transbus Darts were also received in the autumn. They were the first to this useful overall length, and were referred to by Cardiff Bus as LMPDs (Long Mini Pointer Dart). With an unladen weight of 7194kg, these were 34-seaters with 21 standing, and were numbered 221 to 232 (CN53 AJV/X/Y, AKF/G/J/K/O/P/U/V/X). These buses also carried the livery modifications mentioned above, but this time 222 to 232 were branded for routes 8/9/9A (Cardiff Bay to Heath Hospital). At this point in time older MPD Darts 144 to 158 of 1999 lost this branding and were moved on to other services. Number 221 carried an overall advert for Warburtons Bread from new until December 2004.

Number 222 is one of the 10.1m LMP Darts and is noted picking up customers at the County Hall bus stop in Cardiff Bay on 9 June 2006. It will then head off to Heath Hospital on service 8.
(Andrew Wiltshire)

Meanwhile the last of the non-refurbished Leyland Lynx saloons (250 to 255) were withdrawn and sold along with all 13 surviving Plaxton Verde-bodied Scania N113 saloons. 15 Metroriders were also taken out of service, although some were later reinstated. From October 2003 a number of the Optare Metrorider were outshopped in plain white with an orange skirt and Cardiff Bus fleet names. Those eventually receiving this revised livery were 117, 122/4/5/7/8 and 130 to 143.

Memorable services 3: Cardiff to Newport

The Cardiff to Newport service was acquired on 15 April 1924 with the business of G. Vernon Jones of Castleton. Initially the route started from Broadway at the Cardiff end running to a terminus near the Cardiff Road/Commercial Road junction in Newport. From 11 August the Cardiff terminus moved to the Monument in St. Mary Street and by 1929 the service number 30 was being used. This became a joint service with Newport Corporation Transport with effect from 1 July 1945, and it is thought a 20 minute frequency (Monday to Saturday) was in operation from the start. It was a great success from the start and by August 1945 was carrying 35,000 passengers a week.

In 1950 the joint service started from Greyfriars Road, Cardiff, and took 41 minutes to reach Newport where it terminated in Bridge Street. The fare was 1/3d single and 2/- return and Newport supplied three vehicles and Cardiff at least two. By 1956 the 30 service was running from the new Central Bus Station in Cardiff to Dock Street bus station in Newport. From the outset, both undertakings normally used double-deckers, and from the early 1970s, often their latest acquisitions, but by the late 1990s single-deckers had become more common. By 2000 an hourly variation of the 30 was introduced with the service diverting via the Duffryn estate at Newport and numbered 30D. It was worked alternately by both Cardiff Bus and Newport Transport, but Cardiff withdrew from this arrangement in June 2003 leaving Newport to work a two-hourly 30D which ceased in October 2008.

Easy Access Buses, Standardisation and Another New Image

The mutual working arrangement between the two fleets was briefly disrupted between 2 August and 14 November 2010 due to a disagreement by Newport Transport over fares, resulting in that operator running all timings and thus duplicating those of Cardiff Bus. Things then returned to normal and the joint service celebrated its 70th anniversary on 1 July 2015, at which point it was the last remaining joint service between two former municipal fleets still running in the UK. As the Kingsway bus station closed in late 2013, the 30 was transferred to the nearby Market Square bus station, until the new Friars Walk bus station opened in December 2015. From August 2015 the number 30 terminated in Custom House Street, Cardiff, negotiating the Cardiff Bus Box in a clockwise fashion.

On 18 March 2003 Plaxton Verde-bodied Scania 284, now sporting an orange roof, is seen leaving Newport on its run back to Cardiff on the joint 30 service. By early 2016, this area had changed beyond all recognition and the old bus station had also been swept away by the new Friars Walk retail development and a new smaller bus station.

(Andrew Wiltshire)

Vehicles types used by Cardiff over the years on the 30 service included: AEC Regent II, Guy Arab IV, Bristol KW6G, Leyland PD2A, AEC Regent V, Guy Arab V, Daimler Fleetline, Bristol VRT, Leyland Olympian, Leyland Lynx and Scania N113 (double and single deck). In 2016 the 30 can host most vehicle types from the current fleet with the Scania Omnicity saloons being the most common.

Further competition

With effect from 19 April 2004 Cardiff Bus experienced some further competition, this time from 2-Travel of Swansea who used mainly elderly vehicles on a number of core routes, with a curious timetable that was designed to work around existing school contracts. Cardiff Bus responded by rolling out a fleet of Metroriders in plain white, some of which had been taken out of store. The buses involved were 103 to 108/10, 112 to 114/6/8 and 129. It would appear that the 2-Travel services came to an end during October 2004.

Cardiff Bus Optare Metrorider 104 is passed by one of 2-Travel's unusual East Lancs-bodied Volvo B10M double-deckers in St. Mary Street on 20 April 2004. The Metrorider is heading for Llanrumney while the Volvo is off to St. Mellons.
(Andrew Wiltshire)

After the Dart

For 2004, and after trying three demonstrators, Cardiff Bus received a new type of vehicle, the Enviro 300. The Enviro 300 was launched in 2001 as a lightweight semi-integral single-decker and was the first model in the Enviro range. In March 2004 Transbus International went into administration and the Dennis plant at Guildford and Alexander coachworks at Falkirk was acquired by a consortium of investors to create Alexander Dennis Limited. Cardiff Bus ordered a dozen 11.8m Enviro 300s which were considered to be Transbus examples and were delivered in the summer of 2004. They were fitted with Cummins ISBe Euro4 engines of 220bhp and Allison B300 gearboxes. Six of them were laid out internally with extra luggage space, and dedicated to the X91 service to Llantwit Major which serves Cardiff Wales Airport.

The first to arrive were 711 to 716 (CN04 NRJ-L, NRU/V/X) in early July 2004, and were finished in the standard Burges blue and cream livery. These six buses seated 43 passengers with standing for 27. They had an unladen weight of 8460kg and at 2.55m wide, meant they were wider than a SPD Dart, and so drivers had to take extra care. Numbers 711 to 716 were also fitted with tachographs from new, and all six entered service in 2 August 2004. The balance of the order for Enviro300s was completed throughout August with the delivery of 701 to 706 (CN04 NPV/X-Z, NRE/F). They were generally similar to the first six except that they seated 40 with 27 standing and had a large full-height luggage rack on the offside which gave them an unladen weight of 8590kg. These buses were placed into service in late August 2004 (701/2/6) and early September (703 to 705). Numbers 701 to 705 wore a special pale blue livery with large Airbus Xpress lettering in dark blue advertising airline BMI Baby. Number 706 was delivered and entered service in fleet livery, but was given an Air Wales overall advert livery soon after.

Easy Access Buses, Standardisation and Another New Image

Transbus Enviro 300 712 has only been in service 5 weeks when it was photographed passing the Hilton Hotel, Kingsway, on 9 September 2004. The livery suited these buses well, but was not the same after adverts adorned the sides.
(Andrew Wiltshire)

Numbers 711 to 716 soon found themselves on most duties around the City and were popular vehicles on the 30 service to Newport. Numbers 701 to 706 could also be found on city services from time to time, but were intended primarily for use on the Airbus Xpress (Cardiff International Airport) and other services in Barry and the Vale of Glamorgan. They replaced the seven Alexander Strider-bodied Scania saloons 287 to 293, which were withdrawn and sold in late summer 2004.

Number 703 in Airbus Express livery with contravision branding wrap over the windows. It is seen in Westgate Street on 16 February 2005 having worked into Cardiff on an X91.
(Andrew Wiltshire)

Number 704 was involved in a serious accident while working in the Vale of Glamorgan and was subsequently rebuilt, returning to service in December 2007 carrying fleet livery and having had its luggage rack removed making it a 43-seater. In June 2008 702/3 were given a new BMI Baby livery which they retained until June 2011. By this time 705 was in fleet livery together with 706 and had they probably lost their luggage racks too.

The final delivery of Darts for Cardiff Bus consisted of a further dozen 34-seat LMPD 10.1m models which entered service in December 2004. Cardiff had now received a total of 168 Darts over a nine year period. The last examples would be Alexander Dennis models, but identical in most respects to 221 to 232 of 2003. They took fleet numbers 233 to 244 (CN54 NTL/M/T-V/X/Y, NUA-C/E/F).

Number 233 one of the 10.1m Alexander Dennis Darts received in December 2004. On 16 April 2014 it waits at the traffic lights on West Grove before turning right onto Newport Road and making its way into the City Centre. Having been refurbished, it now sports the latest livery.

(Andrew Wiltshire)

Other buses withdrawn during the summer of 2004 were six of the refurbished Leyland Lynx IIs leaving just 262/6/7/8, 270 and 271 in service. The first of the former Fife Scottish Ailsas to be withdrawn was 450 (A970 YSX) which had been in store for some time. In August 2004 it was donated to a charity and became the Urban Sanctuary Community Bus, and maintained at Sloper Road depot as CV3.

Ailsas get another make-over

From the summer of 2004 a number of refurbished Ailsas were repainted into a revised livery, using a slightly darker shade of orange. This featured a single white band, but with the fleet name in white positioned between the wheel arches, and it unofficially became known as the retro livery. The first dealt with was 407 and eventually 15 were repainted as follows: 402/6 to 409, 411/7, 425, 432 and 435 plus ex Fife Scottish examples 449, 452/4/5, with the last being 451 in October 2005.

Easy Access Buses, Standardisation and Another New Image

A new image for a number of the remaining Volvo Ailsas included this retro livery using a slightly darker shade of orange. Number 409 looks very smart for a 25-year old bus. It is heading along St. Mary Street past the Borough Arms on 7 August 2007.

(Andrew Wiltshire)

In October 2004 a Scania OmniCity single-deck demonstrator was taken on loan. Cream-liveried YN04 AHA was briefly put to work on the Newport service as fleet number 007. Another Scania on loan for demonstration purposes was YN54 OBX. This was an East Lancs-bodied Scania N94UD Omnidekka which was allocated fleet number 008. It was not used in normal service, but did appear on at least one contract service which did not require a cash vault to be fitted.

CHAPTER TEN

EVEN BIGGER BUSES AND STRONGER BRANDING

With a new Managing Director in post, future vehicle policies were set to change at Cardiff Bus and the first signs of this occurred in late 2004. Increased patronage on the Ely services 17/18 meant that even with a five minute frequency, a SPD Dart could not provide the required capacity. Low-floor double-deckers and articulated buses were both considered as solutions. Heralded as a European Capital City, Cardiff was keen to improve its image and wished to revamp the bus link between the City Centre and Cardiff Bay. Previously operated by Bebb, the tender for the service 6 Bay Xpress was won by Cardiff Bus, and entailed a new route operated by articulated buses.

The bendy-bus is coming to Cardiff

Mercedes Benz Citaro 0530G demonstrator BX54 EBC was on loan as fleet number 009 from 25 January until 8 February 2005. It was used on Ely routes 17 and 18 as well as doing a spell on service 8 from Grangetown to Wood Street, but not continuing to Heath Hospital.

The impressive Mercedes Benz Citaro articulated bus BX54 EBC was on loan from Evobus Ltd. It is seen crossing Wood Street bridge over the River Taff, on a run from Grangetown on 28 January 2005. This was basically a standard London-specification 3-door vehicle.

(Andrew Wiltshire)

An Alexander Dennis Enviro 300 demonstrator in overall white livery was taken on loan in April 2005 to ease a vehicle shortage caused in part by accident damage suffered to Dart 242. Numbered 010 (PO54 NNM) it stayed until July, and was used exclusively on the Newport service 30, as it did not have a working destination display. Withdrawals during 2005 consisted purely of Metroriders, 14 of which were put to one side pending disposal.

Even Bigger Buses and Stronger Branding

There were no new buses delivered during 2005, but 2006 witnessed the arrival of the very impressive fleet of "bendy-buses". After trials with the Mercedes Benz Citaro 0530G and also inspecting a Scania OmniCity articulated bus, a decision was made to order 19 Scania OmniCity CN94UA models that would be built in Poland at a cost of £4.5 million. These were two-door versions with seating for 53 and a standing capacity of 80; and with an unladen weight of 17320kg, this made them the heaviest buses by far to be operated by Cardiff. They included many extra features such as full air-conditioning, "next bus stop" displays inside the bus, digi-box pre-recorded passenger announcements, internal and external CCTV and "on-bus" screens with local travel information and BBC News 24. The livery and all publicity material including timetables and bus stop flags were designed by Ray Stenning's Best Impressions. Four vehicles 601 to 604 (CN06 GDF/J/O/K) were in a blue livery for the baycar service 6. Numbers 605 to 617 (CN06 GFA/E, GEK,GDU, GEJ/U/Y, GFG/J/K/O, GDV/Z) were in a red and Scarab green livery and branded Capital City Red for the Ely routes. The remaining two buses were numbered 618 and 619 (CN06 GDX/Y) and featured a generic 2-tone green livery with cream fronts, for operation on either service as required.

In the original baycar livery, Scania OmniCity articulated bus 603 makes a stop in High Street on its way to Cardiff Bay on 7 August 2007. Upon closure of High Street and upper St. Mary Street to all through traffic in 2010, the baycar was re-routed via Westgate Street and Wood Street to reach the lower end of St. Mary Street.

(Andrew Wiltshire)

During the early part of 2006 three service pits at Sloper Road garage were lengthened to accommodate the forthcoming 18m bendy-buses. They provided roll-on roll-off access to avoid any reversing. Other work undertaken in preparation for the arrival of these massive vehicles included the upgrading of kerb-side bus-boarding ramps, and even some re-location of bus stops to make the use of bendy-buses more practical and safer. Services 17 and 18 were then re-located from the bus station to the north side of Wood Street in preparation for the planned launch in March. This meant buses would run inbound from Canton via Neville Street and Tudor Street and outbound via Westgate Street and Canton Bridge. However there were delays and the first bus did not arrive until late April. The first few examples started to enter service on 28 May with 614/6/8/9 following in June. The baycar service also commenced on 28 May with a ten-minute daytime frequency.

Capital City Red-liveried bendy-bus 607 has just picked up passengers by the Ty-Pwll Coch pub on the corner of Windway Road on its first day in service, 1 June 2006. It is the morning rush hour and the bus will now continue inbound along Cowbridge Road East through Victoria Park and Canton.

(Andrew Wiltshire)

The bendy-buses buses rarely strayed from these routes in normal service, but could be called upon to help out on Park and Ride duties and for special events. In order to overcome capacity issues at certain times, a small number of term time journeys saw them working from Roath to Western Avenue, Llandaff, on the University of Wales Institute, Cardiff (UWIC) contract, as well as to Colcot Road, Barry, on the 96 serving Cardiff and the Vale College. In September 2006 two of the LMPD Darts. 233 and 234, were allocated to UWIC contract duties to replace Ailsas 445 and 446. They were given UWIC blue vinyls, but retained fleet livery on the front. An interesting demonstrator was then inspected in the autumn in the form of the VDL Electrocity YG52 CCX new in 2002, which arrived on loan from Wrightbus. Based on a DAF SB120 chassis, it was fitted with a 31-seat dual-door body, and was inspected and tested for 7 days in November 2006, but not used in service.

Taken out of service during 2006 were Ailsa 433 and 16 Metroriders. Of these, 104, 117, 122/8, 131 and 141 were then temporarily reinstated by September 2006. The Ailsa was sold for scrap and was believed to be the first of the 56 examples operated by Cardiff Bus to be broken up. Following accident damage MPD Dart 161 was withdrawn in February 2006 and stored. To cover for warranty repairs, Scania OmniCity artic YN54 ALO in all-over red livery was hired from July 2006 until 15 February 2007 with fleet number 600; and was hired again in August 2007.

The 2-axle Scania OmniCity

The 2007 intake of new single-deckers was once again sourced from Scania's bus plant at Slupsk in Poland. The Scania OmniCity was also available as an integrally-constructed saloon with a transverse engine, first appearing on the UK market in right-hand drive layout in 2002. From 2006 the model was designated N270UB and updated to feature a 5-cylinder Euro IV engine. Unlike some low-floor models being offered at the time, the Omnicity featured a low floor beyond the rear axle, and Cardiff Bus placed an order for 15 which entered service during October 2007. They were 41-seaters with an overall length of 11.98m a width of 2.55m and an unladen weight of 11860kg. The first six 721 to 726 (CN57 BHU/Y/W/X/Z, BJE) were branded as Capital City Green and allocated to a revamped service 27 to Thornhill. They were painted in a similar livery layout to the Capital City Red artics, but used lime green in place of red, and until late 2012, these buses rarely strayed from the route 27. The remaining nine buses 727 to 735 (CN57 BJF/J/K/O/U/X/V/Y/Z) wore a similar Scarab green livery but with orange fronts for general service, and this was duly adopted as the new fleet livery.

Even Bigger Buses and Stronger Branding

On the morning of 29 April 2009, Capital City Green-liveried Scania OmniCity 725 is noted heading down Caerphilly Road with an inbound 27 service from Thornhill.

(Andrew Wiltshire)

Similar to 725, but wearing the new standard fleet livery, number 735 turns into Wellfield Road from Ninian Road on an inbound 29B from Parc Ty Glas. It is the morning rush hour on 4 March 2009, there has just been a heavy shower and the sun is still low in the sky. The building behind the bus is the new Roath Community Hall and library.

(Andrew Wiltshire)

Low-floor double-deckers

With the remaining fleet of elderly Volvo Ailsa double-deckers becoming uneconomical to maintain, and with a commitment to the provision of school contracts, Cardiff Bus sought to purchase some new double-deckers for delivery in 2007, the first for 15 years. An un-registered Volvo B9TL double-decker bound for Delaine Coaches was inspected to examine its East Lancs Olympus body. There followed a £2.7M order for 13 Scanias based on the N270UD chassis that featured a Scania EGR Euro4 engine developing 270bhp and driving through a 6-speed fully-automatic ZF gearbox. A black-box engine management system was also installed. They received East Lancs Olympus bodies of Alusuisse construction and finished to a high specification. Seating was for 74 passengers and 3-point seat belts were installed throughout. Other features included an air-chill system on the upper deck, Vultron LED destination displays, a low-bridge warning, and an on-board audio/visual TV system for broadcasting news and notices. Security was provided by a 12-camera CCTV system with three external cameras. The completed bus was 10.86m long, 4.35m high and had an unladen weight of 12840kg. They were numbered 460 to 472 (CN57 BKA/D/E-G/J-L/O/U, FGA/C/D). 460 and 461 were fitted with tachographs, the latter being exhibited at the 2007 Motor Show.

All 13 buses wore a double-deck variation of the new livery, and in addition had special branding to promote Cardiff Bus and the City of Cardiff. They were soon put to work on routes such as the 44/45, 49/50 and 57/58 as well as performing the schools duties. They also provided particularly useful extra capacity on Event Days such as rugby and football matches at the Millennium Stadium, as well as on Park and Ride services in the weeks up to Christmas and the New Year holidays. It is worth noting that both 460 and 461 can operate at up to 60mph, while the others are governed to a maximum speed of 45mph. After some delay, the first ten arrived in November 2007 and entered service at the beginning of December. 470 and 471 then entered service in early 2008, while 472 did so on 11 March, after a visit to Isle of Man between 26 and 28 February. While there it was employed on a school service and also one stage carriage run, and was inspected by local politicians and transport officials.

The East Lancs Olympus body features a large glazed front elevation which is clearly seen here as 463 passes Roath Community Hall and crosses Marlborough Road into Wellfield Road on a 57 service from Pontprennau on 4 March 2011.

(Andrew Wiltshire)

Driving school upgrade

A change in Driving Standards Agency (DSA) regulations meant that from September 2007 all training buses in the United Kingdom would have to be fitted with ABS braking. As a result of this the three Leyland Lynx trainers 257 to 259 had to be replaced. In July it was announced that Transbus SPD Darts 518 and 520 of 2003 would be converted to permanent driver training buses as they met this criteria, and were relatively young vehicles. During July and August they were repainted in a special yellow and dark grey livery as T518 and T520. It is worth mentioning that, having both previously worn overall advert liveries, these buses had never actually been in fleet livery.

End of an era

Towards the end of 2007 and into early 2008 the last of the Leyland Lynx and Optare Metroriders were withdrawn and sold. The final day of normal Ailsa operation was 3 December, while a Special Running Day was organised for Saturday 15 December and utilised 408 and 436 which carried special notices to mark the occasion. Withdrawals at the start of the year saw the official demise of the last ten Ailsas 401/3/4, 406 to 409, 417/9 and 436. The Ailsa was reckoned to have been by far the longest serving type of motor bus with Cardiff. Some of the early Ailsas put in almost 26 years service with the fleet, and the fact that many examples went on to give further service is a fitting tribute to the type and the care they received by Cardiff Bus.

Even Bigger Buses and Stronger Branding

All seven Alexander Dash-bodied Darts (023 to 029) were withdrawn by early 2008, and 025 to 029 were soon sold for further service. Number 024 was reinstated by September 2008 and repainted into blue for use on a UWIC service alongside newer LMP Darts 233 and 234. Accident damaged MP Dart 161 was repaired and converted into a training bus T161 during March 2008, while 023 became training bus T023 in December 2008. Both gained the yellow and grey "training bus" livery.

Dart 024 now in UWIC Rider livery works the U2 service along Albany Road bound for the Llandaff campus on 29 April 2009. On its regular duty the U2 ran from the City Centre to the UWIC Llandaff campus on Western Avenue via Albany Road, Ninian Road and Whitchurch Road (Monday to Friday term-time only.

(Andrew Wiltshire)

Buses from Ballymena

A further seven Scania saloons acquired in 2008 were built as dealer stock for Scania, but were quite different vehicles, being K230UB models. Unlike the Scania OmniCity based on the N270UB chassis, the K-series Scania has a longitudinally-mounted engine in the rear overhang. The K230 has a 9-litre Euro IV Scania engine of 230bhp and Cardiff Bus's examples featured Wright Solar 12.1m bodywork assembled in Ballymena. They took fleet numbers 761 to 767, but the registrations were rather confusingly allocated in reverse order as CN58 FFZ/Y/X/W/V/U/T. The attractive and functional Wright Solar body with its neat uncluttered interior offered seating for 44 passengers and 26 standing, and the completed bus had an unladen weight of 11007kg. When they first entered service these buses did not carry fleet numbers on their front elevation but that was soon remedied.

Wright Solar-bodied Scania K230 number 764 in West Grove on 6 June 2015, on a working from Pontprennau.

(Andrew Wiltshire)

After an initial spell on the Leckwith Park & Ride, these buses began to enter service from 20 November, when they were normally to be found working to Pontprennau, Llanrumney and St. Mellons. Two of this batch, 766 and 767, went on to receive towing brackets so that they could replace SPD Darts 372 and 373, towing bicycle trailers on the Brecon Beacons National Park summer services.

The last new Scanias

A further nine 41-seat Scania Omnicity saloons were purchased in 2009, arriving in two separate batches throughout the summer. 736 to 739 were delivered in May and June and entered service with registrations CN09 EFH/J/K/L. The second consignment was of five buses which were due to be registered CN09 FYY/Z, FZA-C but were delayed and eventually entered service in September 2009 as 740 to 744 and registered CN59 CKU/V/X/Y,CLF. These nine buses differed slightly from 721-35 as they had a large Scania badge below the windscreen and they would be the last new vehicles for four years.

Scania OmniCity 742 enters Newport bus station on 30 April 2011 followed by a Newport Transport example. In 2016 these buses are still regular performers on the 30, but this vantage point has now vanished with the closure of Newport's Kingsway bus station.

(Andrew Wiltshire)

Earlier in the year it was announced that St. David's Travel would start up services in Cardiff in competition with Cardiff Bus using modern vehicles. This operation began in September 2009 serving the Ely area, though using elderly former London Dennis Darts, painted in a striking black and yellow livery. The operation proved to be relatively short-lived and appeared to have ceased by late February 2010. By now a number of early Cardiff Bus Darts including 384 and former demonstrator 861 had been taken out of service and were gradually being cannibalised for spares, and official withdrawal would eventually follow. Withdrawn Dennis Dart 307 passed in November 2009 to charity Safer Cardiff as a non-PSV and was maintained and garaged by Cardiff Bus as CV4.

Changes in the City Centre

In February 2010 a new free bus service was launched with local authority support following the line of the new "bus box" in an anti-clockwise direction around the city centre. Christened "free b" it ran seven days a week on a 10-minute frequency, and MPD Darts 149 to 151 were given a special yellow livery. The "bus box" saw many city routes relocated from the bus station to new termini around the city centre. The buses travelled in an anti-clockwise direction around the centre with Kingsway, Custom House Street, Bute Terrace, Westgate Street (Royal Hotel) and Churchill Way as major boarding points on the circuit. The "free b" service proved to be a short-lived venture due to poor patronage.

Even Bigger Buses and Stronger Branding

Adding a new splash of colour around Cardiff, MPD number 149 is seen in Wood Street on 15 March 2010, and working the "free b" free bus service around the city centre, following the recent introduction of the "bus box."
(Andrew Wiltshire)

A 100% LOW-FLOOR FLEET

The last step-entrance bus in the passenger fleet, Alexander Dash-bodied Dennis Dart 024, latterly dedicated to the UWIC contracts was withdrawn from service and sold in September 2010, therefore resulting in a 100% low-floor passenger fleet. A programme to refurbish and repaint a number of Dennis Darts got under way this year, and the first buses to be dealt with were the 24 10.1m LMPD Darts. From July 2010, 233 to 244 were sent away to Hants and Dorset Trim at Eastleigh where they were re-upholstered and repainted into the new livery of Scarab green and orange, with 221 to 232 following in due course. MPDs 172 to 187 were repainted into the new livery by a contractor at Newport, while SPDs 389 to 399 and 504 to 517 and 519 were further examples sent away to Hants and Dorset Trim for refurbishment, which was concluded in the spring of 2012. Replacement vehicles selected for the UWIC contract were SPD Darts 501 to 503, and they duly received a revised UWIC Rider blue and pink/mauve livery in the October 2010.

From late 2011 through until early 2012, 11 of the Enviro 300s were sent away for repaint into the latest livery. The exception was 703 which briefly received an overall advert livery for KLM Airlines. It was the final Enviro300 to receive fleet colours and in 2016 is the only one to retain its large luggage rack. In September 2011 the baycar service 6 was extended to serve the Welsh Assembly Government (WAG) offices in Cathays Park (Monday to Friday daytime to early evening) and thus provide a link for WAG employees to the WAG offices and headquarters (Senedd) in Cardiff Bay. The service was also extended at the Cardiff Bay end to serve Roath Lock/ Porth Teigr (Tiger Bay) (every day until early evening). The ten minute frequency remained in place, and these changes increased the peak vehicle requirement (PVR) from four to six.

In November 2012 Cynthia Ogbonna was appointed as the new Managing Director at Cardiff Bus, having been in post as Acting Managing Director for a number of months. She had joined Cardiff Bus as Finance Director in 2004.

Buses withdrawn during 2012 saw the demise of a number of heavily cannibalised SPD Darts including 304 and 312, together with Transbus 10.1m Dart 227 (CN53 AKK) which suffered fire damage whilst in service. In November 2011 the University of Wales Institute Cardiff (UWIC) changed its identity to Cardiff Metropolitan University and as a result the three Darts (501 to 503) allocated to the former UWIC contract, received a new blue livery branded Metrider during the summer of 2012. The services serving this university were also revised at this time.

Cardiff's Municipal Buses

FURTHER TESTING TIMES...........INTERESTING BUSES ON TRIAL

By 2012 a new generation of buses was now coming into production from various manufacturers, and with the Scania OmniCity saloon no longer available, Cardiff Bus needed to look for suitable alternatives. There had been no new vehicles for three years and now the matter of fleet renewal had to be addressed. In late 2012 demonstrator trials began, with a view to ordering 60 new buses for delivery over three years.

The stylish Wright Streetlite DF (door forward) demonstrator ERZ 2028 has been given fleet number 798 for its stay with Cardiff Bus. It has picked up a customer on Ty-Gwyn Road, Cyncoed on a bright and crisp 30 January 2013, whilst allocated to the 52A service.
(Andrew Wiltshire)

Also trialled at this time were Mercedes Citaro demonstrator 799 (BN12 CLO), an Alexander Dennis Enviro 200 797 (YX62 FDG) and an MCV-bodied Volvo B7RLE saloon BF62 UYM. Cardiff Bus also took the opportunity to look at alternatives to the conventional diesel-powered bus and a hybrid and two gas buses were evaluated over the coming months. SN62 DNJ was an Enviro 350H hybrid saloon that arrived on loan from Alexander Dennis in April 2013, and returned for further trials in July.

The Caetano-bodied MAN Ecocity gas bus WX13 GHN was used throughout the city and its livery promoted its environmentally-friendly credentials. It is seen here on Plasmawr Road on 4 June while working the 61. It was powered by compressed natural gas (CNG).
(Andrew Wiltshire)

Even Bigger Buses and Stronger Branding

900 (YT13 YUK) was an Alexander Dennis Enviro 300 CNG-powered bus based on a Scania K270UB chassis. It was used extensively throughout the city in the autumn of 2013. Here it is seen on 23 October turning left into Wood Street from Westgate Street and heading off to Pontprennau.

(Andrew Wiltshire)

In the summer of 2013 Alexander Dennis supplied two diesel-powered demonstrators, YN62 AAK, a Scania K230 with an Enviro 300 body and SN61 DFK, an Enviro 400 double-decker, the latter featuring tinted glass and leather seating. Orders were soon placed for ten Alexander Dennis Enviro 200 E20D models and 20 Mercedes Benz Citaro 0530 saloons, for delivery by the end of the 2013.

Commencing in the summer of 2013 the entire fleet of 19 Scania articulated buses began a thorough mid-life refurbishment at Hants and Dorset Trim, which included a full upholstery re-trim. The four baycar buses (601 to 604) were the first dealt with, emerging in a revised blue-based livery. Numbers 605 to 619 followed in random order, and received standard fleet livery with an orange front for the first time. The programme was concluded with the return of 614 in early 2015.

New buses at last

In November 2013 the first new buses for four years began to enter service. The first to arrive were the ten Alexander Dennis Enviro 200 E20D saloons which were numbered from 251 to 260 with registrations CN63 NZF-H/J/K/M-P/R. These buses had an overall length of 10.8m and a width of 2.44m and were fitted with Cummins ISBe 4.5 litre Euro V engines and had Voith 3-speed fully-automatic gearboxes. In addition to the 39 seats they could accommodate 28 standing passengers. Other features included LED destinations displays and next stop bilingual audio-visual information, both produced by Hanover. They soon appeared on the 95/95A routes which served Heath Hospital and Barry Island, and also worked some of the lighter routes around the city such as the 1, 2, 36 and 52. During the latter part of 2013 the option was taken up with Alexander Dennis for a further ten Enviro 200 E20D saloons for delivery in 2014.

Alexander Dennis Enviro 200 256 waits in Canal Street at the rear of Cardiff's Central Library with a working to Channel View, Grangetown, on 28 May 2014. Note the emergency exit positioned in the low-floor area of the bus.

(Andrew Wiltshire)

The final deliveries for 2013 were 20 splendid Mercedes Benz Citaro 0530 saloons. These were standard single-door 11.95m vehicles with Cardiff Bus's choice of upholstery. Numbered 101 to 120 with out of sequence registrations CN63 NYU-Z, NZA-D, NZS/T, NYL-P/R-T, they entered service from early December. With seating for 40 and additional room for 30 standing, the Citaros featured the 6-cylinder horizontal Mercedes Benz OM906 6.37 litre diesel of 286bhp to meet Euro V emissions regulations. They featured the same Hanover destination screens and next-stop bilingual audio and visual information systems as the ten Enviro E20Ds.

Mercedes Benz Citaro 119 waits in the rain at the Cardiff East Park and Ride site at Pentwyn on 26 January 2014. This is the inaugural day of operation, and 119 complete with X59 branding is about to undertake the first departure at 10.00.

(Gareth Stevens)

Even Bigger Buses and Stronger Branding

A number of Dennis Darts were officially removed from fleet strength during 2013, including 317, 320, 384 and 861 which had been gradually cannibalised for spare parts over a long period of time, and were sold for scrap. Training bus T023, the last step-entrance bus owned, passed into preservation while the sale of Darts 144 to 159, 166 and 168, 187 was a direct result of new vehicles entering service.

In January 2014 Mercedes Citaros 117 to 120 were branded for the X59 Cardiff East Park and Ride service which Cardiff Bus had just taken over from First Bus. Cardiff Bus also took responsibility for managing the site at Pentwyn. The service, which runs into Churchill Way, takes advantage of numerous bus-priority schemes and has become a major success. It is popular with commuters, shoppers and people attending major events in the city, and by early 2015, heavy loadings meant that it required the use of double-deckers on Saturdays. On certain special event days, bendy-buses are often employed.

New buses received in November 2014 were the follow up batch of Enviro 200 E20D saloons, 261 to 270 (CN64 FWJ-M/O/P/R-U). All had entered service by December and unlike 251 to 260, these featured Voith 4-speed gearboxes. They were similar to the first batch, except that the entire roof area was painted Scarab green, 251 to 260 had white roof centres. In addition 270 was fitted with a tachograph. With 20 of this type of bus now in service, their duties became more widespread across Cardiff, although a good number can usually be found on the Penarth and Barry area services. Further Darts were taken out of service during 2014 and included 162 and 183 plus the last SPD examples from the initial batch, 316 and 319.

Euro 6

With 20 vehicles yet to be ordered from the original plan to order 60, and the desire to acquire vehicles that conformed to Euro 6 emission legislation, further demonstrator trials began in November 2014. The first vehicle taken on loan was an Alexander Dennis Enviro 400MMC E40D double-decker YY64 GWX painted in a dark blue livery. It was given temporary fleet number 794, and remained on loan for about 6 weeks appearing on a number of different routes. The year 2015 got off to an interesting start with the arrival of more Euro 6 compliant demonstrators. In January a Mercedes Benz Citaro 0530K 10.5m single-decker (BV14 TZY) was used exclusively on the Cardiff West Park and Ride for a week or so as fleet number 793. In early February a Wright Gemini 3-bodied Volvo B5TL arrived on a two-week loan and was allocated fleet number 792 (BX14 SYT) being used on a variety of services. The 73 seat bus was previously registered 141 D 19194 as a demonstrator with Dublin Bus. A full size 41-seat Mercedes Citaro 0295 was also taken on loan for about ten days. It was 791 (BP14 FJZ) and returned again briefly in May. Number 790 (YX64 VOO) was another Alexander Dennis Enviro 400MMC E40D double-decker on loan during March and wore a silver livery.

The shape of things to come. In March 2015 Cardiff Bus tried a second Enviro 400MMC demonstrator YX64 VOO, but this time with a higher seating capacity of 80. Given temporary fleet number 790, it is seen on 20 March returning from a trip to Thornhill on the 27.
(Andrew Wiltshire)

In 2015 free 4G WiFi was initially introduced on Mercedes Citaros 101 to 120 from January, and had been installed throughout the entire fleet by the end of March. This month also saw the Wayfarer ticket machines replaced by the Ticketer system which has an integrated GPS system to relay Real Time Information via bus stop displays or smartphone apps. Early in 2015 the remaining MP Darts numbered below 188 were withdrawn and all but one were sold, while the first W-registration SPD Dart 368, was withdrawn in April and sold for scrap.

Double-deck makeover

In April 2005 East Lancs Olympus-bodied Scania double-decker 460 was the first of the type to be sent away for refurbishment at Hants and Dorset Trim. This involved the installation of new seats throughout, which gave the vehicle a revised and more useful seating capacity of 78 plus 5 standing. Seat belts were no longer a feature, and 460 re-entered service in July 2015 sporting a slightly revised livery and a reduced unladen weight of 12060kg, a saving of 780kg. Next in line for similar treatment were 461 to 466. In early May an order for ten Mercedes Citaro 0295 12m saloons and ten Alexander Dennis Enviro 400MMC 11.4m double-deckers was announced, all to Euro 6 specification.

460 was the first of the East Lancs Olympus bodied Scanias to be refurbished in 2015. Visible detail differences in this view include the orange painted front bumper and the new seats with their orange head rests. The bus is passing City Link retail park, Newport Road, inbound on 19 September 2015.

(Andrew Wiltshire)

Once again there was further competition for Cardiff Bus as local and rapidly expanding operator New Adventure Travel (NAT) entered the arena on 11 May, with a new cross-town service numbered X1. This followed a route from Culverhouse Cross (Tesco) to Pontprennau (Asda) running via the City Centre, and unlike earlier operators that competed with Cardiff, NAT deployed a fleet of ten new livery-branded buses.

At 23.20 on 1 August 2015 the last bus departed from Cardiff's Central Bus Station which was then subsequently closed for demolition and redevelopment. There had been a bus station on this site for 61 years. Services were moved to other locations across the city centre.

Even Bigger Buses and Stronger Branding

Large double-deckers

In 2014 Alexander Dennis re-launched its very successful Enviro 400 double-deck model christened the MMC (Major Model Change), which would continue to be available in both hybrid and conventional diesel form. It was lighter and more fuel efficient and featured a completely revised style of body to allow a greater seating capacity, and an interior that incorporated a new heating and ventilation system. The diesel version was powered by the Cummins 6.7-litre engine that conforms to Euro 6 emission standards. Much thought had been put into the design of the driver's cab area, which is more spacious, with improved visibility. Cardiff's ten Enviro 400MMC E40Ds were delivered in late August into early September, and numbered 301 to 310 (CN65 AAE/F/J/K/O/U/V/X/Y/Z). They have an unladen weight of 11365kg and seating for 85 passengers with an additional space for 14 standing, making an impressive total of 99 persons. The first examples entered service on 5 September and all were in service within three weeks. They became regular performers on routes to Pontprennau, St. Mellons and Pentrebane, and of course would provide useful capacity on the Cardiff East Park and Ride at busy times. These are the largest double-deckers ever operated by Cardiff.

The new Mercedes Benz Citaro 0295 (Euro 6) introduced a revised body style with a deeper glazed area at the front of the bus and a waist rail that followed the contours of the wheel arches. The seating trim was to Cardiff's standard specification, and the layout was much neater over the rear axle, compared to the first 20 Citaros 101 to 120. Nine of these smart 41-seat buses arrived in Cardiff from 16 September to form the batch numbered 121 to 130 (CN65 ABF/K/O/U/V/X/Z, ACF/J/O). The outstanding vehicle 125 (CN65 ABV) was exhibited in the demonstration park at Coach and Bus Live at the NEC on 30 September and 1 October 2015, before making its way to Cardiff. They are powered by a Mercedes OM936h 6-cylinders (Euro 6) engine developing 220kw and transmission is by way of a 6-speed ZF Ecolife automatic gearbox. They have an unladen weight of 10855kg and all were in service by the week ending 16 October 2015. Fleet numbers appeared in cream as opposed to white. All 20 new buses feature 4G Wi-Fi, USB charging points and next stop audio-visual information.

The 306, one of the ten 85 seat Alexander Dennis Enviro 400MMC models new in 2015. Seen here on the X59 Cardiff East Part and Ride route, 19 September 2015 when still quite new.
(Andrew Wiltshire)

As a result of these new vehicles, a number of SPD type Dennis Darts were withdrawn and disposed of, including the remaining W-registered examples dating from 2000.

In January 2016 a 37-seat Alexander Dennis Enviro 200 demonstrator in overall white livery, SN15 LLA, was taken on loan to cover for Enviro 200 262 which had suffered accident damage. It featured a ZF gearbox and was given fleet number 789 seeing service on the City Circle and X91 during its stay.

CHAPTER ELEVEN

SOME OTHER ASPECTS OF THE UNDERTAKING

THE WHO'S WHO IN CHARGE AT CARDIFF

There have been just 12 periods of leadership in the Cardiff fleet since municipal operations began back in 1902. As can be seen from the table below a number of managers remained in post for long periods of time. The title General Manager was used up until the retirement of David Smith in 1986, since when the title Managing Director was used to describe the senior post at the undertaking.

FROM	UNTIL	MANAGER
1902	1920	Arthur Ellis
1920	1928	Robert L Horsfield
1928	1940	William Forbes (died in post 31 May 1940)
1940	1946	Jointly managed by W J Evans (Engineer) and J W Dunning (Traffic Manager)
1946	1948	John W Dunning
1948	1962	John F Siddall
1962	1971	Edwin G A Singleton
1971	1986	David R Smith
1986	1998	Frank Yates
1998	2004	Alan Kreppel
2004	2012	David Brown
2012	Present	Cynthia Ogbonna (she was stand-in MD from July to November 2012)

OFFICIAL TITLES FOR THE UNDERTAKING

The title of the operator and the legend or fleet name that appears on the vehicles have changed on a number of occasions over the years. This has in part been due to local political changes, but can also be attributed to the desire to create new bold images for the fleet.

Period	Official title	Fleet name carried
1902 to 1933	Cardiff City Tramways (trams and buses) Cardiff Corporation Tramways (trams) Cardiff City Tramways and Motors (buses)	Any of these would be carried on vehicles. The first one was soon abandoned. 'Cardiff Corporation Tramways and Motors' was used on literature.
1933 to 1964	Cardiff Corporation Transport Department (trams, buses and trolleybuses)	The word 'Department' was soon dropped from vehicles, which then carried Cardiff Corporation Transport as a fleet name.
1964 to 1986	City of Cardiff Transport	From 1972 the fleet name Cardiff Buses was trialed but City of Cardiff/Dinas Caerdydd was adopted. 'Cardiff Buses' was however used on timetables.
1986 to present	Cardiff City Transport Services Limited	The fleet name Cardiff Bus/Bws Caerdydd was most commonly used.

Some Other Aspects of the Undertaking

THE LIVERIES

The livery used from the initial introduction of the electric tramcars in 1902 was crimson lake and cream with black lining on the cream and gold lining on the crimson. Crimson lake was the official description and has been used throughout this book, but many also refer to it as maroon. The various titles for the fleet were found along the bottom edge of the lower panels, large gold letters on trams and small gold letters on trolley and motor buses. The only variation to this livery was a special ivory scheme on AEC Regal saloons 149 and 150 in 1937, for their use on sightseeing tours.

New in 1938, Northern Counties-bodied AEC Regent 184 (BBO 69) is a good example of the pre-war crimson lake and cream livery with full lining-out and a cream roof.

(Roy Marshall collection courtesy of The Omnibus Society)

Prior to 1939 cream roofs had become standard. During the war an all-grey primer livery was adopted and surprisingly after hostilities ceased, vehicles continued to be turned out in all-grey for a number of years, many lasting until at least 1950. Following the war some of the AEC trolleybuses received a smart streamlined crimson lake and cream livery for a few years. The gold lining was gradually phased out by 1953, and it is thought that AEC Regal 148 was the last example to be so adorned. Black lining on the cream was not used post-war, black now being confined to separate the crimson lake and cream areas as well as enhancing the mudguards. In 1963 Leyland PD3As 402 to 407 were the last new buses delivered with black lining. Black mudguards then disappeared too, and from 1964 the new title City of Cardiff began to appear on the cream area just below the lower saloons windows.

From late 1963 the cream areas of the livery were gradually reduced, though the paint shops at Sloper Road and Roath each had their own ideas of exactly how the fleet livery should be interpreted. Towards the late 1960s Roath began applying an acceptable proportion of cream while Sloper Road on the other hand sought to reduce it even further. Livery experiments were undertaken in early 1972 with the intention of introducing a fresh new image for the fleet. Both aquamarine and dark orange were rejected as primary colours in the summer of 1972 in favour of light orange (tangerine) with a white band which remained in use until the late 1990s.

What might have been. The aquamarine experimental livery is seen to superb effect on Guy Arab V 461. The bus is negotiating the Caerphilly crossroads roundabout and heading for Templeton Avenue in the evening rush hour of 30 August 1972.
(John Wiltshire)

Special and advert liveries aside (these are listed elsewhere), in later years there were other variations to the fleet livery. In 1976 two open-top buses appeared in overall white with orange bands, while the following year saw the introduction of a new coach livery of overall white with a deep orange band. Black relief was experimented with on five Leyland Olympians in 1981/83 but not adopted. The low-height (coach-seated) Olympians delivered in 1985/86 had their own distinctive livery using a larger area of white, while from 1987 Metrorider midibuses carried a special and distinctive Clipper livery. The slogan "Pick an Orange" was in use by Cardiff Bus from October 1986 appearing on vehicles and literature, and finally disappeared around 2000. From 1990 the double-deck livery was generally enhanced with additional white paint, but this was not applied to the Bristol VRTs. The Leyland Lynx launched a new livery in 1989 of white with a brown roof and orange skirt, and variations of this appeared on many subsequent deliveries of saloons and midibuses until 1998.

A complete change of image occurred in 1999 when a new livery of Burges blue and cream with a narrow orange band was adopted for all new low-floor vehicles, but also appeared on the refurbished Leyland Lynx IIs as well. Further changes in 2006/07 witnessed the introduction of branded liveries for specific routes using a base colour of Scarab green. A new bold and modern Scarab green-based livery with the front of the bus in orange was designed by Best Impressions. This began to appear on all new and some existing buses from late 2007. On the side of the bus the legend Cardiff Bus appeared in cream while Bws Caerdydd appeared in yellow. This was repeated on the front of the vehicle with Cardiff Bus in white and Bws Caerdydd in light green. This livery remains in use in 2016.

Some Other Aspects of the Undertaking

122 one of the new Euro6 specification Mercedes Benz Citaro saloons, passes the Urban Tap House on Westgate Street on 20 November 2015. The bus is inbound from Pontprennau and the destination display has already been reset for a return working on the 58.

(Andrew Wiltshire)

The Coat of Arms

The coat of arms and motifs as carried on vehicles was subject to many changes over the years.

Before 1905	Original specification before City status
1905 to 1969	Much more elaborate
1969 to 1972	A much smaller design and simplified style using more pastel shades
1972 to 1986	Simplified style, gold on a black disc or black on a white disc
1986 to 1988	Coat of arms not used post-deregulation
1988 to 1991	Traditional multi-coloured coat of arms
1991 to 1997	New Cardiff motif featuring a red dragon is adopted
1997 to 1999	None
1999 to 2007	Cardiff County Council's dancing dragon logo in green
2007 to date	Cardiff County Council's dancing dragon logo in yellow or green

The fleet numbering system

Trams

The original electric trams introduced from 1902 were numbered from 1 to 130 with 131 being the Brush rail-cleaning service car. The second generation trams commenced with 101 and then took random fleet numbers vacated by withdrawn first generation tramcars. The second generation saloons cars were slightly more ordered being allocated random numbers between 41 and 54, then blocks from 116 to 124 and 126 to 137.

Motor buses and trolleybuses

The allocation of fleet numbers to buses over the years is interesting. Originally the licence number allocated to vehicles by the Watch Committee (Cardiff's police force) was the number adopted by Cardiff Corporation as a fleet number. By 1935 this system had become misleading and so a new fleet number scheme based upon type of bus was introduced.

1 >	Double-deckers, oil engined, high-bridge (except 23)
51 >	Double-deckers, petrol engined, low-bridge (53 to 62 soon became oil engined.)
101>	Single-deckers

The motor bus fleet expanded rapidly from 1935 and the new system was soon found to be inadequate. A new series for high-bridge, oil engined double-deckers commenced from 151 in 1937, while the handful of single-deckers acquired, occupied the sequence 143 to 150. During and after the Second World War new additions took fleet numbers vacated by withdrawn vehicles. Trolleybuses however were all numbered from 201 upwards from the outset. In 1956 a new series for motor buses began at 301 and continued until 605 was reached in early 1974. From 1974 fleet numbers were allocated by vehicles types as set out below.

1 to 99	Coaches, open-toppers and experimental buses
101 to 199	Midi-buses
201 to 299	Full-size single-deckers
301>	Double-deckers (Bristol VRTs)
401>	" (Volvo Ailsas)
501>	" (Leyland Olympians)
601>	" (Scania N113)

Exceptions to this were Dennis Darts 023 to 029.

From 1998 this was revised as older types were eliminated and the double-deck fleet was greatly reduced in strength.

144 to 250	Dart midi-buses
301> then 501>	Dart full-size saloons
601>	Articulated buses
460>	Double-deckers
701>	Full-size saloons (Enviro 300 and Scanias)

The latest series for new vehicles dates from late 2013.

101>	Mercedes Citaro full-size saloons
251>	Alexander Dennis Enviro 200 full-size saloons
301>	Alexander Dennis Enviro 400MMC double-deckers

Since the 1980s, service and ancillary vehicles have usually been allocated fleet numbers randomly between 021 and 099. It is interesting to note that since 2003, demonstrators taken on loan were often numbered in a temporary series upwards from 001, while from late 2013 they took temporary fleet numbers downwards from 799.

Depots and garages

Tram sheds

Three small horse-tram sheds were acquired with the Cardiff Tramway operation in January 1902, these being at Wood Street, Lucas Street and Severn Road. The Wood Street shed was adapted to house about ten single-deck electric tramcars and opened as such on 31 March 1904. Another small depot in Clive Street came with the Cardiff District and Penarth Harbour Company in February 1903. Part of the Roath depot on Newport Road officially opened 18 September 1902 serving the eastern area tram routes. It eventually housed up to 100 trams. This building featured a 4-track entrance leading to 12 roads inside the shed. There was a traverser and a number of repair shops.

The 31 single-deck cars received from Brush in 1925/26 were attractive-looking trams. This is thought to be car number 50 and is seen on Newport Road outside Roath depot.
(The late Dave B. Thomas collection)

Located in the Grangetown area, the smaller Clare Road site also opened as a tram shed in 1902 and could house 32 tramcars. Its entrance was modified in 1923 and the shed was extended in December 1927 to accommodate a further 36 trams.

Trolleybus garages

The first trolleybuses were initially based at Clare Road which was adapted to house them from March 1942, and closed to trams completely on 28 August 1946. In October 1948 Roath was modified so that it could overhaul trolleybuses, and following the closure of the tram system in 1950, trolleybuses were also based at this site. Finally on 25 October 1953 the Clare Road depot closed and its allocation of trolleybuses was transferred to Roath to join the others. The building was transferred to the Public Works Department and remained in use for many years, but had closed by 2012. Appropriately named the Tramshed, a portion of the building opened as a live music venue in late 2015, and remains a Grade II listed structure. All trolleybuses remained at Roath until closure of the system in January 1970. The former trolleybus routes then continued to be operated from Roath by motor buses. For many years there was a small in-house foundry at Roath depot that produced trolley-heads, bus stop signs and radiator caps amongst other things.

Motor bus garages

The first motor buses were garaged in small premises at Andrews Road in Llandaff North, and also in the old tramway shed at Wood Street in the town centre while others were often housed at the Roath depot and Clare Road sites. In 1929 the disused Lucas Street horse-tram shed was re-opened to accommodate some motor buses. This unsatisfactory situation was resolved on 29 July 1931 when the Lord Mayor of Cardiff (Alderman R G Hill-Snook) opened a modern garage and workshop facility at Sloper Road, Leckwith. Capable of housing 106 vehicles, all motor buses would now be garaged here, and the Llandaff North and Wood Street sites were sold off. In March 1938 an extension opened at Sloper Road which could now house 150 vehicles.

In 1935 some brake-testing apparatus for the motor bus fleet was installed at Sloper Road, while in 1949 a Weaver steam jenny was installed for cleaning chassis and engines. The following year an Essex bus washing machine was installed and a chassis cleaning ramp was built at one end of the main west yard. From 1951 Roath became the central works and stores for the overhaul of both motor and trolleybuses. In 1964 diesel fuel tanks were installed at Roath for the first time and motor buses were subsequently based here for service as the rundown of the trolleybus system began. By 1965 a Widney "drive-through" bus-washing machine was installed at Sloper Road. By 1968 a Dawson "drive-through" bus-washing machine had been installed at Roath while in 1969/70 the blacksmith's shop was converted into a fibreglass preparation shop. Roath depot closed as an operational garage in 19 April 1980, but remained open as the main engineering works. Even in 1980 there were many telltale signs such as visible tram rails set into the floor, as a reminder of the depot's origins as a tram shed.

This splendid cartoon of wartime activity at Roath depot was thought to have been created by Peter Arch, who was later foreman coach painter at the site.
(Courtesy of Glyn Bowen)

Sloper Road was initially rebuilt from 1977 being completed in February 1979. The undercover accommodation was enlarged by building over the yard adjacent to Newton Road. A new signing-on office and first floor canteen and kitchen were built at the front of the garage. A second phase from 1982 saw the relocation of the body shop and bus wash. In February 1985 the front of the garage was extended outwards onto the forecourt which was much reduced in area leaving just a lane width. A new office block was constructed on former railway land and both the undercover and open parking areas were also extended, all being completed during early 1986. Roath depot was closed completely in September 1986, when all remaining engineering operations were concentrated on Sloper Road. Roath was subsequently demolished in June/July 1987, and a retail outlet later appeared on this site. In early 2012 Cardiff Bus purchased an annexe, situated almost opposite the main garage on Sloper Road. This provides additional secure overnight parking for around 40 buses and is referred to as "Sloper Road 2".

Some Other Aspects of the Undertaking

A nice study of Bristol KW6G number 127, which is seen standing in the sun at Sloper Road depot. It has been rebuilt, but without any rubber-mounted windows though it does have a revised destination box. The chassis-cleaning ramp is clearly visible behind the bus.

(Glyn Bowen courtesy Chris Taylor CTPG)

The services

Map of routes in 1951

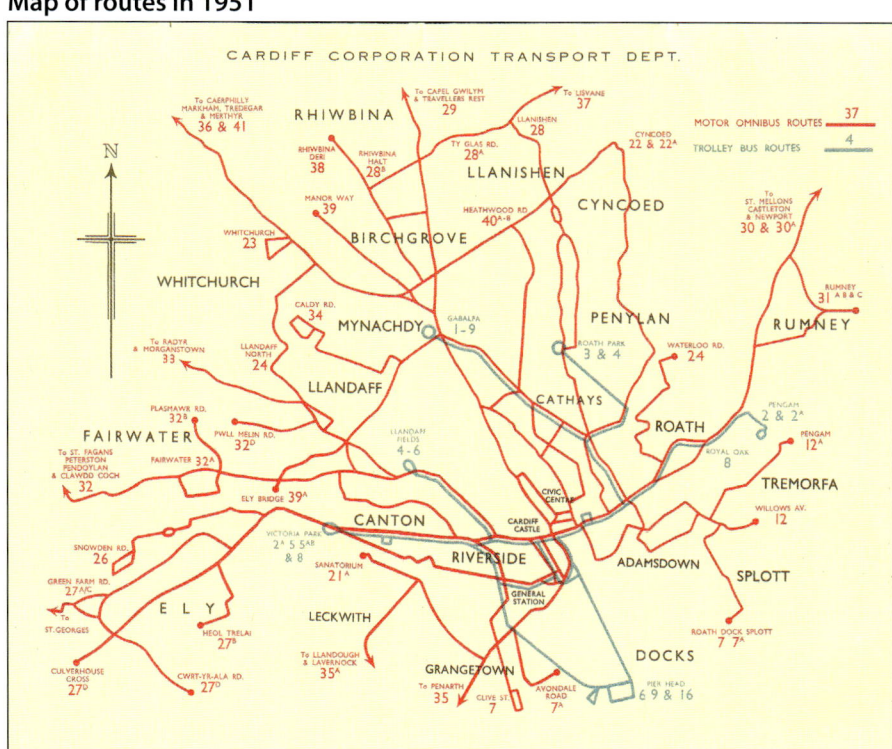

The evolution of the early tram and motor bus routes has already been briefly described in the text, as have the chain of events which saw the decline of the tramway network in Cardiff, and progressive introduction of trolleybuses in their place. The motor bus services continued to evolve as the city grew in size geographically, and its population increased from about 173,000 in 1902 to approximately 350,000 by 2016. Today services are regularly revised and improved to meet changes in demand as well as addressing timing issues. One of the major headaches for Cardiff Bus in recent years has been congestion in and around the city, and in particular unpredictable congestion, which appears with little warning and can cause havoc with time-keeping. Many bus-priority measures such as bus lanes have been introduced in the last couple of decades, which can greatly reduce journey times for Cardiff Bus's customers.

\multicolumn{3}{c}{SUMMARY OF SERVICES IN JUNE 1956}
\multicolumn{3}{c}{TROLLEYBUS SERVICES}
Route no.	Area served	Comments
1	St. Mary St. to Gabalfa	
2	St. Mary St. to Pengam	
3	St. Mary St. to Roath Park	
4	Roath Park to Llandaff Fields	
5	Victoria Park to Windsor Lane	
5A	Victoria Park, Castle St., High St., Wood St., Neville St., Victoria Park	
5B	Victoria Park, Neville St., Wood St., High St., Castle St., Victoria Park	
6	Llandaff Fields to Pier Head	
8	Victoria Park to Royal Oak	
9	Gabalfa to Pier Head	
10A	Wood St. to Green Farm Rd. (Ely) via Grand Avenue	Return via Cowbridge Road
10B	Wood St. to Green Farm Rd. (Ely) via Cowbridge Rd West	Return via Grand Avenue
16	Monument to Pier Head (via Bute St)	Single-deck service
\multicolumn{3}{c}{MOTOR BUS SERVICES}
7	Roath Dock and Splott to Clive St. (Grangetown)	
7A	Roath Dock and Splott to Avondale Rd. (Grangetown)	
12	Monument to Tweedsmuir Rd (Tremorfa)	
12A	C.B.S. to Splott Rd via Sanquhar St.	
12B	C.B.S. to Splott Rd via Constellation St.	
22	St. John Square to Cyncoed via Penylan	
22A	St. John Square to Cyncoed via Rhydypennau	
22B	Greyfriars Rd to Llanedeyrn (Heol Pant Glas school)	Tuesday and Friday only
23	C.B.S. to Whitchurch	
24	Kingsway, Whitchurch, Llandaff North, Castle St to Waterloo Rd.	
26	General Station to Snowden Rd (Ely)	
27	General Station to St. Georges-super-Ely	Monday to Saturday
27B	Victoria Park to Heol Trelai (Ely)	
27D	General Station to Culverhouse Cross	
28	Greyfriars Rd. to Llanishen Church	
28A	Kingsway to Templeton Avenue via North Rd **or** Lake Rd West	
28B	Kingsway to Rhiwbina Halt	
29	Kingsway to Thornhill (Travellers' Rest) (connects with C.U.D.C. bus)	Monday to Saturday
30	C.B.S. to Newport	Joint with Newport C.T.
31	Greyfriars Rd to Llanrumney Avenue (Llanrumney)	
31A	C.B.S. to Countisbury Avenue (Llanrumney)	
31B	Greyfriars Rd. to Greenway Rd. via Cross Inn	

	MOTOR BUS SERVICES cont.	
31C	Greyfriars Rd. to Greenway Rd. via New Rd.	
32A	C.B.S. to Fairways Crescent (Fairwater) via Chargot Rd.	
32B	C.B.S. to Keyston Rd. (Fairwater) via Plasmawr Rd.	
32D	C.B.S. to Cosheston Rd. (Fairwater) via Pwllmelin Rd.	Monday to Saturday
33	C.B.S. to Radyr and Morganstown	
34	Kingsway to Caldy Rd (Gabalfa)	
35	C.B.S., Cogan, Penarth Centre to Lower Penarth	
35A	C.B.S., Llandough, Redlands Rd, Lower Penarth	Joint with Western Welsh
36	C.B.S., Caerphilly, Markham to Tredegar	Joint with C.U.D.C. or W.M.O.B.
37	Sanatorium Rd, Sloper Rd, Wood St., Llanishen to Lisvane	Monday to Saturday
39	Pier Head, Mill Lane, Gabalfa to Manor Way	
39A	Pier Head, Mill Lane, Gabalfa to Ely Bridge	
40A	C.B.S. to Heathwood Rd. via Whitchurch Rd. and North Rd.	
40B	C.B.S. to Heathwood Rd. via Allensbank Rd.	
41	C.B.S. to Merthyr Tydfil	Joint with M.T.C. and R.T.C.
-	Fitzalan Rd. and Llandough Hospital special journeys	Monday to Friday (evenings) Saturday and Sunday (pm)
-	General station to East Moors Rd. (Steel works service)	Monday to Saturday
-	General station to Lewis Rd./ East Tyndall St. (Steel works service)	

C.B.S. is Central Bus Station. C.U.D.C. is Caerphilly Urban District Council. WMOB is West Mon Omnibus Board.

M.T.C. is Merthyr Tydfil Corporation. R.T.C. is Rhondda Transport Co. Newport C.T. is Newport Corporation Transport.

A number of terminus locations in the above table such as Royal Oak and Llandaff Fields, which dated back to the tram era, will not be found in the following table, as most routes these days extend well beyond these points. New names such as Cardiff Bay, Sports Village and Parc Ty Glas are based on sites that have been re-developed over the years while Drope, Thornhill, Danescourt and Pontprennau are examples of more recent housing developments on the outer fringes of the city. Cardiff General Station was renamed Central Station in the 1970s.

	SUMMARY OF SERVICES IN AUGUST 2015	
Route no.	Area served	Comments
1	City Circle (serving Cardiff Bay, Canton, UHW, Tremorfa)	Monday to Saturday
2	City Circle (serving Tremorfa, UHW, Canton, Cardiff Bay)	Monday to Saturday
6	baycar Cathays Park to Porth Teigr	Monday to Friday (office hours)
6	baycar City Centre to Cardiff Bay	Evenings and weekends
7	City Centre, Cardiff Bay and Sports Village	Monday to Saturday
8	City Centre, Grangetown, County Hall and Pier Head	
9	City Centre, Grangetown, Ferry Rd and Sports Village	
9A	City Centre, Grangetown and Channel View	Monday to Saturday
11	City Centre to Pengam Green via Tremorfa	

\multicolumn{3}{c}{SUMMARY OF SERVICES IN AUGUST 2015 cont.}
12	Leckwith Retail Park, Canton, Caerau and Drope	Monday to Friday
13	City Centre to Drope via Victoria Park	
15	City Centre, Ely and UHW	Monday to Saturday
17	City Centre to Ely (via Heol Trelai and on to Grand Ave)	
18	City Centre to Ely (via Grand Ave and on to Heol Trelai)	
21	City Centre, Rhiwbina, Pantmawr, Whitchurch	
23	City Centre, Whitchurch, Pantmawr, Rhiwbina	
21A	City Centre, Rhiwbina, Pantmawr, Whitchurch, UHW and Rhydypennau	Monday to Saturday
23A	Rhydypennau, UHW, Whitchurch, Pantmawr, Rhiwbina and City Centre	Monday to Saturday
24	City Centre, Whitchurch Library	
25	City Centre, Pontcanna, Llandaff North, Whitchurch, City Centre	
24A	City Centre to Whitchurch Library	Monday to Saturday
25A	Whitchurch Library to City Centre	Monday to Saturday
27	City Centre to Thornhill and Llanishen	
28	City Centre, Lake Rd West, Llanishen, Thornhill, Parc Ty Glas and Fishguard Rd	Monday to Saturday
28A	City Centre, Lake Rd West, Fishguard Rd, Parc Ty Glas, Thornhill, Llanishen	Monday to Saturday
28B	City Centre, Lake Rd West, Llanishen, Thornhill	
30	Cardiff to Newport via Castleton	Joint with Newport Bus
35	City Centre to Gabalfa (via Cathays Terrace)	
36	City Centre to Gabalfa (via North Rd)	
38	City Centre to UHW (via City Rd, Gabalfa Interchange and Rhydhelig Ave)	
38A	City Centre to UHW (via City Rd, Gabalfa Interchange)	
41	Pontprennau, Penylan, City Rd to Cardiff & Vale College (Canal Parade)	Monday to Friday (term time)
44/44B	City Centre to St. Mellons (via New Rd and Brynbala Way)	44B extends to Business Park
45/45B	City Centre to St. Mellons (via Cae Glas Rd)	45B extends to Business Park
46	City Centre to St. Mellons (via New Rd)	Peak times only
49	City Centre to Llanrumney (via Llanrumney Ave)	
50	City Centre to Llanrumney (via Ball Rd)	
51	City Centre, Llanedeyrn, Pentwyn, Cyncoed, UHW return via Cathays	Monday to Saturday
52	City Centre to Cyncoed MET and Cyncoed Village (via Albany Rd)	
54	City Centre to Lakeside and Cyncoed Village	
57	City Centre to Pontprennau (via Hollybush Inn)	

Some Other Aspects of the Undertaking

\multicolumn{3}{|c|}{SUMMARY OF SERVICES IN AUGUST 2015 cont.}		
Route no.	Area served	Comments
58	City Centre to Pontprennau (via Holiday Inn)	
X59	City Centre to Cardiff East park and ride, Asda Pontprennau and Cardiff Gate Business Park	Saturday (P&R and Asda only)
61	City Centre to Pentrebane (via Wyndham Cres and Fairwater Green)	
62	City Centre to Danescourt (via Pontcanna and Llandaff)	
63	Radyr (via Llandaff and Danescourt)	
64	Ely, Pentrebane, Llandaff North, Whitchurch, Birchgrove, UHW, New Rd, St.Mellons and Llanrumney	Monday to Saturday
65	Ely, Pentrebane, Llandaff North, Whitchurch, Birchgrove, UHW, Llanrumney, St. Mellons and New Rd	Monday to Saturday
66	City Centre to Danescourt (via Canton and Llandaff)	Monday to Saturday
86	City Centre to Lisvane (via Cathays, Heath and Llanishen)	Monday to Saturday
X91	Cardiff to Llantwit Major (via Ely Link Rd, Wenvoe and St. Athan)	Monday to Saturday
92	City Centre to Penarth (St. Lukes Ave) (via Cogan)	
92B	City Centre to Penarth (St. Lukes Ave) (via Bessemer Rd & Cogan)	Monday to Friday
93	City Centre to Penarth, Dinas Powys and Barry Waterfront	Monday to Saturday
94	City Centre to Penarth, Sully and Barry Waterfront	
94B	City Centre to Penarth, Sully and Barry Waterfront (via Bessemer Rd)	Monday to Friday
95	UHW, City Centre to Barry and Barry Island	
95A	City Centre to Penarth Town Centre (via Leckwith Retail Park)	Monday to Saturday
96	City Centre to Barry Waterfront (via Ely, Wenvoe, Colcot)	Monday to Saturday
96A	City Centre to Barry Hospital & Waterfront (via Ely, Wenvoe, Colcot)	
97	Barry Town Circular (clockwise)	Monday to Saturday
97A	Barry Town Circular (anti-clockwise)	Monday to Saturday
98	Highlight Park, Barry Waterfront to Kings Square (Barry)	Monday to Friday
-	City Centre to Cardiff West park and ride	Monday to Friday
M1	*Metrider* Plas Gwyn halls, Cardiff MET Llandaff, Cardiff MET Cyncoed	Monday to Friday (term time)
M2	*Metrider* Cardiff MET Llandaff, Albany Rd and City Rd	Monday to Friday (term time)
M3	*Metrider* Cardiff MET Llandaff, Pontcanna, City Centre, North Rd to Cardiff MET Llandaff	Monday to Friday (term time)
M4	*Metrider* Cardiff MET Llandaff, North Rd, City Centre, Pontcanna to Cardiff MET Llandaff	Monday to Friday (term time)

UHW is University Hospital of Wales, Heath.

Metrider is the brand name for Cardiff Metropolitan University (Cardiff MET) services.

Facts and Figures

YEAR	MILES OPERATED	PASSENGERS CARRIED	INCOME	CITY POPULATION
1903	1,824,072	18,038,525	£78,073	164,333
1933	6,802,520	45,918,238	£381,409	226,937
1963	8,638,673	80,395,135	£1,559,880	260,640
1973	6,507,766	45,595,624	£2,528,504	276,880
1984	6,231,659	32,830,661	£10,464,706	279,800

Destination and Route Number Blinds

Over the years the destination displays on Cardiff's buses have evolved from sign-written boards to a variety of roller blind arrangements that adopted a number of different layouts and with varying amounts of information. Possibly the neatest arrangement was that used on new vehicles delivered from 1964 to 1970. However like all the previous arrangements, it did not give much scope for flexibility when services were revised or routes renumbered. This problem was partly addressed from 1971 when 2-track route numbers blinds meant changes could be made very quickly. From 1973 single-line displays now showing the ultimate destination, made for a neater and easier to read blind. The real benefits came with the electronic digital displays which allowed customised displays which could be updated with relative ease and no material cost.

TRAMS		
Era	Design	Comments
1902	Single-line blind in destination box. Separate route number box later appeared above this.	Black blind, white upper case letters
1923	Closed-top trams. Destination blind box above cab with route number box at roofline.	As above

TROLLEYBUSES		
Era	Design	Comments
1942 (201 to 210)	3-piece destination box with route number on offside.	Black blind, white upper case letters
1947 (231 to 237)	These former Pontypridd vehicles had a very small destination aperture.	As above with text diagonally split
1948 to 1962	Integral one-piece destination blinds on front and rear. Apertures later rebuilt and reduced in size while rear display was gradually phased out from 1962 and replaced by route numbers only.	Black blind, white upper case letters

MOTOR BUSES		
1920 to 1924	Fixed board above cab in white	Black upper case on 4 lines.
1925 to 1929	Single line blind in a separate box on front veranda or above cab.	Black blind, white upper case letters
From about 1929	3-piece integral destination box located between decks or above cab, and also first evidence of route numbers. All subsequent displays are integral with body.	As above

MOTOR BUSES cont.		
From 1932 to 1937	Two destination boxes side by side located between decks or above cab, with integral route number box above. Usually a 2 or 3-piece intgral box at rear.	As above
From 1937 to 1947	3-piece 2-line destination box located between decks or above cab, with route number on left-hand side.	As above
1947 to 1964	One-piece display with some examples later reduced in size after rebuild. Many pre-1947 deliveries get a similar display after rebuild. From 1961 only a route number box appeared on the rear of the vehicle. Nearside displays continue to be specified.	As above with 3 lines of information.
1964 to 1973	One-piece display with separate route number box on the offside front of the bus. By 1973 rear and nearside blinds had fallen out of use and were later painted or panelled over.	By 1973 vehicles 372 to 419 had apertures masked to single line and route numbers were carried in the front n/s bulkhead window.
1971 to 1972	2-track route number blinds and 2 single-line destination blinds.	Black blind, white upper case letters.
1973 to 1993	3-track route number blinds and a single-line destination blind usually with masking.	Black blind, white upper and lower case letters, later upper case. From 1992 black on white for inbound/Cardiff-bound journeys.
1993 to 1999	3-track route number blinds and a single-line destination blind usually with masking.	Black blind, yellow upper case letters and black on yellow for inbound/Cardiff-bound journeys. Later upper and lower case letters.
1996 to 2001	Flip-disc electronic digital displays first appeared on the ex Merseybus Volvo Ailsas. The Optare Excels were first new deliveries with this type of display.	The flip-disc type were yellow or lime green upper case letters and were difficult to read under certain conditions. Nearside destination and rear route number displays were re-introduced from 2000.
2001 onwards	Vultron LED displays were then adopted across much of the fleet. Currently Hanover displays are specified for new vehicles.	The LED displays were a big improvement. The bendy buses introduced scrolling legends in 2006. In 2015 the Enviro 400MMCs and Citaros introduced rear display with both route number and destinations.

Ticket machines and fare collection

MECHANICAL MACHINES		
Era	Ticket issuing system	Comments
1902 to circa 1950	Bell Punch Co. Ltd.	Hired by CCT at a cost of 15/- per annum.
By February 1936 and probably in use until 1950	Willebrew	Used on Merthyr service by this date. Several machines were loaned to Merthyr Tydfil Corporation at this time, to aid accounting and administration on the joint service.
During 1930s	Verometer	Used experimentally in this period
1930s to 1960s	Bellgraphics	Used on the joint 36 route with C.U.D.C. and W.M.O.B. and on service 41/20 to Merthyr.
From 1930s	T.I.M.	Used on the Newport route probably. Used on the Merthyr route from august 1946. Once again several machines were loaned to Merthyr Tydfil corporation, to aid accounting and administration on the joint service.
01/3/42 to 12/11/50	No ticket issued	PAYE flat fare system on trams and trollybuses.
12/11/50 to April 1978	Bell Punch Co. Ltd. Ultimate (5-roll type)	Until April 1978 and could also be used on one-man buses until there were sufficient Almex machines available.

The 5-roll Ultimate ticket machine from Bell Punch that could be carried and worn using a leather strap or secured to a mount for one-man operation.
(Mac Winfield courtesy CTPG)

Some Other Aspects of the Undertaking

MECHANICAL MACHINES cont.		
Era	Ticket issuing system	Comments
Late 1960s/ early 1970s	Bell Punch Co. Ltd. Solomatic (6-roll type)	AEC Swifts 506 to 525 and Fleetlines 526 to 550 batch for the early omo conversions.
1973 until 1975/76	T.I.M. Videmat Self Service	Trialled in 1973 and adopted as a secondary system on certain vehicles only. Fitted to most Willowbook-bodied Fleetlines, all ECW-bodies VRTs from new but only some of the K-reg Fleetlines. They were used on services 7/8 and 9 (from Roath depot) and on the 21, 23, 24 and 25 (from Sloper Road).
1973 to circa 1988	Almex Ticket Machine Company. (at least 4 models including Almex A)	This became the norm on one-man services. Long-range machines first appeared on the 36 service gradually followed by short-range machines on city routes. Later they worked in conjunction with Almex Fastfare using cash vaults. Fastfare was trialled from October 1979 on Fleetline 557, and introduced from June 1981. 100% by April 1983.
ELECTRONIC MACHINES		
Era	Ticket issuing system	Comments
By May 1988	Wayfarer II	Replaced in 1999
From 1999 to 2006	ERG TP5000	Cardiff Bus may have also tried the earlier AES Prodata electronic ticket machine.
2006 until March 2015	Wayfarer TGX150	Smart card sign-on and with card reader.
From March 2015	Corvia Ltd Ticketer ETM.	This has an integrated GPS system to relay Real Time Information via bus stop displays or smartphone apps. An on-line ticket system with card reader and PIN sign-on.

The Wayfarer TGX150 was a bulky electronic ticket machine that featured an LCD screen and card reader.
(Mac Winfield courtesy CTPG)

Cardiff's Municipal Buses

Tickets

A selection of tickets by the Bell Punch Co.

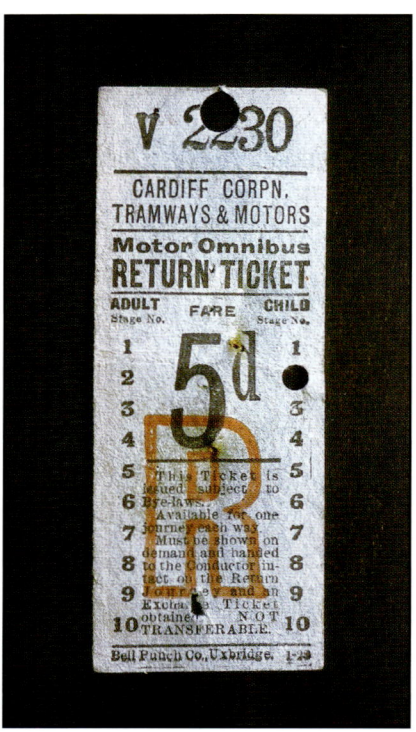
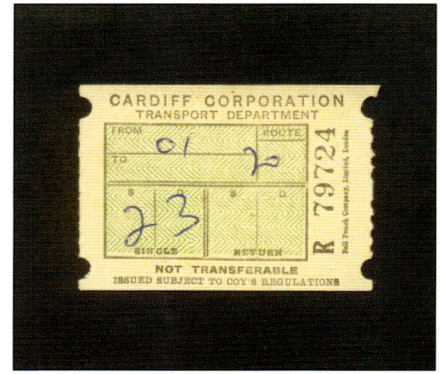

The service vehicle fleet

The service vehicle fleet has always existed in the background and even today forms an important part of operations. Over the years many buses have seen a further lease of life as training vehicles, while others have been rebuilt for more specialist roles such as tower wagons and pole-carriers for the tram and trolleybus overhead infrastructure. Others have been rebuilt into lorries or vans while one former double-decker became a permanent tree-lopper.

Some Other Aspects of the Undertaking

A number of wartime utility Bristol K6As joined the ancillary fleet. Formerly fleet number 83, CKG 650 became a tower wagon in 1961, and is seen here on North Road in June 1965.
(John Wiltshire)

Many vehicles included in the service vehicle fleet over the years were based on standard production commercial vehicles and have included a number of Land Rovers and more recently vans, both large and small. We must not however forget the recovery vehicles that served the fleet for many years. The AEC Matador new in 1944, was obtained in May 1948 and registered DKG 601. It was formerly with the British Army, and initially, its main purpose was to tow new trolleybuses from the coachbuilders East Lancs at Blackburn and Bridlington, and Bruce in Cardiff. In 1956 a coach-built body and towing winch was fitted, while in the 1970s the Matador was painted yellow and received a 2-way radio. Another vehicle regularly used for recovery work was Leyland Mastiff KBO 35P, which was new in 1975 and was taken out of service in October 1986.

Another Bristol K6A rebuilt was CKG 667 which was cut down to become a pole-carrier in 1959. It is seen here in action on Cowbridge Road West at the Amroth Road Junction, on 2 December 1969. It is on trade plates 419 BO, while Bedford J2 tower wagon 911 BUH of 1962 is also in attendance.
(Mike Street)

The AEC Matador DKG 601, now on trade plates 048 BO, is seen in the Cardiff Civic Centre on 26 June 1983.
(Andrew Wiltshire)

The Matador was sold in July 1986 and replaced by an ERF 24GTR B-series tractor unit NUT 344W that was new in January 1981. This was rebuilt into a fine-looking recovery vehicle by West Midlands Trucks of West Bromwich and entered service in October 1986. The ERF originally carried the orange and white livery but later received Scarab green and cream and fleet number 073. With recovery of disabled buses passing to a private contractor, the ERF eventually became surplus to requirements and was withdrawn and sold to the Cardiff Transport Preservation Group in 2013, and is now based at The Bus Depot at Barry.

Unusual additions to the driver training vehicle fleet in 1991 were a pair of MoD-specification Bedford NJMs that had previously been with the Royal Air Force. Q346 NTM was later given fleet number 046, and continued as a training vehicle until 1996. It is seen in the yard at Sloper Road depot.
(The late Dave B. Thomas)

CHAPTER TWELVE

PRESERVATION

In my younger days I often asked why so few of Cardiff Corporation's buses saw further service. This was usually met with the reply from my father that "they were only fit for scrap when Cardiff had finished with them". This may well have been true in many cases, and as we have seen in the earlier chapters, many buses were rebuilt often several times to get the very last bit of life out of them. Bus bodywork needed regular attention, especially as early bodywork incorporated many wooden components, often poor quality, which deteriorated rapidly in the damp British climate. Over time the running units such as engines, gearboxes and brakes gradually became much more reliable, and often outlived bodies by many years. From the late 1960s, and with the rapid introduction of one-man operation, half-cab double-deckers became obsolete. Upon withdrawal, those with open rear platforms had little value other than for their engines which were often exported, and the vast majority of Cardiff's half-cabs fell into this category. Consequently most of Cardiff's motor buses withdrawn during the 1950s, 1960s and 1970s went straight for scrap, which meant very few survived long enough to be considered worthy of preservation. In more recent years a number of former Cardiff vehicles have been saved, some of which have been restored to full working order. Unlike many former municipal fleets, the interest in actively preserving Cardiff motor buses did not really get underway until 1979, and this is reflected in the relatively few early motor buses to have survived. This was also true for most of the South Wales fleets.

Trams

No-one was able to save one of the electric tramcars that plied the streets from 1902 until 1950, such was the haste to rid the city of this tired and unloved form of transport. I understand there was a desire to do so, but no-one had the necessary finance or facilities to undertake such a task at that time, and the Corporation was never very enthusiast-friendly. However the Brush electric water-carrier/rail-cleaner car was put into store at Roath depot in the early 1950s and preserved, but was pushed out relatively quickly. It eventually became part of the National Tramway Museum at Crich, where, in 1959, it was the first tram to arrive on site. Number 131 would however have to wait 50 years until 2009, before it was restored to full working order.

Beautifully restored 131, the Brush water-carrier/rail cleaner of 1905, is seen in action in this wonderful setting at the Crich Tramway Village near Matlock in Derbyshire.

(Mike Ballinger)

Trolleybuses

The trolleybuses were a little more fortunate and the first example to be sold for preservation was AEC number 203 way back in 1963. The table below shows the initial survivors.

FLEET NO.	REG NO.	CHASSIS	BODY	SEATING	YEAR	STATUS
203	CKG 193	AEC 664T	NCME	H38/32R	1942	Working order
215	DBO 475	B.U.T. 9641T	East Lancs	H38/29D	1948	Restored
262	EBO 919	"	Bruce	"	1949	Under restoration
243	KBO 961	"	East Lancs	B40R	1955	"
277	KBO 950	"	"	H40/32R	1955	Since scrapped

The chassis of 277 was saved for exhibition purposes at Carlton Colville, but was later scrapped by July 1996.

Number 203 was eventually restored to working order and made its debut in 1994 in wartime grey livery at The Black Country Museum though it is now based at Sandtoft near Doncaster. B.U.T. trolleybus 215 passed to the National Museum of Wales in 1970 and was duly allocated to the Welsh Industrial and Maritime Museum for display at Cardiff. Following the closure of this museum in 1998, the vehicle remains in their ownership, but is now in secure storage. Number 262 was purchased locally before the Cardiff system closed and then passed to local bus dealer Bill Way. It was rescued by a group from West Sussex and stored in a quarry near Crawley, eventually moving to the Sandtoft museum. It was acquired by the Cardiff & South Wales Trolleybus Project in 1995. In October 1997 the C&SWTP was given single-deck trolleybus 243, which had originally been sold to the National Trolleybus Association in May 1965, and subsequently stored at a number of locations, eventually ending up at Sandtoft. Both 243 and 262 were returned to South Wales for restoration, which soon began. Since the Cardiff system closed in 1970, only 203 has operated so far whilst in preservation.

AEC trolleybus 203 resplendent at Sandtoft on 30 May 2010, the day it was re-launched following a lengthy restoration. It has been repainted into the streamlined livery which it wore in the early post-war years.

(Glyn Bowen)

Preservation

MOTOR BUSES

In 1966 Crossley 46 was the first motor bus from the Cardiff Corporation fleet to pass into preservation, and gradually as time passed the numbers slowly increased, but not before many significant types had become extinct. In more recent years an effort has been made to secure important representatives of the Cardiff fleet as soon as their useful working life was over, and this is an on going process. The majority of the motor buses listed in the table below have been saved since 1990.

FLEET NO.	REG NO.	CHASSIS	BODY	SEATING	YEAR	STATUS
46	EBO 900	Crossley DD42/7	Alexander	L27/26R	1949	Restored
135	GKG 52	Leyland PSU1/15	East Lancs	B44F	1952	Unrestored
368	XUH 368	" PD2A/30	Metro-Cammell	H36/28R	1961	"
408	408 DBO	AEC Regent V	East Lancs	H35/28R	1963	Restored
424	ABO 424B	Guy Arab V	Neepsend	O38/32R	1964	Unrestored
434	ABO 434B	"	"	O37/28R	"	Operational
497	JKG 497F	Daimler CRG6LX	Park Royal	H42/33F	1968	Restored
512	MBO 512F	AEC Swift	Alexander	B47D	"	Operational
532	PKG 532H	Daimler CRG6LX	Willowbrook	H44/30D	1969	Unrestored
570	WUH 570K	" CRL6-30	MCW	H43/31F	1971	"
584	WUH 584K	" "	"	"	1972	"
585	WUH 585K	" "	"	"	"	Restored
587	PKG 587M	Bristol VRTSL6G	ECW	H43/31F	1973	Unrestored
105	LUH 105P	" LHS6L	"	DP27F	1976	Restored
2	WTG 902T	Leyland PSU3C/4R	Plaxton	C51F	1978	Unrestored
360	WTG 360T	Bristol VRT/SL3	Alexander	O44/31F	1979	Operational
375	WTG 375T	"	"	H44/31F	"	Unrestored
396	CTX 396V	"	"	"	"	"
407	NDW 407X	Volvo B55-10	NCME	H39/35F	1982	Operational
412	NDW 412X	"	"	"	"	For sale
415	NDW 415X	"	"	"	"	Operational
436	A436 VNY	"	"	"	1984	Under repair
238	F238 CNY	Leyland Lynx	"	DP47F	1989	Unrestored
258	G258 HUH	"	"	B49F	1990	Restored
262	J262 UDW	Leyland Lynx 2	"	"	1991	"
267	J267 UDW	"	"	"	1991	Operational
023	N23 OBO	Dennis Dart	Alexander	B40F	1995	"
143	N143 PTG	Optare Metrorider	Optare	B31F	1996	"
302	S302 SHB	Dennis Dart SLF	Plaxton	B41F	1998	"

The Cardiff Transport Preservation Group

The Cardiff Transport Preservation Group (CTPG) was formed in 1992 to bring together enthusiasts who were keen to acquire, restore and operate vehicles that reflected the transport heritage of Cardiff and the surrounding area. To this end the CTPG has acquired a number of buses formerly operated by City of Cardiff Transport/ Cardiff Bus and other local operators. Many vehicles are owned by the CTPG while others are owned by individual or groups of members. The earliest additions to the CTPG collection were 368, the 1961 Leyland PD2A, and 512 the 1968 AEC Swift. By 2003 a temporary restoration base was occupied at Wenvoe near Cardiff, and from 2004 the CTPG began attending a number of bus rallies. The year 2005 saw the Group's fortunes prosper in terms of members, events and fund-raising with Daimler Fleetline 497 and Optare Metrorider 174 added to the collection. Annual bus rallies were now being held at both Barry and Merthyr Tydfil, and by 2006, the Group had relocated to a yard in Bonvilston, and more vehicles were added to the collection. A significant move took place in 2008 when the CTPG obtained a lease on the former Western Welsh bus garage in Barry, and was now able to house many of its collection under cover. Dating from the late 1930s, the garage provides ideal facilities for restoring, maintaining and operating vehicles. Referred to as The Bus Depot, by 2016 the collection housed within was open to the public on Fridays and Saturdays between 10am and 4pm. An additional and secure storage facility on Barry docks was leased from 2014, which acts as an overflow facility to The Bus Depot. Around 55 preserved vehicles are housed between the two facilities at Barry, of which 20 are former Cardiff examples including a recovery vehicle.

CTPG OWNED FORMER CARDIFF VEHICLES					
Fleet no.	Reg. No	Chassis	Body	Year	Livery
368	XUH 368	Leyland PD2A/30	Metro-Cammell	1961	Crimson lake and cream
434*	ABO 434B	Guy Arab V	Neepsend	1964	White and orange
497	JKG 497F	Daimler CRG6LX	Park Royal	1968	Orange and white
512	MBO 512F	AEC Swift	Alexander	"	Crimson lake and cream
532	PKG 532H	Daimler CRG6LX	Willowbrook	1969	Cream (previous owner)
587	PKG 587M	Bristol VRTSL6G	ECW	1973	Blue (previous owner)
360*	WTG 360T	Bristol VRT/SL3	Alexander	1979	Yellow (previous owner)
396	CTX 396V	"	Alexander	1980	Red (previous owner)
407	NDW 407X	Volvo B55-10	NCME	1982	Orange and white
258	G258 HUH	Leyland Lynx		1990	Cardiff Bus training livery
262	J262 UDW	Leyland Lynx II		1991	Yellow (previous owner)
267	J267 UDW	"		"	Brown, white and orange
023	N23 OBO	Dennis Dart	Alexander	1995	Cardiff Bus training livery
143	N143 PTG	Optare Metrorider	Optare	1996	Orange and white "Clipper"
073	NUT 344W	ERF 24GTR	Recovery vehicle	1981	Burges blue and cream

* 434 and 360 are open top vehicles

From 1973 until 1982 Leyland PD2A number 368 (XUH 368) saw service in South Wales as a school bus with Kenfig Motors. It then passed in 1983 to AUTEC Transport Training of Llandow near Cowbridge as a driver training vehicle where it lost its seats. By late 1990 the bus was showing signs of its age, suffering from a lot of corrosion after years parked out in the open. It subsequently passed to bus dealer Carl Ireland of Hull in early 1991 and was rescued for preservation by the British Bus Preservation Group later that year. This vehicle was the first to be delivered to the Cardiff Transport Preservation Group after the latter had been formed in March 1992. The bus is now safely under cover at the Barry depot and will be a major restoration project.

Preservation

Guy Arab open-topper ABO 434B was taken out of service by Cardiff in 1983, and duly passed to the National Museum of Wales. It was subsequently kept at the Industrial and Maritime Museum at Bute Street, Cardiff, and was occasionally made serviceable for an outing. The Museum donated 434 to the CTPG in 2008 and it forms part of the operational fleet.

After withdrawal by Cardiff in December 1982, Daimler Fleetline 497 (JKG 497F) passed straight into preservation locally in February 1983 and was repainted into crimson lake and cream. It was rallied for a number of years, eventually passing to another preservationist in the Cardiff area. Around 1994 it was sold out of preservation passing to an owner in Cheltenham who planned to convert it to a mobile caravan. Fortunately little work was undertaken and in 1998, after several subsequent owners, 497 was rescued by a small band of Cardiff enthusiasts. It joined the CTPG collection in early 2005 and by the end of 2013, had been fully repainted in orange and white livery in 2016. Restoration is now more or less complete, with just a few mechanical issues remaining.

For its age 497 is in remarkably good condition externally and internally, a fine example of an earlier Daimler Fleetline. Here it is seen on 28 June 1987 at the Cardiff bus rally on Museum Avenue. The Daimler badge on the front is not an original feature of this bus.

(Andrew Wiltshire)

By 1990 only two of Cardiff's 20 AEC Swifts were known to still exist, 512 and 520, and were to be found with Percival's of Oxford where they had been re-registered EDL 249F and EDL 248F respectively. The Swifts were inspected by the CTPG and 512 was acquired as it was the better of the pair, although a replacement engine was required. Moved to South Wales, restoration was then undertaken including a complete professional repaint in Newport Transport's paint shop. A replacement engine was eventually found, and was overhauled by Cardiff Bus in 2002. Restoration was completed, and after overcoming a few minor mechanical issues, the bus is now part of the CTPG's serviceable fleet based at The Bus Depot in Barry.

Beautifully restored AEC Swift 512 is caught arriving at the Rhydycar rally site for the Bus and Coaches Wales bus rally near Merthyr Tydfil in September 2012.
(Richard Field)

Daimler Fleetline 532 (PKG 532H) was withdrawn by Cardiff in September 1982 and passed to the Rubettes Jazz Band in Stoke-on-Trent. It returned to South Wales in 1990 to become a staff bus/mobile billboard for the Savemore Discount Store of South Cornelly. At this point it was still in more or less original condition. In 1992 it was sold to a charity for conversion into a mobile exhibition unit and the bodywork was altered. Eventually 532 was laid up and stripped of its engine and gearbox. It was rescued by the Cardiff Transport Preservation Group in 1998 and in 2016 remains a major restoration project.

Bristol VRT number 587 (PKG 587M) was withdrawn by Cardiff in 1984 and converted to an exhibition unit. In 1987 it was sold by Cardiff and had a number of subsequent owners. It was eventually purchased for preservation by the Bristol VR Enthusiasts Society (BVRES) in 2001, passing to the CTPG in January 2007 for continued preservation. It now awaits its turn in the queue of vehicles to be restored. Series-3 Bristol VRT 360 (WTG 360T) was one of the two convertible open-top examples sold by Cardiff Bus in 1999. Subsequent owners included Bath Bus Company and Solent Blueline (who scrapped its roof). It ended its working days with Classic Bus of Blackpool who used the vehicle at Weston-super-Mare as recently as 2012, and it passed to the CTPG in late 2013. After withdrawal by Cardiff Bus in June 1999, 396 (CTX 396V) spent 15 years with Cole (TRC Coaches) of Treorchy as a school bus, joining the CTPG collection in 2014. It is a good example of one of the 71 Alexander-bodied Bristol VRTs and is in more or less original condition

On 30 January 2008 Cardiff Bus donated three vehicles to the CTPG for preservation. These were Volvo Ailsa 407 (NDW 407X), Leyland Lynx 258 (G258 HUH) and Optare Metro-rider 143 (N143 PTG). Number 407 is in working order and is one of the 36 Northern Counties Ailsas purchased by Cardiff in the years 1982 to 1984. It was refurbished by Cardiff Bus in March 1999 and carries the orange and white retro livery. Number 143 was numerically the last Metrorider delivered to Cardiff Bus, and now repainted into its original Clipper livery, it is also part of the active fleet. The Leyland Lynx 258 has been in store since joining the collection, but in 2015 was receiving attention to get it back on the road. It was previously one of the three Lynx that were used for driver training by Cardiff Bus until 2007. Two of the Mark II Lynx are also in the collection. 262 (J262 UDW) arrived from Abertawe Travel of Swansea in April 2015, and was joined by 267 (J267 UDW) the following month which had previously been in preservation with Neil Gardner in Kent. Number 267 is considered to be in excellent condition and is operational.

Preservation

Leyland Lynx 2 267 (J267 UDW) was acquired in 2015 and is seen near Ogmore on an evening outing in July 2015. It has been restored to its original livery as acquired in 1991.

(Paul Hamley)

Further new additions to the collection from Cardiff Bus in September 2013 included Dennis Dart 023 (N23 OBO) and ERF recovery vehicle 073 (NUT 344W). The Dart had latterly been in use as a training bus and was in full working order, while the ERF had been with Cardiff Bus for around 30 years having replaced the AEC Matador.

Alexander Dash-bodied Dennis Dart 023 in action at the Barry Transport Festival in June 2015. It is wearing the Cardiff Bus driver trainer livery, in which it was acquired.

(Paul Hamley)

Non-CTPG owned vehicles

The table below is a breakdown of vehicles which are preserved in private ownership. Many are actually owned by members of the CTPG and reside at Barry, while 412 and 415 are owned by a member but are not kept in the South Wales area.

PRIVATELY OWNED VEHICLES					
Fleet no.	Reg. No	Chassis	Body	Livery	Owner
46	EBO 900	Crossley DD42/7	Alexander	Crimson lake	National Museum of Wales
135	GKG 52	Leyland PSU1/15	East Lancs	Brown & cream	A. Brewer *
408	408 DBO	AEC Regent V	"	Crimson lake	Cardiff Regent V Group *
424	ABO 424B	Guy Arab V	Neepsend	Dark green	Mardens Commmercials, Essex
570	WUH 570K	Daimler CRL6-30	MCW	Playbus livery	A. Brewer
584	WUH 584K	"	"	Crimson lake	"
585	WUH 585K	"	"	"	Cardiff K-Liner Group *
105	LUH 105P	Bristol LHS6L	ECW	Orange & white	M. Taylor *
2	WTG 902T	Leyland PSU3C/4R	Plaxton	Red and cream	" *
375	WTG 375T	Bristol VRT/SL3	Alexander	Cream	M. Carroll and I. Barlow
412	NDW 412X	Volvo B55-10	NCME	Yellow	Patrickson, Wigan #
415	NDW 415X	"	"	"	" "
436	A436 VNY	"	"	Orange & white	M. Carroll and I. Barlow*
238	F238 CNY	Leyland Lynx	"	Light green	A. Jeenes and S. Morgn
302	S302 SHB	Dennis Dart SLF	Plaxton	Green/orange	K. Edwards

* Indicates vehicle kept at either The Bus Depot or the annexe site at Barry.

\# indicates vehicle for sale in 2015.

Upon withdrawal in September 1966 Crossley 46 (EBO 900) was saved by a group of enthusiasts, and it had the distinction of being the first Cardiff Corporation motor bus to pass into preservation. By June 1977 it had passed from the Cardiff 46 Group to the National Museum of Wales. Unfortunately it has not seen the light of day for many years but, after being vandalised, is now in secure storage.

The story of Leyland Royal Tiger 135 (GKG 52) is an interesting one since its days at Cardiff Corporation. In 1969 it passed to the Board Na Mona (Irish Turf Board), Eire for conversion to a non-powered rail vehicle. It was mounted on a railway underframe, but had become redundant during the late 1980s. It was eventually rescued for preservation in 2000, and currently resides at the CTPG's annexe in the Barry area.

AEC Regent V 408 (408 DBO) was saved in 1979 passing to the Cardiff Regent V Group shortly after Cardiff withdrew the last of its half-cabs. It was subsequently kept in running order and regularly rallied over the years, and is now based at The Bus Depot in Barry.

Open top Guy Arab 424 (ABO 424B) was withdrawn by Cardiff in 1980 and sold in September that year to a private owner at the West of England Transport Collection, Winkleigh in North Devon. It later passed to Topdeck of Dadford near Buckingham as a hospitality unit, until laid up in the open from May 1994. By 2009 it was in a very sorry state and was rescued for preservation in South Wales. Latterly at the Swansea Bus Museum, 424 was sold on, and is currently with Mardens Commercials of Benfleet, Essex, and pending restoration.

Daimler Fleetline 570 (WUH 570K) had latterly been a training bus with Cardiff until its sale in 1986. It was eventually exported to Dublin in 1990 for conversion into a playbus, its interior having been much altered in the process. It was rescued for preservation in 2001, being repatriated in 2007. Number 584 (WUH 584K) had been withdrawn along with 585 in late 1984. 584 passed to Wilson, Carnwath and was eventually rescued for preservation from an operator in Skegness in 1992. It is now partially restored and currently resides in the Lydney area with 570. Number 585 (WUH 585K) was the first of the K-reg Fleetlines to be preserved being saved in June 1990 after seeing out its days in the Surrey and Kent areas. The restoration of 585 is more advanced and benefits from being housed at Barry.

Leyland Lynx F238 CNY is one of the dual-purpose seated examples. It is seen at the Barry Transport Festival on 14 June 2009, not long after entering preservation.
(Andrew Wiltshire)

Bristol LHS midibus 105 (LUH 105P) and Leyland Leopard coach 2 (WTG 902T) were both acquired by CTPG member Mike Taylor in 2002/3 and represent the more specialist vehicles that operated for Cardiff in the 1970s and 1980s. Number 105 has been restored and was active on the rally scene in 2004 and 2005, however the coach still awaits restoration. In addition to the CTPG's own Ailsa 407 (NDW 407X), three others are considered preserved, although only 415 (NDW 415X) is known to be in operational condition. Leyland Lynx 238 (F238 CNY), the only survivor of the four dual-purpose seated examples, was operational when acquired for preservation, but is now out of use. Finally, the newest former Cardiff vehicle in preservation is SPD Dennis Dart 302 (S302 SHB) which, after seeing some service in the West Midlands area, returned to South Wales, and is currently a regular participant at rallies.

No longer in preservation

For a number of reasons buses that have been purchased for preservation are often sold on, either for scrap or to perform a new role. The following former Cardiff motor buses were preserved at one time.

Fleet No.	Reg No.	Chassis	Bodywork	Seating	Year
(91)	CKG 667	Bristol K6A	Pole-carrier	n/a	1946
423	ABO 423B	Guy Arab V	Neepsend	H38/32R	1964
542	PKG 542H	Daimler CRG6LX	Willowbrook	Playbus	1970
104	LUH 104P	Bristol LHS6L	ECW	Caravan	1976
348	WTG 348T	Bristol VRT/SL3/6LXB	Alexander	H44/31F	1978
397	CTX 397V	" "	"	"	1980
408	NDW 408X	Volvo Ailsa B55-10	NCME	H39/35F	1982
409	NDW 409X	"	"	"	"
419	RKG 419Y	"	"	"	1983
510	RBO 510Y	Leyland ONLXB	East Lancs	H43/31F	"
240	F240 CNY	Leyland Lynx	"	DP47F	1989
174	H174 RBO	Optare Metrorider	Optare	B31F	1991

Bristol K6A 91 (CKG 667) was cut down to a pole-carrying lorry and served in the service vehicle fleet from 1959 until about 1972. It was eventually sold to the WETC at Winkleigh for preservation, but was later scrapped. Number 423 (ABO 423B) was rescued as an intact vehicle, but unfortunately suffered at the hands of vandals and was sold for scrap. Fleetline 542 (PKG 542H) on the other hand had been converted into a playbus and was reluctantly sold for scrap in July 1993 due to lack of suitable storage. Bristol LHS 104 had latterly been a caravan, but was eventually sold for spare parts. Bristol VRT 348 (WTG 348T) was initially preserved locally by an enthusiast, and along with VRT 397 (CTX 397V), was considered for long-term preservation by the CTPG. Both were sold on for scrap as their overall condition was poor.

Upon their final withdrawal at the beginning of 2008 a number of other Volvo Ailsas were snapped up by preservationists, although most did not last long. The three listed in the table passed to Edwards Coaches and 408 (NDW 408X) and 409 (NDW 409X) went back into PSV service, while 419 (RKG 419Y) was broken up for spares. Olympian 510 (RBO 510Y) was rescued by a South Wales enthusiast, but is now owned by a theatrical group based in the London area, while Leyland Lynx 240 (F240 CNY) was restored to full working order in Cardiff livery, but broken up at very short notice. Finally Optare Metrorider 174 (H174 RBO) was part of the CTPG collection, but was badly damaged after being struck by another vehicle while stored in a yard.

THE FUTURE

Willowbrook-bodied Fleetline PKG 535H of 1969 had a number of owners after sale by Cardiff in 1982 including DeCourcey of Coventry. These were latterly non-PSV roles, and by 1991 it had been converted into a caravan in the Winkleigh area of North Devon. It was later driven across to France by a group of travellers and was last heard of in 2000 near Chateaureu in central France. Thought to have subsequently been scrapped, it was discovered in 2015 still remarkably intact. Shortly afterwards, an appeal was set up by the CTPG to raise funds to purchase and repatriate the bus.

Meanwhile the excellent work of the Cardiff Transport Preservation Group at Barry will see efforts being made to restore a number of former Cardiff vehicles to working order over the next few years. These include Bristol VRTs 587 and 396 and Leyland Lynx 258.

APPENDIX 1

CARDIFF'S OVERALL ADVERT BUSES AND SPECIAL LIVERIES SINCE 1970

Daimler Fleetline 585 is in a special livery promoting Cardiff with its German twin city Stuttgart. The bus is seen approaching Pengam Bridge from Tremorfa in early evening sunshine on 2 July 1973.

(John Wiltshire)

OVERALL LIVERIES WITH FLEET COLOURS ON THE FRONT					
Vehicle	Type	Description of livery	From	To	Comments
550	Fleetline	Silexine paints	04/70	07/72	
461	Arab V	Aquamarine & white	03/72	10/73	Experimental livery
488	Fleetline	Dark orange & white	03/72	05/73	" "
524	Swift	Light orange & white	03/72	-	" "
550	Fleetline	Aquamarine & white	07/72	05/73	" "
476	"	Barclaycard	07/72	03/74	
565	"	Light orange & white	06/72	-	Experimental livery
585	"	Stadt Stuttgart twin city	09/72	07/73	Between deck branding
526	"	Nantes twin city	01/73	12/74	" "
488	"	"Steel must stay" campaign	05/73	03/75	" "
480	"	British Rail campaign	06/73	10/74	" "
556	"	Hill House Insurance	06/73	09/74	
570	"	Rediffusion TV rentals	07/73	09/74	
532	"	John Lee Motor Group	10/73	04/76	
549	"	Barclaycard	03/74	05/76	
566	"	H. M. Silver Jubilee	05/77	06/78	

Number 367 sets down opposite the Hollybush Inn on Glyn Coed Road, Pentwyn, on 10 August 1989. This is a good example of an overall advert livery that retains basic fleet livery on the front elevation.

(Andrew Wiltshire)

OVERALL LIVERIES WITH FLEET COLOURS ON THE FRONT					
Vehicle	Type	Description of livery	From	To	Comments
578	Fleetline	Multiride tickets	07/77	05/79	
566	"	National Eisteddfod	06/78	07/79	
587	VRT	Bellevue Discount Stores	06/79	04/82	
311	"	Nash/ Carmo car dealer	09/79	11/82	
532	Fleetline	Ace Windows	02/80	09/82	
317	VRT	Allders store	02/80	12/81	
305	"	Phoenix Assurance	05/80	07/83	
343	"	Cardiff City Tramways	08/80	03/83	With a grey roof
327	"	Debenhams	06/81	07/83	
359	"	Cardiff City Tramways	02/83	05/86	
360	"	" "	02/83	04/86	
85	Fleetline	" "	02/83	10/86	Open-top
340	VRT	Jockey Shorts	03/84	04/85	
218	L. National	The New Exchange Restaurant	05/84	07/85	
213	"	Sall's Crisps	06/84	04/85	
387	VRT	Asda Stores	11/84	08/86	
329	"	Bildapower	03/85	05/87	
340	"	Ken Thorne Cars/Daihatsu	04/85	1988	
339	"	Randall Cox	05/85	11/87	
218	L. National	Super Ted Pantomime	08/85	02/86	
567	Olympian	Caine's Furnishers	02/86	06/88	
502	"	Woolworths	05/86	10/86	
502	"	B&Q Autocentres	10/86	09/88	
391	VRT	Debenhams	12/87	?	

Commencing with 361 most overall advert liveries carried fleet colours on the front of the bus.

\multicolumn{6}{c}{OVERALL LIVERIES WITH FLEET COLOURS ON THE FRONT}					
Vehicle	Type	Description of livery	From	To	Comments
361	VRT	Thomsons Directories	02/88	1992	
347	"	Workforce Employment Agency	05/88	?	
367	"	Clive Ranger	06/88	09/90	
502	Olympian	B&Q Superstores	09/88	10/90	
350	VRT	Welsh Bitter	07/89	10/91	
364	"	"	08/89	10/90	
363	"	Senator Windows	07/89	10/90	
355	"	Queens West Shopping Centre	10/89	07/01	
171	Metrorider	South Glamorgan TEC	09/94	09/96	blue and white
362	VRT	National Museum of Wales	05/95	11/97	
607	Scania	Bryant Homes	04/96	05/98	
434	Ailsa	Darlows Estate Agents	08/96	1997	
407	"	Talking Pages	09/96	02/99	
171	Metrorider	South Glamorgan TEC	10/96	09/98	red and blue
174	"	Co-operative Stores	05/97	09/98	
362	VRT	Edwards Sports House	11/97	01/99	
186	Metrorider	Knights of Barry	02/98	08/00	
601	Scania	South Wales Echo	05/98	12/99	
603	"	"	05/98	12/99	
607	"	"	05/98	02/00	
602	"	Acorn Recruitment	08/98	07/00	
608	"	Peter Allan Estate Agents	05/99	07/00	Advert also on front
443	Ailsa	George Street Furnishers	08/99	08/02	
601	Scania	Arthur Llewellyn Jenkins	12/99	08/00	
603	"	Cardiff Professional Sports Club	12/99	08/00	
607	"	Ken Thorne Cars	02/00	08/00	
439	Ailsa	Peter Allan Estate Agents	08/00	04/02	
441	"	Arthur Llewellyn Jenkins	08/00	08/02	
442	"	Acorn Recruitment	09/00	04/02	
444	"	UWIC blue	10/00	04/02	
445	"	"	09/00	09/06	
446	"	"	08/00	02/07	
129	Metrorider	Beacon's Bus	05/01	04/03	
291	Scania	Airbus	03/02	8/04	
292	"	"	03/02	8/04	
293	"	"	03/02	8/04	
289	"	"	04/02	8/04	

OVERALL LIVERIES WITH FLEET COLOURS ON THE FRONT cont.					
Vehicle	Type	Description of livery	From	To	Comments
290	Scania	Airbus	04/02	08/04	
287	"	"	12/02	08/04	
288	"	"	12/02	08/04	
320	Dart	Centenary livery	05/02	?	
399	"	Education and Learning Wales	06/02	by 05/07	Advert also on front of bus
451	Ailsa	Peter Allan Estate Agents	10/02	by 05/06	
456	"	Western Mail	by 08/03	by 04/06	
518	Dart	St, Davis Hall	10/03	08/07	Advert also on front of bus
519	"	Coleg Glan Hafren	10/03	11/07	" "
520	"	Cardiff Events	09/03	05/05	" "
520	"	Cardiff in bloom	05/05	08/07	" "
701	Enviro 300	BMI Baby	09/04	12/07	
702	"	"	09/04	2008	revised in 2008
703	"	"	09/04	2008	"
704	"	"	09/04	11/07	
705	"	"	09/04	by 06/11	
706	"	Air Wales	late 2004	04/06	Advert also on front of bus
714	"	Acorn People	08/05	2007	
221	Dart	Warburtons	09/04	12/05	
193	"	Future Inns	06/05	03/09	
302	"	B&Q	5/07	03/09	
399	"	Acorn People	by 05/07	?	
233	"	UWIC blue	09/06	08/10	
234	"	"	09/06	09/10	
024	"	"	09.08	09/10	
702	Enviro 300	BMI Baby (revised)	2008	06/11	
703	"	" "	2008	06/11	
149	Dart	FreeB	02/10	2010	Special free bus livery
150	"	"	02/10	2010	" "
151	"	"	02/10	2010	" "
501	"	UWIC	10/10	08/12	Mauve and blue livery
502	"	"	10/10	08/12	" "
503	"	"	10/10	08/12	" "
472	Scania	IFF Card	10/10	2013?	Advert also on front of bus
703	Enviro 300	KLM	10/11	12/12	" "
501	Dart	Cardiff Met Metrider	08/12	Current	All over blue livery
502	"	" "	08/12	Current	" "
503	"	" "	08/12	Current	" "
721	Scania	Heart FM	12/14	Current	Advert also on front of bus

468 to 470 briefly carried an overall advert wrap for Nat West bank during November 2015.

SPECIALLY DECORATED TROLLEYBUSES.

Year	Fleet number	Occasion
1955	208	50th anniversary of City status
1958	Many carried bunting on trolley booms	British Empire and Commonwealth Games in July 1958
1960	Many carried bunting on trolley booms.	National Eisteddfod of Wales in August 1960
The following were decorated with colour lights		
1962	201 and 206	Cardiff Shopping Festival and Christmas
1963	201/2/4 & 207	Cardiff Shopping Festival and Christmas
1964	201/2/4 & 207	Cardiff Shopping Festival and Christmas
1965	220/1/7/8, 230/55/62 & 269	Christmas
1966	220/7/8 & 230	Christmas
1967	227/30, 262 and 269	Christmas
1968	218, 220/8 & 255	Christmas

APPENDIX 2

LIST OF ALL BUSES OWNED

Explanation of seating codes:

B = single-deck bus, **C** = coach, **H** = high-bridge layout double-deck bus, **L** = low-bridge layout double-deck bus with sunken upper deck gangway
DP = bus with dual-purpose type seating, **O** = open-top bus, **CO** = Convertible open-top bus, **AB** = articulated bus

Numbers indicate seating capacity and for double-deckers upper deck is given before lower deck if the split is known. eg: H43/31F

F = front entrance, **R** = rear entrance with open platform, **RD** = rear entrance with platform doors, **RO** = rear entrance with an open staircase
D = dual entrance/exit, **T** = toilet fitted

MOTOR BUSES

FLEET NO.	REGISTRATION NO.	CHASSIS TYPE	BODY	SEATING	YEAR NEW	YEARS WITHDRAWN
48-53	BO 3638-43	Dennis-Stevens	Dodson	B28R	1920	1925 (50) 1929 (others) (a)
61-6	BO 5221-6	"	"	O52RO	1922	1929/30
76-80	BO 5862-6	Dennis 30hp	"	B20F	1923	1931 to 1933
1-6	BO 6741-6	Dennis 4-ton	See below (b)	O52RO	1924	1934
7-11/7	BO 7921-6	"	See below (c)	"	"	1934
113-5	BO 8249-51	Dennis 2½-ton	See below (d)	B25F	"	1932
16	BO 8402	"	Dennis	"	"	1932
	AX 2083	W. & G. du Cros 22hp	?	B20-	1920	1926 (e)
	AX 2931	"	?	"	1921	1926 (e)
	AX 5716	"	?	"	1924	1926 (e)
67-70, 81	BO 8746-50	Dennis 4-ton	NCME	O52RO	1925	1932 (67) 1934 (others)
152	BO 8751	"	Dodson	H52RO	"	1934
117-22	BO 8752-7	Dennis 2½-ton	NCME	B30R	"	1932
50	UH 80	Dennis 4-ton	Dodson	B28R	1926	1932
150	UH 81	"	"	H50RO	"	1934
155-61	UH 1351-7	Dennis 2½-ton	"	B28-	"	1934 to 1935
	BO 1844	Trafford	?	?	1917	By 1927 (f)
	BO 4282	Leyland	?	?	1921	By 1927 (f)
	NR 1145	Daimler CB	(Charabanc)	-26-	1922	By 1927 (g)
	AU 8316	Daimler Y	?	-24-	1923	By 1927 (g)

FLEET NO.	REGISTRATION NO.	CHASSIS TYPE	BODY	SEATING	YEAR NEW	YEARS WITHDRAWN
	BO 8199	AEC 2-ton	?	?	1924	By 1927 (g)
	BO 8552	"	?	?	1925	By 1927 (g)
	UH 1563	Morris	?	?	1926	By 1927 (g)
164-73	UH 2191-2200	Dennis E	See below (h)	B32D	1927	1936 to 1939
174-9	UH 3130-5	"	See below (i)	"	"	1936 to 1939
44	BO 6190	Palladium YEC	Rich	O52RO	1922	1930 (j)
43	BO 6921	"	"	"	1924	1930 (j)
13	BO 7424	"	"	"	"	1930 (j)
29	BO 8871	Commer 3P	Commer?	"	1925	1930 (j)
87	UH 1058	"	"	"	1926	1930 (j)
89	UH 2190	"	Rich?	"	1927	1930 (j)
180-3	UH 4461/2/4/5	Bristol B	Buckingham	B34R	1928	1937
184-6	UH 4463/6/7	Albion PM28	"	"	"	1937
210-29	UH 6980-99	Dennis HS	Brush	L22/24R	1929	1938/39
179	PK 3347	Dennis H	Hall Lewis	L28/20R	1928	1936 (k)
234-6	FE 8518-20	Dennis E	Bracebridge	B32R	1926	1939/40 (l)
237-9	FE 8625-7	"	"	"	"	1939/40 (l)
240/1	FE 8870/1	"	"	"	1927	1939/40 (l)

(a) Body on 50 (BO 3640) was fitted to new chassis UH 80 in 1926 and retained fleet number 50.
(b) Bodies on 1-6 (BO 6741-6) were by Dodson (4), W. Lewis (1) and J. Norman (1)
(c) Bodies on 7-11/7 (BO7921-6) were by Buckingham (3), Dodson (1), W. Lewis (1) and J. Norman (1)
(d) Bodies on 113-115 (BO 8249-51) were by W. Lewis (2) and J. Norman (1)
(e) AX 2083, AX 2931 and AX 5716 were three of four vehicles acquired from GV Jones, Castleton in 1924.
(f) BO 1844 and BO 4282 were two of five vehicles acquired from G. Worrel in 1926.
(g) These were acquired from J. Worrel in 1926.
(h) Bodies on 164-73 (UH 2191-5) were by Dodson (6) and W. Lewis (4).
(i) Bodies on 174-9 (UH 3130-5) were Dodson (5) and W. Lewis (1)
(j) 44, 43, 13, 29, 87 and 89 were acquired from J.A. Rich, Cardiff in early 1927.
(k) 179 (PK 3347) was a former demonstrator acquired from Dennis Bros, Guildford in October 1929.
(l) 234-241 were acquired from Lincoln Corporation in November 1929. The exact order of fleet numbers is not actually confirmed.

FLEET NO.	REGISTRATION NO.	CHASSIS TYPE	BODY	SEATING	YEAR NEW	YEARS WITHDRAWN
251-4	UH 8231-4	Thornycroft LC	Hall Lewis	H26/26R	1930	1943 (a)
255-60	UH 9001-6	"	NCME	B32R	1931	1944 to 1945
	UH 7535	Crossley Condor	Crossley	L50R	1930	1941 (b)
66	UH 7175	Leyland TD1	Leyland	L24/24R	1929	1945 (c)
75-80	KG 1141-5	Leyland TS4	NCME	B29R	1932	1947 to 1958
113-22	KG 1146-55	Leyland TD2	"	L24/24R	"	1948 to 1950
	OU 4028	Thornycroft BC	Strachans	H26/26R	1931	1941 (d)
	UB 4935	Daimler CP6	Park Royal	H26/24R	"	1937 (e)
	MV 529	AEC Regent	Brush	H56R	1932	1941 (f)
1-10	KG 3701-10	"	NCME	H50R	1934	1949/50
	TF 6821	Leyland TD1	Leyland	L27/24R	1931	1944 (g)
76	KG 1251	AEC Regent	Weymann	L25/25R	"	1945 (h)
21/22	KG 5001/2	Crossley Mancunian	NCME	H30/26R	1935	1949
11-20	KG 5003-12	AEC Regent	"	"	"	1950
30	KG 7750	AEC Q	English Electric Co.	H29/27F	1936	1943
31-5	KG 8904/5/3/2/1	Leyland TD4c	NCME	H28/25R	"	1949
36-41	KG 8906-11	AEC Regent	"	H30/26R	"	1949 to 1957
42	UA 5850	Crossley Condor	Dodson	H24/24R	1930	1938 (i)
43-5	UA 5851/2/4	"	Roe	"	"	1938 (i)
46	UB 2857	"	Crossley	"	"	1938 (i)
47-50	KG 9801-4	AEC Regent	NCME	H30/26R	1937	1950 to 1956
151-66	KG 9805-20	"	"	"	"	1950 to 1957
167-81	ABO 970-84	"	"	"	"	1950 to 1958
143-7	ABO 985-9	AEC Regal	Lewis	B32R	"	1950 to 1953
148-50	AKG 418-20	"	NCME	"	"	1956/57
182-91	BBO 67-76	AEC Regent	"	H30/26R	1938	1956 to 1958
192-8	CBO 701-7	"	East Lancs	"	1940	1953 to 1958

(a) 251-4 (UH 8231-4) were new as 41 to 44.
(b) UH 7535 was a former demonstrator acquired from Crossley, March 1931.
(c) 66 (UH 7175) was a former demonstrator acquired from Leyland, April 1931.
(d) OU 4028 was a former demonstrator acquired from Thornycroft, Basingstoke, March 1932.
(e) UB 4935 was a former demonstrator acquired from Daimler Motors, Coventry, July 1932.
(f) MV 529 was a former demonstrator acquired from AEC, Southall in 1933.
(g) TF 6821 was a former demonstrator acquired from Leyland Motors in March 1934 and became 51.
(h) 76 (KG 1251) was a former demonstrator acquired from AEC in March 1934.
(i) 42-6 were all acquired from Leeds City Transport (L100-2/4/5) in 1936.

FLEET NO.	REGISTRATION NO.	CHASSIS TYPE	BODY	SEATING	YEAR NEW	YEARS WITHDRAWN
199	CKG 325	AEC Regent	East Lancs	H30/26R	1942	1958
29/63	CKG 377/422	Guy Arab I 5LW	Park Royal	"	"	1958
42/3	CKG 405/6	Bedford OWB	Duple	B32F	1943	1943
64	CKG 465	Guy Arab I 5LW	Park Royal	H30/26R	1943	1958
65-7	CKG 407-9	Guy Arab II 5LW	"	"	"	1960/61
71-3	CKG 516-8	"	"	"	"	1958 to 1961
74-6	CKG 519-21	"	"	"	1944	1958 to 1961
77-9	CKG 581-3	Bristol K6A	"	"	"	1958 to 1962
80-2	CKG 584-6	"	"	"	1945	1958 to 1962
83-9	CKG 650-6	"	"	"	"	1958 to 1962
90-4	CKG 666-70	"	Duple	"	1946	1958 to 1963
95-100	CUH 371-6	AEC Regent II	Air Dispatch	"	1947	1962 to 1964
101-4	CUH 377-80	"	East Lancs	L27/26R	"	1963
105-13	DKG 829-37	"	Air Dispatch	H30/26R	1948	1962 to 1964
23	GDF 58	Crossley DD42/3	Scottish Commercial	"	1947	1961
24	GDG 458	"	"	"	"	1961
25	EBO 103	Crossley DD42/5	"	"	1948	1961
114-33	DUH 311-20	Bristol KW6G	Bruce	H33/26R	"	1964 to 1968
52-4	EBO 7/10,6	Daimler CVD6	East Lancs	H30/26R	"	1964 to 1966
55-8	EBO 5/8/4/1	Guy Arab IV	"	"	"	1964 to 1966
59-61	EBO 3/9/2	"	D.J. Davies	"	"	1965/66 (a)
42-6,51	EBO 896-901	Crossley DD42/7	Alexander	L27/26R	1949	1963 to 1966
1-20	EUH 733-52	AEC Regent III	Bruce	H33/26R	1950	1966 to 1968 (b)
134-8	GKG 51-5	Leyland PSU1/15	East Lancs	B44F	1952	1966 to 1968
26-40	GUH 931-45	Guy Arab IV	East Lancs	H32/28R	1953	1967 to 1969
301-15	LBO 511-25	Daimler CVG6	East Lancs	H35/28R	1956/57	1970/71
316-30	MUH 316-30	Guy Arab IV	"	"	"	1971 to 1974
143-6	NKG 143-6	Leyland PSUCI/1	Longwell Green	B44F	1957	1969/70
331-42	OBO 331-42	Daimler CVG6	East Lancs	H35/28R	"	1970/71
343-54	OUH 343-54	Guy Arab IV	"	"	1958	1971
355-60	SKG 355-60	Daimler CSG6	"	"	1959	1971

(a) 52 to 61 received Longwell Green H32/28R bodies in 1957.   (b) 11,14,15,16 and 20 were bodied by East Lancs at Bridlington.

FLEET NO.	REGISTRATION NO.	CHASSIS TYPE	BODY	SEATING	YEAR NEW	YEARS WITHDRAWN
361-6	TUH 361-6	AEC Bridgemaster	Park Royal	H41/27RD	1960	1971/72
367-71	XUH 367-71	Leyland PD2A/30	Metro-Cammell	H36/28R	1961	1971/72
372-81	XUH 372-81	AEC Regent V 2D3RV	East Lancs	H35/28R	"	1973/74
382-91	382-91 BUH	AEC Regent V 2D3RA	"	"	1962	1974/75
392-401	392-401 BUH	Leyland PD2A/30	"	H37/28R	1963	1973/74
402-7	402-7 CKG	Leyland PD3A/1	"	H38/32R	"	1975
408-13	408-13 DBO	AEC Regent V 2D3RA	"	H35/28R	"	1979
414-9	414-9 DBO	"	Neepsend	"	1964	1979
420-4	ABO 420-4B	Guy Arab V	"	H38/32R	"	1979
425-30	ABO 425-30C	"	"	H37/28R	1965	1976/77
431/3/4	ABO 431/3/4B	"	"	"	1964	1976/77 & 1983 (34)
432/5/6	ABO 432/5/6C	"	"	"	1965	1977
437-51	EUH 437-51D	"	Alexander	H38/32R	1966	1977/78
452-73	EUH 452-73D	"	"	H37/28R	"	1977 to 1979
474-89	JKG 474-89F	Daimler CRG6LX	MCW	H42/33F	1967	1979/80 & 1986 (85)
490-505	JKG 490-505F	"	Park Royal	"	1968	1980 to 1982
506-25	MBO 506-25F	AEC Swift MP2R	Alexander	B47D	"	1975 to 1977
526-50	PKG 526-50H	Daimler CRG6LX	Willowbrook	H44/30D	1969/70	1980 to 1982
551-85	WUH 551-85K	Daimler CRL6-30	MCW	H43/31F	1971/72	1980 to 1985
101-3	RNY 101-3M	Seddon Pennine IV-236	Pennine	DP25F	1973	1984 to 1988
586-605	PKG 586-605M	Bristol VRTSL6G	ECW	H43/31F	1973/74	1983 to 1989
201	RUH 201M	Leyland National 10351/2R		B40D	1974	1984
202-10	GBO 137-46N	"		"	"	1981 to 1989
212-21	JBO 352-4/45-51N	"		"	1975	1984 to 1989
104/5	LUH 104/5P	Bristol LHS6L	ECW	DP27F	1976	1988
1	NWO 901R	Leyland PSU3B/4R	Duple Dominant	C51F	"	1989
106	MJK 94L	Seddon Pennine IV-236	Pennine	DP25F	1973	1988 (a)
301-26	SWO 301-26S	Bristol VRT/SL3/6LXB	Willowbrook	H43/31F	1977	1988 to 1991
506-9	WJY 749/54/6/7	Leyland PD3/1	Metro-Cammell	H44/31F	1962	1978 to 1979 (b)
510-2	16/9/24 JVK	"	Weymann	"	1963	1979 (c)
513/4	30/41 JVK	"	Alexander	"	1964	1979 (c)

FLEET NO.	REGISTRATION NO.	CHASSIS TYPE	BODY	SEATING	YEAR NEW	YEARS WITHDRAWN
515/6	ETN 89/97C	Leyland PDR1/1	Weymann	H44/31F	1965	1979 (c)
517	KBB 111D	"	Metro-Cammell	"	1966	1979 (c)
518	ETN 74C	"	Alexander	"	1965	1979 (c)
519	ETN 103C	"	Weymann	"	"	1979 (c)
2	WTG 902T	Leyland PSU3E/4R	Plaxton Supreme III	C51F	1978	1989
51	WTX 51T	Dennis Dominator DD110	East Lancs	H43/31F	"	1986
327-58	WTG 327-58T	Bristol VRT/SL3/6LXB	Alexander AL	H44/31F	"	1993 to 1998
359/60	WTG 359/60T	"	"	CO44/31F	1979	1999
361-81	WTG 361-81T	"	"	H44/31F	"	1992 to 1999
382-97	CTX 382-97V	"	"	"	1980	1994 to 1999

(a) 106 ex Eastbourne BT in 1977. (b) 506 to 509 ex Plymouth CT in 1977. (c) 510 to 519 ex Tyne & Wear PTE in 1977.

FLEET NO.	REGISTRATION NO.	CHASSIS TYPE	BODY	SEATING	YEAR NEW	YEARS WITHDRAWN
3,4	GTG 633/4W	Leyland PSU3E/4R	Duple Dominant II	C53F	1980	1989 (3) and 1994 (4)
501	LBO 501X	Leyland ONLXB/1R	East Lancs	H43/31F	1981	1998
401-18	NDW 401-18X	Volvo Ailsa B55-10	NCME	H39/35F	1982	2000 to 2007
502-10	RBO 502-10Y	Leyland ONLXB/1R	East Lancs	H43/31F	1983	1998/99
419-27	RKG 419-27Y	Volvo Ailsa B55-10	NCME	H39/35F	"	2001 to 2007
107-10	GPD 299,306/15/7N	Bristol LHS6L	ECW	B35F	1974/75	1988 (a)
511-9	A511-9 VKG	Leyland ONLXB/1R	East Lancs	H43/31F	1984	1998/99
428-36	A428-36 VNY	Volvo Ailsa B55-10	NCME	H39/35F	"	2001 to 2007
551-9	B551-9 ATX	Leyland TRCTL11/3R	East Lancs	CH43/27F	1985	1999
5,6	B905/6 DHB	"	Duple Caribbean 2	C53FT	"	1995
560-7	C560-7 GWO	Leyland ONLXB/1R	East Lancs	CH43/27F	1986	1999
111/2	D111/2 LTG	Mercedes Benz L608D	PMT	B20F	"	1994
120-9	E120-9 RDW	MCW Metrorider MF150	MCW	B23F	1987	1994 to 1995
130-41	E130-41 SNY	"	"	"	1987/88	1994 to 1996
142-9	E142-9 TBO	"	"	"	1988	1994 to 1996
150-5	F150-5 AWO	"	"	"	"	1997
156-65	F156-65 AWO	MCW Metrorider MF154	"	B31F	1988/89	1997 to 1999
231-6	F231-6 CNY	Leyland Lynx LX112L10ZR1R		B49F	1989	2000 to 2002
237-40	F237-40 CNY	"		DP47F	"	2000

FLEET NO.	REGISTRATION NO.	CHASSIS TYPE	BODY	SEATING	YEAR NEW	YEARS WITHDRAWN
241-8	F241-8 CNY	Leyland Lynx LX2R11C15Z4R		B49F	1989	2002
7	F907 DHB	Scania K113CRB	Plaxton Paramount III	C49FT	"	1995
066/067	D107 NOJ, D131 NON	Freight Rover 350D	Carlyle	B18F	1987	1991 (b)
249-59	G249-59 HUH	Leyland Lynx LX2R11C15Z4R		B49F	1990	2002/03
166/7	G166/7 HWO	Optare Metrorider MR01	Optare	B31F	"	1999
601-7	G601-7 KTX	Scania N113DRB	Alexander RH	H47/33F	"	2000
168-71	H168-71 OTG	Optare Metrorider MR01	Optare	B31F	"	1999 to 2000
172-5	H172-5 RBO	"	"	"	1991	2000
260	H49 NDU	Leyland Lynx 2 LX2R11C15Z4S		B49F	"	2004 to 2007
261-71	J261-71 UDW	"		"	"	2004 to 2007
101-4	D138/58/60/1 LTA	Dodge S56	Reebur	B23F	1986	1993 (c)
105-7	D162/4/5 LTA	"	"	"	"	1993 (c)
108-10	D177/8/81 LTA	"	"	"	"	1993 (c)
272-9	J272-9 UWO	Scania N113CRB	Plaxton Verde	B51F	1992	2003
281-6	J281-6 UWO	"	"	"	"	2003 (283 in 1998)
608-10	J608-10 VDW	Scania N113DRB	Alexander RH	H47/31F	"	2000
176-82	J176-82 WAX	Optare Metrorider MR01	Optare	B31F	"	2000
183-7	K183-7 YDW	"	"	"	"	2000
287-93	L287-93 ETG	Scania N113CRB	Alexander Strider	B50F	1994	2004
188-97	L188-97 DDW	Optare Metrorider MR15	Optare	B31F	"	2000 to 2001
101-6	L101-6 GBO	"	"	"	"	2001 to 2007
107-9	M107-9 JHB	"	"	"	"	2003 to 2006
2	972 SYD	Scania K113CRB	Jonckheere Jubilee P50	C51FT	1988	1995 (d)
110/2-33	M110/2-33 KBO	Optare Metrorider MR15	Optare	B31F	1994/95	2003 to 2007
023-9	N23-9 OBO	Dennis Dart 9.8SDL	Alexander Dash	B40F	1995	2008 to 2010
134-43	N134-43 PTG	Optare Metrorider MR15	Optare	B31F	1996	2005 to 2007
437-46	A151/2/4/6/8-63 HLV	Volvo Ailsa B55-10	Alexander RV	H44/37F	1984	2001 to 2006 (e)
447/8	DEM 821/2Y	"	"	H44/35F	1982	2001 (e)
201-15	R201-15 DKG	Optare Excel I1150	Optare	B42F	1997	2000
301-20	S301-20 SHB	Dennis Dart SLF	Plaxton Pointer SPD	B41F	1998/99	2007 to 2014
010	E830 ATT	Mercedes 709D	Reebur	DP25F	1988	2000 (f)

FLEET NO.	REGISTRATION NO.	CHASSIS TYPE	BODY	SEATING	YEAR NEW	YEARS WITHDRAWN
011	F714 ADV	Mercedes 709D	Reebur	DP25F	1988	2000 (f)
012/3	F405/8 KOD	"	"	"	"	2000 (f)
449-56	A969-74/67/8 YSX	Volvo Ailsa B55-10	Alexander AV	H44/37F	1984	2001 to 2007 (g)

(a) 107 to 110 ex London Country B.S. in 1983. (b) 066/067 ex Carlyle, Birmingham in 1988 (c) 101 to 110 ex Plymouth Citybus in 1992. (d) 2 (972 SYD) was originally registered E701 NNH and was ex Midland Fox in 1994. (e) 437 to 448 ex Merseybus in 1996. (f) 010 to 013 ex Stagecoach Devon (401/2, 436/8) in 1998. (g) 449 to 456 ex Stagecoach Fife Scottish in 1998/99.

FLEET NO.	REGISTRATION NO.	CHASSIS TYPE	BODY	SEATING	YEAR NEW	YEARS WITHDRAWN
144-50	T144-50 DAX	Dennis Dart SLF	Plaxton Pointer MPD	B30F	1999	2013/14
151-8	V151-8 JKG	"	"	"	"	2013/14
361-9/71	W361-9/71 VHB	"	Plaxton Pointer SPD	B41F	2000	2015
159/61-9	W159/61-9 EAX	"	Plaxton Pointer MPD	B30F	"	2006 to 2014
171/2	W171/2 EAX	"	"	"	"	2014
173/4/6-9	X173/4/6-9 CTG	"	"	"	"	2014
181-7	X181-7 CTG	"	"	"	"	2014
372-4/6-9	Y372-4/6-9 GAX	"	Plaxton Pointer SPD	B41F	2001	
381-8	Y381-8 GAX	"	"	"	"	2010 (384)
389-91	CE02 UVD/G/H	Transbus Dart	Transbus Pointer SPD	"	2002	
392-9	CE02 UVJ-P/R	"	"	"	"	
188-96	CE02 UUG/H/J-P	"	Transbus Pointer MPD	B29F	"	
197-9	CE02 UUR-T	"	"	"	"	
211-5	CE02 UUV-Z	"	"	"	"	
216-8	CE02 UVA-C	"	"	"	"	
861	S861 VAT	Dennis Dart SLF	Plaxton Pointer SPD	B41F	1998	2010 (a)
501-8	CA03 VRD-G/J-M	Transbus Dart	Transbus Pointer SPD	"	2003	
509-11	CN53 AKY/Z, ALO	"	"	"	"	
512/3	CN53 ALU,AMK	"	"	"	"	
514-7	CN53 AMO/U/V/X	"	"	"	"	
518-20	CN53 ANF/P/R	"	"	"	"	2007 (518/20 to trainers)
221-3	CN53 AJV/X/Y	"	Transbus Pointer 10.1m	B34F	"	
224-7	CN53 AKF/G/J/K	"	"	"	"	2012 (227)
228/9	CN53 AKO/P	"	"	"	"	

FLEET NO.	REGISTRATION NO.	CHASSIS TYPE	BODY	SEATING	YEAR NEW	YEARS WITHDRAWN
230-2	CN53 AKU/V/X	Transbus Dart	Transbus Pointer 10.1m	B34F	2003	
701-4	CN04 NPV/X-Z	Transbus	Enviro 300	B40F	2004	(b)
705/6	CN04 NRE/F	"	"	"	"	(b)
711-3	CN04 NRJ-L	"	"	B43F	"	
714-6	CN04 NRU/V/X	"	"	"	"	
233-7	CN54 NTL/M/T-V	Alexander Dennis Dart	Alexander Dennis Pointer 10.1m	B34F	"	
238/9	CN54 NTX/Y	"	"	"	"	
240-4	CN54 NUA-C/E/F	"	"	"	"	
601-4	CN06 GDF/J/O/K	Scania OmniCity CN94UA		AB53D	2006	Articulated bus
605/6	CN06 GFA/E	"		"	"	"
607/8	CN06 GEK,GDU	"		"	"	"
609-11	CN06 GEJ/U/Y	"		"	"	"
612-5	CN06 GFG/J/K/O	"		"	"	"
616-9	CN06 GDV/Z/X/Y	"		"	"	"
721-4	CN57 BHU/Y/W/X	Scania OmniCity N270UB		B41F	2007	
725-8	CN57 BHZ,BJE/F/J	"		"	"	
729-32	CN57 BJK/O/U/X	"		"	"	
733-5	CN57 BJV/Y/Z	"		"	"	
460-4	CN57 BKA/D/E-G	Scania N270UD	East Lancs Olympus	H47/27F (c)	"	
465-9	CN57 BKJ-L/O/U	"	"	"	"	
470-2	CN57 FGA/C/D	"	"	"	2008	
761-4	CN58 FFZ/Y/X/W	Scania K230UB	Wright Solar	B44F	"	
765-7	CN58 FFV/U/T	"	"	"	"	
736-9	CN09 EFH-L	Scania OmniCity N270UB		B41F	2009	
740-3	CN59 CKU/V/X/Y	"		"	"	
744	CN59 CLF	"		"	"	
251-6	CN63 NZF-H/J/K	Alexander Dennis	Enviro E20D	B39F	2013	
257-60	CN63 NZM/N/P/R	"	"	"	"	
101-6	CN63 NYU-Z	Mercedes Citaro O530		B40F	"	
107-10	CN63 NZA-D	"		"	"	
111/2	CN63 NZS/T	"		"	"	

FLEET NO.	REGISTRATION NO.	CHASSIS TYPE	BODY	SEATING	YEAR NEW	YEARS WITHDRAWN
113-20	CN63 NYL-P/R-T	Mercedes Citaro O530		B40F	2013	
261-5	CN64 FWJ-M/O	Alexander Dennis	Enviro E20D	B39F	2014	
266-70	CN64 FWP/R-U	"	"	"	"	
301-5	CN65 AAE/F/J/K/O	"	Enviro E40D MMC	H51/34F	2015	
306-10	CN65 AAU/V/X/Y/Z	"	"	"	"	
121-7	CN65 ABF/K/O/U/V/X/Z	Mercedes Citaro O295		B41F	"	
128-30	CN65 ACF/J/O	"		"	"	

(a) 861 ex Plaxton demonstrator in 2002. (b) 701/2, 704-6 later became B43F when their luggage racks were removed. (c) 460 to 466/72 are now rebuilt to H51/27F.

TROLLEYBUSES

FLEET NO.	REGISTRATION NO.	CHASSIS TYPE	BODY	SEATING	YEAR NEW	YEARS WITHDRAWN
201/2	CKG 191/2	AEC 664T	NCME	H38/32R	1941	1965
202-10	CKG 193-9	"	"	"	1942	1962 to 1965
210	CKG 200	"	"	"	1943	1962
231-7	TG 379/81/3/5/7/9/91	E.E.C. SD6WTB	English Electric Co.	B32C	1930	1949: 232/3/5/7 1950: 231/4/6 (a)
211-20	DBO 471-80	B.U.T. 9641T	East Lancs	H38/29D (b)	1948	1966 to 1970
221-30	DUH 716-725	"	"	"	"	1966 to 1970
238-242	EBO 891-5	"	"	B38D (c)	1949	1964 to 1966
248/51-64	EBO 905/8-15	"	Bruce	H38/29D (b)	1949/50	1966 to 1969
245-7/9/50	EBO 902-4/6/7	"	Yorkshire Equipment Co.	"	1950	1965 to 1968 (d)
265-74	FBO 85-94	"	Bruce	"	"	1965 to 1968
275-87	KBO 948-60	"	East Lancs	H40/32R	1955	1968 to 1970
243	KBO 961	"	"	B40R	"	1964

(a) 231-7 were ex Pontypridd U.D.C. (1-7) in 1947. (b) Were later rebuilt to H38/29R. (c) Were later rebuilt to B38R
(d) 245-7, 249/50 were those built at Bridlington using East Lancs frames.

APPENDIX 3

FORMER BUSES IN THE SERVICE VEHICLE FLEET

FLEET NO.	REGISTRATION	CHASSIS TYPE	ROLE	FROM	TO	COMMENTS
	BO 3638	Dennis-Stevens	Tower wagon	?	?	
	BO 3639	"	"	05/29	1947	Sold 1947
	BO 5225	"	Welding plant wagon	12/29	By 11/41	
	BO 8746	Dennis 4-ton	Breakdown lorry	07/32	??	Sold 1956
	HB 2244	Leyland A13	Training vehicle	1936	??	(a)
	UH 9004	Thornycroft BC	Pole-carrier	194x	1958	
	KG 1143	Leyland TS4	Mobile canteen	1949	1950	
	KG 1144	"	Training vehicle	1956	1958	
	OU 4028	Thornycroft BC	"	1941	1950	
	UB 4953	Daimler CP6	Tower wagon	1937	1950	
	MV 529	AEC Regent	Training vehicle	1941	08/48	(see next entry)
	MV 529	"	Utility/generator van	1948	1950	
	KG 3703	"	Lorry	1949	1950	
	KG 3706	"	Trainer chassis	1950	-	
	KG 3706	"	Utility van	-	1960	Sold 1960
No.2	KG 8904	Leyland TD4c	Tower wagon	11/49	1961	
	ABO 988	AEC Regal	Mobile canteen	1950	?	Sold 1956
199	CKG 325	AEC Regent	Training vehicle	08/58	06/62	
77	CKG 581	Bristol K6A	"	03/58	07/58	Sold March 1962
	CKG 582	"	"	11/61	12/67	(See next entry)
	CKG 582	"	Temporary canteen	08/64	-	Temporary role only.
	CKG 650	"	Tower wagon	09/61	1969	
	CKG 667	"	Pole wagon	03/59	03/72	
	CKG 669	"	Training vehicle	04/64	09/67	
	CKG 670	"	"	04/62	04/64	
	CUH 372	AEC Regent II	"	04/64	07/64	
	CUH 380	"	"	06/64	01/67	
	DUH 302	Bristol KW6G	"	10/67	05/69	

FLEET NO.	REGISTRATION	CHASSIS TYPE	ROLE	FROM	TO	COMMENTS
	DUH 305	Bristol KW6G	Training vehicle	02/67	03/70	
	DUH 308	"	Trainer/tree-lopper	07/66	03/70	Partial open-top layout.
	FBO 91	B.U.T. 9641T	Training vehicle	02/68	10/68	
	GKG 55	Leyland PSU1/15	"	01/68	06/69	Sold June 1970
	GUH 932	Guy Arab IV	"	01/69	02/72	Special livery later applied
	GUH 939	"	"	01/69	02/72	"
	GUH 940	"	"	03/68	02/72	"
	MUH 319	"	Exhibition bus	1972	03/72	(see next entry)
324	MUH 319	"	Training vehicle	03/72	by 01/76	
327	MUH 324	"	"	03/72	by 06/76	
345	MUH 327	"	"	1972	03/75	
382 (21)	OUH 345	"	"	09/71	03/75	
382 (21)	382 BUH	AEC Regent V	"	04/74	09/77	(b)
	382 BUH	"	Crew rest room	09/77	02/78	
383 (22)	383 BUH	"	Training vehicle	12/74	08/78	(b)
385 (23)	385 BUH	"	"	04/74	06/79	(b)
386 (24)	386 BUH	"	"	02/75	09/75	(b)
387	387 BUH	"	Crew rest room	11/74	06/77	
390 (25)	390 BUH	"	Training vehicle	06/75	04/79	(b)
508	MBO 508F	AEC Swift	"	06/75	08/79	Renumbered T522 in 1977.
425	ABO 425C	Guy Arab V	"	04/77	06/79	
427	ABO 427C	"	"	08/77	08/79	
430	ABO 430C	"	"	04/77	06/79	
446	EUH 446D	"	"	12/78	11/79	
450	EUH 450D	"	"	01/79	02/80	
464	EUH 464D	"	"	02/79	05/80	
469	EUH 469D	"	Crew rest room	04/78	03/80	
470	EUH 470D	"	Training vehicle	04/79	03/80	
471	EUH 471D	"	"	04/79	03/80	
472	EUH 472D	"	"	05/79	05/80	
494	JKG 494F	Daimler Fleetline	"	04/80	07/83	Renumbered 94 in 3/82

FLEET NO.	REGISTRATION	CHASSIS TYPE	ROLE	FROM	TO	COMMENTS
495	JKG 495F	Daimler Fleetline	Training vehicle	02/80	02/83	Renumbered 95 in 3/82
537	PKG 537H	"	Temporary office	02/82	03/82	Damaged by fire
568	WUH 568K	"	Training vehicle	02/83	04/86	As fleet number 068
570	WUH 570K	"	"	03/83	04/86	As fleet number 070
591	PKG 591M	Bristol VRT	"	04/87	07/91	Renumbered 091 in 11/87
592	PKG 592M	"	"	03/86	07/90	Renumbered 092 in 11/87
593	PKG 593M	"	"	07/86	07/90	Renumbered 093 in 11/87
046	Q346 NTM	Bedford NJM2BZ0	"	06/91	02/96	Ex MoD
047	Q347 NTM	"	"	06/91	04/95	Ex MoD
319	SWO 319S	Bristol VRT	Office and rest room	12/91	01/93	Sold in 1994.
357	WTG 357T	"	Office bus	11/92	08/94	
363	WTG 363T	"	"	01/93	09/95	
145	E145 TBO	MCW Metrorider	"	03/96	04/99	Then 045 from 3/96.
011	F714 ADV	Mercedes 709D	Staff bus	03/01	05/01	
509	RBO 509Y	Leyland Olympian	Training vehicle	12/99	05/02	
512	A512 VKG	"	"	12/99	05/02	
553	B553 ATX	"	"	06/99	02/00	
561	C561 GWO	"	"	06/99	11/99	
566	C566 GWO	"	"	06/99	06/02	
257 to 259	G257-9 HUH	Leyland Lynx	"	04/02	07/07	
010	E830 ATT	Mercedes 709D	Staff bus	10/00	05/01	
166	G166 HWO	Optare Metrorider	Training vehicle	1999	2000	Then 066 from 8/00.
088	L188 DDW	"	"	09/00	05/01	
092	L192 DDW	"	"	03/01	05/01	
096	L196 DDW	"	"	05/01	08/01	
097	L197 DDW	"	"	05/01	08/01	
101	L101 GBO	"	"	c08/01	05/06	Reinstated as PSV
122	M122 KBO	"	"	c01/05	04/06	Returned to normal service
028	N28 OBO	Dennis Dart	"	11/00	05/01	Returned to normal service
029	N29 OBO	"	"	11/00	05/01	
T518	CN53 ANF	Transbus Dart SLF	"	07/07	current	

FLEET NO.	REGISTRATION	CHASSIS TYPE	ROLE	FROM	TO	COMMENTS
T520	CN53 ANR	Transbus Dart SLF	Training vehicle	07/07	current	
T161	W161 EAX	Dennis Dart SLF	"	03/08	current	
T023	N23 OBO	Dennis Dart	"	12/08	09/13	
184	X184 CTG	Dennis Dart SLF	Engineering dept.	2015	current	

Note that prior to 1972, many vehicles did not carry fleet numbers upon entry to the service vehicle fleet.

(a) HB 2244 was acquired from Merthyr Corporation (7) in 1936. (b) Fleetnumbers 21 to 25 were allocated on paper only.

APPENDIX 4
DEMONSTRATORS INSPECTED AND/OR EVALUATED IN SERVICE OR PURCHASED

SUPPLIER	REG. NO.	CHASSIS	BODY	SEATING	YEAR NEW	FROM	TO	COMMENTS
Dennis	PK 3347	Dennis H	Dennis	L28/20R	1928	07/29	10/29	Acquired as 179.
Crossley	UH 7535	Crossley Condor	Crossley	L50R	1930	02/30	03/31	Acquired and later 63.
Leyland	UH 7175	Leyland TD1	Leyland	L24/24R	1929	11/29	03/31	Acquired as 66.
Thornycroft	OU 4264	Thornycroft 3-axle	Brush	H68R	1930	01/30	c07/30	In service
"	OU 4028	Thornycroft BC	Strachans	H26/26R	1931	05/31	03/32	Acquired and later 29.
Dennis	PL 3078	Dennis Lance		H54R	1930	03/31	05/31	In service
Daimler	UB 4953	Daimler CP6	Park Royal	H26/24R	1931	01/31	07/32	Acquired and later 85.
AEC	MV 529	AEC Regent	Brush	H56R	1932	02/32	03/33	Acquired and later 24.
Leyland	TF 6821	Leyland TD1	Leyland	L27/24R	1931	11/32	03/34	Acquired and later 51.
AEC	KG 1251	AEC Regent	Weymann	L25/25R	"	07/32	03/34	Acquired as 76.
Crossley?	RG 1676	Crossley Condor	Crossley	H24/24R	1930	01/33	06/33	
AEC	AMV 433	AEC Q	Park Royal	H31/29F	1933	09/34	-	Inspection only?
Sentinel	AUX 296	Sentinel HSG	Cowieson	B32R	1939	03/39	-	In service
Foden	KMA 575	Foden PVD6	Willowbrook	L27/28R	1948	04/50	-	Tredegar & Newport routes
Daimler	PHP 220	Daimler CVG6	NCME	H33/28R	1954	02/55	04/55	In service
ACV Sales	88 CMV	AEC Regent V	Park Royal	"	"	01/56	-	In service
Daimler	VKV 99	Daimler CVG6-30	Willowbrook	H41/33R	1957	05/58	-	Inspected
Guy Mtrs.	OHL 863	Guy Wulfrunian	Roe	H45/32F	1959	01/60	-	Ran in service to Newport
Western Welsh	TUH 306	Leyland PDR1/1	Weymann	L36/34F?	1960	1960	-	In service on route 24
Albion Motors	(TCS 151)	Albion LR1	Alexander	H41/31F	1961	1962	-	Inspected and on trade plates.
ACV Sales	7552 MX	AEC Renown	Park Royal	H39/32F	1962	02/63	-	In service
Leyland	SGD 669	Leyland PDR1/1	Alexander	H44/34F	1963	06/63	07/63	In service
"	RCS 380	Leyland PD3A/3	"	L35/32RD	1961	01/65	-	Inspected
Aberdare	FTX 228C	AEC Reliance	Strachans	B44D	1965	1966	-	To evaluate an omo bus
Daimler	FNE 747D	Daimler CRG6LX	MCW	H43/33F	1966	08/67	09/67	Manchester CT 4747.
Br Leyland	FRM 499K	Leyland National	1151/2R	B44D	1972	1973	-	Loan in 3/73.
MCW	NVP 533M	Scania BR111DH	MCW	H45/29D	1974	10/74	-	Inspected only.

SUPPLIER	REG. NO.	CHASSIS	BODY	SEATING	YEAR NEW	FROM	TO	COMMENTS
Br Leyland	RCN 165N	Bristol VRTSL	ECW	H43/27D	1974	10/74	-	Inspected 11 Oct 1974 (a)
(CIE)(D694?)	(694 ZO)?	Leyland AN68/1R	VHMA	H45/29D	1975	1975	-	Inspected 6 Jan 1975 at Roath.
Tayside RC	SSN 247S	Volvo Ailsa B55 MkI	Alexander	H44/31D	1978	04/78	10/78	In service as 54
MCW	TOJ 592S	MCW Metrobus	MCW	H43/28D	1977	03/79	06/79	In service as 52
BL UK Ltd	FHG 592S	Leyland B15	Park Royal	H47/26F	1975	02/79	07/79	In service as 55 (b)
Tayside RC	WTS 275T	Volvo Ailsa B55 MkII	Alexander	H44/31D	1979	06/79	07/79	It saw some service.
BL UK Ltd	UWW 11X	Leyland ONLXB	Roe	H47/29F	1980	02/83	-	In service to Tredegar
Derby CT	A129 DTO	Volvo B10M-50	East Lancs	H45/31F	1984	05/84	08/84	
Leyland	B263 AMG	Leyland TRCTL	Plaxton	C51F	1985	02/85	-	
Volvo (GB)	B100 CCS	Volvo B10M-61	Jonckheere	C52F	1984	02/85	-	Inspected
Optare	E95 RWR	Mercedes 811D	Optare StarRider	B33F	1987	10/88	-	Inspected
Leyland	E709 MFV	Leyland Lynx		B51F	1988	10/88	-	Inspected
Optare	G688 KNW	VW LT55	Optare CityPacer	B25F	1989	12/89	03/90	Used in service
"	G837 LWR	Daf SB220	Optare Delta	B49F	1990	07/91	-	Inspected for 4 days
Scania UK	H912 HRO	Scania N113CRB	Plaxton	B47F	1991	07/91	-	Inspected for 6 days
V.L. Bus	K114 PRV	Volvo B10B	NCME	B51F	1993	06/93	-	Inspected for 4 days
Arriva (dlr)	YD02 RDY	Daf SB200	Wright	B44F	2002	08/02	09/02	Used in service
Optare	YK02 SKU	Optare Solo M850	Optare	B29F	"	02/03	03/03	Used in service as 223
Transbus	SK52 USS	Transbus	Enviro 300	B44F	"	08/03	10/03	Used in service
"	SN03 LFU	"	"	B50F	2003	08/03	09/03	Used in service
MAN	PN03 OWA	MAN 14.220	East Lancs	B35F	2003	10/03	-	To service (1 week)
Transbus	SN53 KKZ	Transbus	Enviro 300	B44F	"	12/03	02/04	Used in service as 006.
Scania UK	YN04 AHA	Scania CN94UB	OmniCity	B41F	2004	10/04	-	Used in service as 007 (3 days).
Transbus	SN54 GRU	Transbus	Enviro 200	B27D	2002	10/04	-	Inspected.
Volvo Bus	BX54 XPU	Volvo B7TL	Wright	H43/29F	2004	10/04	11/04	Inspected.

SUPPLIER	REG. NO.	CHASSIS	BODY	SEATING	YEAR NEW	FROM	TO	COMMENTS
Scania UK	YN54 OBX	Scania N94UD	East Lancs	H47/33F	2004	12/04	01/05	As 008 (Park & Ride & contracts only)
Evobus	BX54 EDC	Mercedes Citaro 0530G		AB49T	2005	01/05	02/05	Used in service as 009.
Scania UK	YN54 ALO	Scania CN94UBA	OmniCity	AB48T	2004	02/05	-	And again in 7/05.
TWest Mid	YN55 PXB	Scania N94UD	"	H45/27F	2006	01/06	-	Inspected.
Scania UK	YN54 ALO	Scania CN94UBA	"	AB48T	2004	07/06	02/07	As 600
"	YN06 TGE	Scania N230UB	East Lancs	B33F	2006	01/06	-	Inspected for 2 days
"	YN06 TGE	"	"	B33F	"	08/06	-	Inspected for 4 days
Wrightbus	YG52 CCX	Daf SB120 electric	Wright	B31D	2002	11/06	-	Inspected and tested (7 days)
Volvo Bus	Un-reg	Volvo B9TL	East Lancs	H47/31F	2006	12/06	-	Inspected (in Delaine livery)
Scania UK	YN54 ALO	Scania CN94UBA	OmniCity	AB48T	2004	08/07	01/08	As 600

(a) This bus appeared at the 1974 Commercial Motor Show as Northern General 165N and was the second series III Bristol VRT to be built. It later entered service with Northern General in 1975 as 3239 and registered HUP 441N.
(b) This period included one month spell with the Borough of Newport Transport who loaned Cardiff Leyland Atlantean 99 (PDW 99H) in exchange.

SUPPLIER	REG. NO.	CHASSIS	BODY	SEATING	YEAR NEW	FROM	TO	COMMENTS
Evobus	BN12 CLO	Mercedes Citaro 0530		B39F	2012	11/12	12/12	As 799
Wrightbus	ERZ 2028	Wright Streetlite DF		B41F	"	11/12	02/13	As 798
A Dennis	YX62 FDG	A Dennis E20D	Enviro 200	B39F	"	02/13	-	As 797
Volvo	BF62 UYM	Volvo B7RLE	MCV	B44F	"	02/13	-	As 796 (not carried)
A Dennis	SN62 DNJ	A Dennis	E350H hybrid	B41F	"	03/13	04/13	As 800 (not carried)
MAN	WX13 GHN	MAN A69 gas	Caetano	B43F	2013	05/13	06/13	-
A Dennis	YN62 AAK	Scania K230UB	Enviro 300	"	2012	07/13	-	Carried number 01
"	SN62 DNJ	A Dennis Enviro	E350H hybrid	B41F	"	07/13	-	Carried number 02
"	YX62 EEY	A Dennis E20D	Enviro 200	B29F	"	08/13	-	As 795

SUPPLIER	REG. NO.	CHASSIS	BODY	SEATING	YEAR NEW	FROM	TO	COMMENTS
"	YX62 FDG	A Dennis E20D	Enviro 200	B39F	2012	08/13	-	As 797 (second visit)
"	SN61 DFK	A Dennis E40D	Enviro 400	H45/33F	2011	08/13	09/13	Carried number 9136
"	YT13 YUK	Scania K270UB	Enviro 300 gas	B42F	2013	10/13	12/13	As 900
"	YX62 FDG	A Dennis E20D	Enviro 200	B39F	2012	09/13	12/13	Third visit, but as a trainer.
Evobus	BF60 OEZ	Mercedes Citaro 0530		"	2011	10/13	11/13	For driver training.
A Dennis	YY64 GWX	A Dennis E40D	Enviro 400 MMC	H43/30F	2014	11/14	12/14	As 794
Evobus	BV14 TZY	Mercedes Citaro 0530K		B30F?	"	01/15	-	As 793
Volvo	BX14 SYT	Volvo B5TL	Wright Gemini3	H45/28F	"	02/15	-	As 792
Evobus	BP14 FJZ	Mercedes Citaro 0295		B41F	"	02/15	-	As 791
A Dennis	YX64 VOO	A Dennis E40D	Enviro400MMC	H47/33F	"	03/15	-	As 790
Evobus	BP14 FJZ	Mercedes Citaro 0295		B41F	"	05/15	-	-
A Dennis	SN15 LLA	A Dennis E20D	Enviro 200	B37F	2015	01/16	-	As 789
A Dennis	YX65 RKK	"	Enviro 200 MMC	B41F	"	04/16	-	As 788

BIBLIOGRAPHY

Books

Cardiff's Electric Tramways	David Gould	Oakwood Press 1996
The Cardiff Trolleybus	Bowen & Callow	National Trolleybus Association 1970
Blue Triangle – AEC buses	Alan Townsin	Venture Publications 1994
Alexander Coachbuilders	Gavin Booth	Transport Publishing Co 1980
Park Royal Coachworks	Alan Townsin	Transport Publishing Co 1980
Air Dispatch Ltd and Bruce Coachworks Ltd of Cardiff	Glyn Bowen	CTPG 2002
All Aboard	Roger Davies	Cardiff Bus 2002
Dennis – 100 Years of Innovation	Stewart J Brown	Ian Allan 1995
Bus Monographs 2: Leyland National	Stephen Morris	Ian Allan 1984
Bus Monographs 4: The Bristol K type	Geoff Green	Ian Allan 1984
PSV Circle fleet history PG1 City of Cardiff Transport and Newport Corporation Transport		PSV Circle/Omnibus Society 1973
Guy Motors Ltd and the Wulfrunian	R N Hannay	Transport Publishing Co 1978

The Best of British Buses series:

1. Leyland Titans 1927-1942	Alan Townsin	Transport Publishing Co 1981
2. The AEC Q Family	Alan Townsin	Transport Publishing Co 1981
3. Leyland Tigers 1927-81	Alan Townsin	Transport Publishing Co 1981
6. AEC Regals	Alan Townsin	Transport Publishing Co 1982
7. AEC Regents 1929-42	Alan Townsin	Transport Publishing Co 1982
8. Utilities	Alan Townsin	Transport Publishing Co 1983
9. Post-war Titans 1945-1984	Alan Townsin	Transport Publishing Co 1986
10. Post-war Regents 1945-1968	Alan Townsin	Transport Publishing Co 1986
11. Post-war Daimlers 1942-1981	Alan Townsin	Transport Publishing Co 1986

Magazines etc

Buses Illustrated/Buses
Commercial Motor (various articles from very old copies)
Cardiff City Council: Transport Committee minutes (various pre 1986)
Cardiff Transport Preservation Group newsletter and articles therein
The archives and records of the late Dave B. Thomas
The archives and records of the late Chris Taylor
The archives and records of John Jones

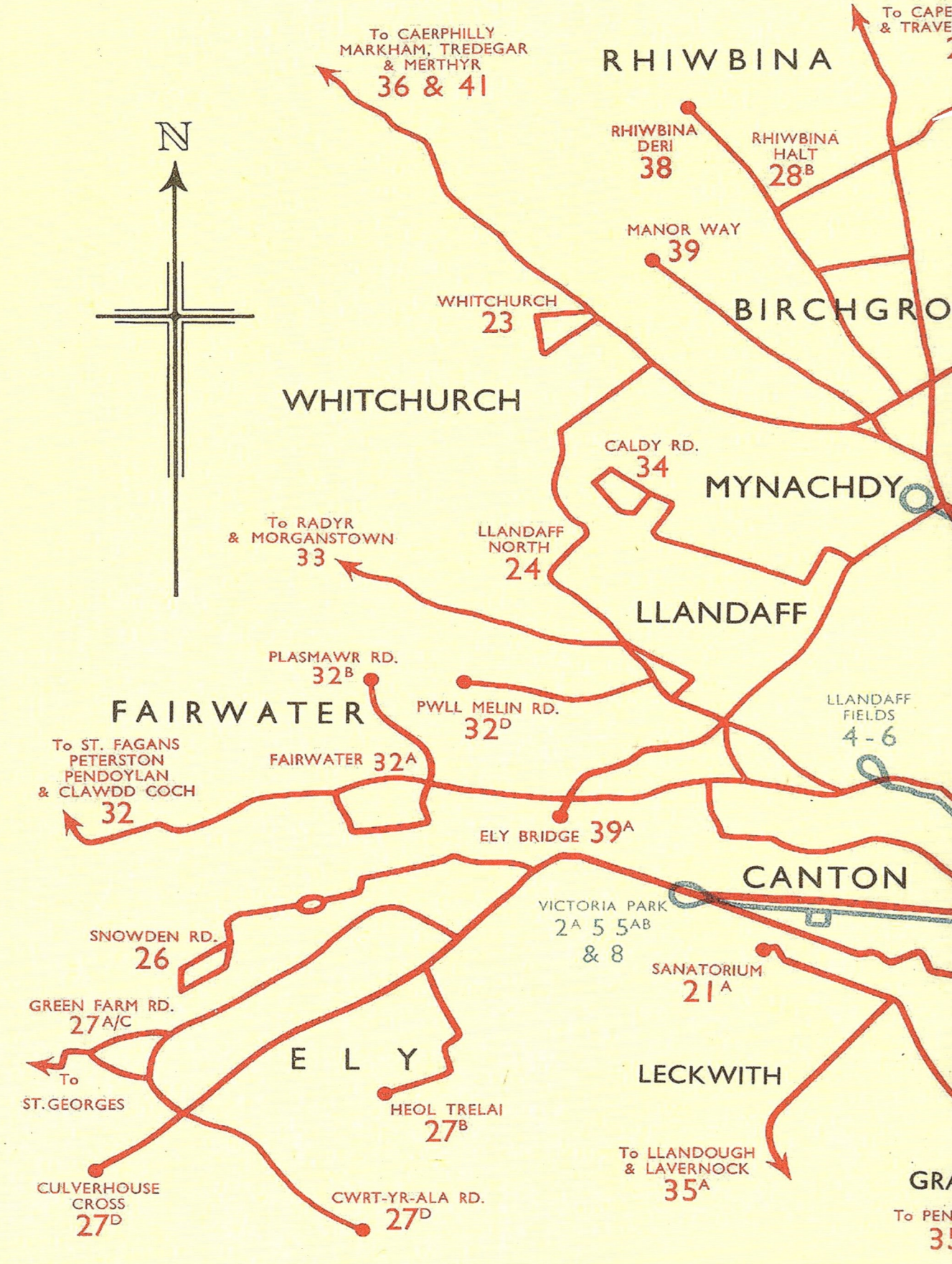